IMPERIAL RESTORATION
IN MEDIEVAL JAPAN

STUDIES OF THE
EAST ASIAN INSTITUTE
COLUMBIA UNIVERSITY

H. PAUL VARLEY

IMPERIAL RESTORATION IN MEDIEVAL JAPAN

1971
COLUMBIA UNIVERSITY PRESS
NEW YORK & LONDON

H. Paul Varley, author of
*The Ōnin War: History of Its Origins and Background,
with a Selective Translation of* The Chronicle of Ōnin,
and *A Syllabus of Japanese Civilization,*
is Associate Professor of Japanese History
at Columbia University.

12-11-78

TO IVAN MORRIS

The East Asian Institute of Columbia University

The East Asian Institute of Columbia University was established in 1949 to prepare graduate students for careers dealing with East Asia, and to aid research and publication on East Asia during the modern period. The faculty of the Institute are grateful to the Ford Foundation and the Rockefeller Foundation for their financial assistance.

The Studies of the East Asian Institute were inaugurated in 1962 to bring to a wider public the results of significant new research on modern and contemporary East Asia.

Acknowledgments

I must first acknowledge my indebtedness to Professor Kuroda Toshio of Osaka University, whom I have never met but whose ideas have strongly influenced me in my analysis of political history in early Japan in terms of competition for power among family or family-like entities. Two of the studies in which Professor Kuroda discusses such competition are "Chūsei no Kokka to Tennō," in Iwanami Shoten, *Iwanami Kōza Nihon Rekishi*, VI (Tokyo, 1963) and *Shōen-sei Shakai* (Tokyo, 1967).

Those who have read and commented on the manuscript before publication include Professors Donald Keene, Ivan Morris, Herschel Webb, and Burton Watson. Herschel Webb in particular spent many hours discussing with me the problems of interpretation I encountered during the course of writing.

I would like to thank Professor John Lindbeck of the East Asian Institute of Columbia University for providing a grant that enabled me to go to Japan during the summer of 1968 to complete research on the chapter "History Revised."

Finally, may I express my personal appreciation for the assistance of my editor, Miss Elisabeth L. Shoemaker, who has now worked with me on each of the three manuscripts that I have had published by Columbia University Press.

H. PAUL VARLEY

Columbia University, 1970

Table of Contents

IMPERIAL RESTORATION
IN MEDIEVAL JAPAN

Introduction

IN SEPTEMBER, 1945, shortly after the Japanese surrender in World War II, a shopkeeper from the city of Nagoya sent an extraordinary letter to General Douglas MacArthur, newly designated supreme commander of the Allied occupational forces in Japan. The shopkeeper, whose name was Kumazawa Kandō, claimed no less than that he, and not the reigning sovereign, was the rightful emperor of Japan. Kumazawa based his extravagant claim on the grounds that he was a direct descendant of the "southern" line of emperors who, during the only major dynastic schism of Japan's imperial family some six centuries earlier, had been deprived of its rulership by an illegitimate "northern" line, which was supported by the dominant Ashikaga warrior family of that age.

Kumazawa Kandō (or Emperor Kumazawa, as he called himself) received a great deal of publicity; yet in fact he was only one of at least seventeen pretenders who about this time asserted their descent from the fourteenth-century line of southern emperors.[1]

It is highly unlikely that General MacArthur and his aides noted with more than passing curiosity any of these royal claims. Nevertheless their assertion was acutely embarrassing to many people in Japanese ruling quarters at a time when the continuance of the imperial institution itself—which had been made the focal point of militaristic ultranationalism in the prewar and wartime periods—was in question and when a freshly liberated Japanese press was eager to exploit sensational news.

The dynastic division to which Kumazawa Kandō and the others referred had its origins in a succession dispute that began in the thirteenth century after most of the central ruling powers, which had previously been the sole prerogative of Japan's ancient imperial court at Kyoto, had been assumed by the country's first military govern-

[1] A good discussion of the Emperor Kumazawa incident may be found in Murata Masashi, *Namboku-chō Ron*, pp. 256–63.

ment or shogunate (*bakufu*) at Kamakura in the eastern provinces. When in 1333 the then tottering Kamakura Shogunate was overthrown by a coalition of warriors and courtiers, an emperor of one branch of the imperial family, Godaigo (1288–1339), attempted to restore the lost authority and prestige of the throne. But his "restoration," known after the calendrical era as the Kemmu Restoration, was an unequivocal failure. As it became increasingly clear that Godaigo was unalterably bent upon reviving outmoded and impractical ways of governance, many former allies abandoned his cause.

In 1336 the leading warrior chieftain of the day, Ashikaga Takauji (1305–58), forced Godaigo to flee from the capital, placed a member of the other branch of the imperial family on the throne and established a new shogunate in Kyoto. Godaigo, however, still regarded himself as the legitimate emperor and set up a rival court at Yoshino in the province of Yamato to the south. For the next half century, from 1336 until 1392, there were two courts in Japan: the northern court, supported and dominated by the Ashikaga, and the southern court of Godaigo and his successors. In 1392 the Ashikaga succeeded in unifying the courts with the promise of a return to the practice that had been followed before the Kemmu Restoration. But the Ashikaga never honored this promise and the southern branch was from this time denied all claims to the imperial succession.

The Kemmu Restoration was noteworthy as the last time during the premodern period when the court took an active part in national affairs. Its collapse marked the completion of a process, begun with the establishment of the Kamakura Shogunate in the 1180s, of political displacement by warrior leaders of the court nobles of Kyoto, who had formerly constituted the governing class of the land.

Although the restoration failed utterly, the attempt itself had a tremendous impact on the minds of contemporary observers and later historians. It brought into focus certain attitudes and conflicts of attitude concerning the theory of rule in Japan that were fundamental to affairs of the medieval age.[2] To Japanese before World

[2] The medieval age of Japanese history is generally taken to mean the period from the founding of the Kamakura Shogunate in 1185 until the end of the Muromachi or Ashikaga Shogunate in 1573.

War II the Kemmu Restoration and the war between the courts created a difficult problem of interpretation: which of the courts during this period should in fact be regarded as legitimate or rightful? What criteria should be used to judge the legitimacy of one or the other? As recently as 1911 these questions were raised at the highest levels of the Japanese government and an orthodox line of interpretation was laid down for presentation to Japanese youth through primary school history textbooks.

This study will deal both with the Kemmu Restoration, within the context of transition from rule by courtiers to rule by warriors in the early medieval age, and with the fourteenth-century dynastic schism as a topic of Japanese historiography.

I

Court and Military
in the Early Kamakura Period

THE EARLIEST WRITTEN ACCOUNTS of Japan, which are to be found in the Chinese Dynastic Histories that deal with the period from the first through the third century A.D., describe the country as a land of numerous "communities" or tribal groupings, probably concentrated in the northern part of Kyushu. We know, chiefly from archaeological remains, that sometime between the mid-third and the fifth century a process of amalgamation and a shift in the political center of gravity took place which resulted in a hegemony of extended families (*uji*) centered in the Kansai region of the main island of Honshu. By the early sixth century this hegemony was presided over by one kinship group that became the Japanese imperial family of historic times.

The relatively small group of families (perhaps 120 or so, if we are to believe the Chinese accounts) that comprised the emergent ruling aristocracy of the sixth century controlled territorial domains in which they were the possessors of superior proprietary rights over the agricultural lands that overwhelmingly constituted the economic wealth of Japan. Each family, including the imperial family, claimed mythical descent from a different tutelary deity or Shinto *kami* and one of the principal functions of each family head was to lead his family in rites to its *kami*. Leaders of the more important families, especially those located geographically near the imperial seat in the central provinces of the Kansai Plain, held hereditary ranks and positions at court. By the middle of the sixth century several of these leaders appear to have acquired a degree of political power comparable, if not superior, to that of the emperor.

Sometime shortly after the mid-century a dispute arose at court over whether or not to "accept" Buddhism, which according to tradition was officially introduced into Japan from Korea in 552. The

[4]

real issue at this time was over the desirability of investigating the systems and institutions of Chinese civilization, including Confucianism as well as Buddhism, for the purpose of using them to centralize and strengthen the Japanese state. The family that emerged as the foremost proponent of Buddhism, and therefore the leading advocate of reform and progress, was the Soga. Its chief adversaries were the Mononobe and the Nakatomi, families that served respectively as elite guards and Shinto ritualists at court and were opposed to any radical change in the status quo. In 587 the Soga defeated the Nakatomi and Mononobe in battle and established themselves as indisputably the most powerful family in the land. Even before this date the Soga had strengthened their position by marrying into the imperial family and in 592 they placed their niece, Empress Suiko (r. 592–628), on the throne.

Suiko, the first reigning empress of Japan, appears to have been essentially a figurehead for the Soga. Certainly she was not as politically prominent as some of her recent predecessors on the throne. Yet quite likely it was during Suiko's reign that an important step was taken, as part of a prelude to reform, to increase the prestige of the imperial institution. This was the adoption of the Chinese-style designation of *tennō* for the Japanese sovereign. Previously the latter had been known as *ōkimi*, a title that may originally have meant simply that its holder was *primus inter pares* in relation to the other clan leaders of early Japanese society. A number of scholars have hypothesized that it was during the sixth century that the tutelary deity of the imperial family, the Sun Goddess (Amaterasu Ōmikami), was consciously elevated to the highest position in the Shinto pantheon and was made the ancestress of the nation. The *tennō*, whose symbols of office were the three regalia (a mirror, sword, and jewel, which were gifts from the Sun Goddess),[1] was alone qualified to conduct the rites to his ancestress that were deemed essential to the proper conduct of central government.

Although Suiko remained mostly in the background during her reign, the imperial family was in no sense deprived of all its political powers by the Soga. One of the leading figures in national affairs of this age was Prince Shōtoku (574–622), an intellectual and statesman

[1] See Appendix 3 for a discussion of the imperial regalia.

who has been highly idealized in later history. Shōtoku's name is associated with several significant measures—including the adoption of a system of ministerial ranks and the writing of a "constitution" —that were aimed at fostering ethical government in Japan and at paving the way for creation of a new centralized bureaucracy. Shōtoku was also the first to dispatch students to the continent to acquire firsthand knowledge of Chinese civilization. Several of the more prominent of these students became, after their return to Japan, the main theoreticians of the great Taika Reform of 645.

By the mid-seventh century the Soga, who had been the progressives of the sixth century, became the most formidable obstacle to further reform. By constructing pretentious homes and mausolea for themselves and by assuming certain of the *tennō*'s ritual functions,[2] they even gave signs that their aim was to usurp the throne. Such behavior threatened to destroy the balance of power among the great clans which earlier Soga leaders had carefully maintained; and in 645 a clandestine faction at court, headed by Prince Naka (626–71) and Nakatomi Kamatari (614–69), overthrew the Soga in a brief but bloody coup.

The Taika Reform, which the new leaders of the court inaugurated, was in its early stages primarily a land reform. Prince Naka and his advisers emulated the "equal-field" system of T'ang China by declaring all land of the realm to be public domain and by setting up a scheme for the allotment of agricultural holdings by the throne to its subjects. Unfortunately the records do not tell us how widely the Taika land system was enforced; but the aim was to give each peasant an equal plot and to grant special allotments to members of the ruling aristocracy for offices and ranks held and for meritorious service and the like.

During the second half of the seventh century the court sought to construct the kind of centralized bureaucracy envisioned by Prince Shōtoku in which ministerial appointments would be made more on the basis of rational than on that of status criteria and the functions of government would be differentiated, regularized, and clearly

---

[2] E.g., praying for rain and personally undertaking the entertainment of envoys from Emishi tribes in the north. See Naoki Kōjirō, *Kodai Kokka no Seiritsu*, in Chūō Kōron Sha, *Nihon no Rekishi*, II, 159.

defined by law. The final stages in completion of this half century of reform were the issuance in 701 of the Taihō Code, a comprehensive formulary designating the offices and the rules for the conduct of imperial government, and the establishment in 710 of a new capital at Nara in Yamato Province.

The inclination among scholars today is to regard the Taika Reform as less a revolution than the continuation or acceleration of certain processes, leading toward greater public control over land and toward bureaucratic rationalization, that had begun in the previous century. In addition to the steps they took to establish a centralized bureaucracy during this period, the reformists made deliberate efforts to strengthen the authority and real power of the throne at its apex. Prince Naka, who guided the Reform as crown prince and regent from 645 until 667 and then as Emperor Tenji (r. 667–71), and his brother, Emperor Temmu (r. 672–86), were among the most powerful sovereigns in Japanese history. The records describe Tenji's assumption of imperial authority in strongly Confucian terms, citing various portents and omens as proof that he enjoyed Heaven's blessing or mandate.[3] Yet, significantly, they make no mention of the concomitant Chinese idea that Heaven could withdraw as well as grant such a mandate to rule. The Japanese stopped short of acceptance of this rationale for dynastic change and tacitly affirmed that kingship was the exclusive domain of the imperial family, whose members were descended from the Sun Goddess and who were themselves regarded as living *kami*.

Temmu, who ascended the throne in 672 after an armed struggle with his nephew and who was looked upon by some as a usurper, sought to enlist Buddhism in support of his acquisition of imperial prerogatives. He asserted that he had become sovereign because of personal merit acquired in previous existences and because of his devotion to Buddhism, a devotion that had earned him the protection of the Deva, or guardian, kings.[4] Temmu completely dominated affairs at court. He placed members of his immediate family in

[3] Aston, W. G., *Nihongi, Chronicles of Japan From the Earliest Times to A.D. 697.* See Book XXIV, pp. 171–94.
[4] Tsunoda, Ryusaku, Wm. T. de Bary, and Donald Keene, eds., *Sources of Japanese Tradition*, pp. 99–101.

all the key ministerial positions and maintained careful control over the leading courtier families.

Temmu's reign was, for other reasons as well, one of the most important in Japanese history. In the view of present-day scholars it was Temmu who eliminated the remaining opposition to the policies of the Taika Reform.[5] He also appears to have elevated the imperial family to a level of sanctity which virtually precluded the possibility that any other family in the future might seek, as perhaps the Soga did, to dispossess it of the throne.

During the Nara period (710–84) the country was, by and large, governed by the sovereign with the assistance of his chief ministers in the department of state (*dajōkan*), the principal administrative body below the throne. The new central government was of substantial size, employing some 10,000 ministers and functionaries in Nara alone.[6] Yet, despite many outward similarities, Japan had not really become a small-scale bureaucratic state on the model of China. The principle of ministerial selection on the basis of rational criteria— e.g., by means of an examination system—never fully took hold in Japan. Family status remained the most important prerequisite for official appointment. Moreover, the aristocratic families of the central provinces, which had been most active in the Reform period, held a distinct advantage over those in the outlying regions. One family in particular, the Fujiwara, gradually emerged as a powerful new force at court. The Fujiwara name had been created by Emperor Tenji, who bestowed it on Nakatomi Kamatari, his chief ally in the overthrow of the Soga in 645, in appreciation for distinguished service to the throne. From the early Nara period Kamatari's descendants became ever more prominent in governing circles.

In 794 the capital was moved some twenty-six miles northward to the city of Heian or Kyoto in Yamashiro Province. The age from 794 until the founding of the Kamakura Shogunate in 1185 is commonly designated the Heian period, although the imperial seat remained at Kyoto until the mid-nineteenth century. It was during the early centuries of the Heian period that the Fujiwara firmly con-

---

[5] Naoki, *Kodai Kokka*, pp. 333–35.

[6] Aoki Kazuo, *Nara no Miyako*, in Chūō Kōron Sha, *Nihon no Rekishi*, III, 22.

solidated their position at court. They married into the imperial family, as had the Soga earlier, and established an imperial regency by means of which they assumed the actual controls of government. The Fujiwara reached their highest point of power and prestige under Michinaga (966–1027) about the year 1000. At the time they held nearly all the ranking ministerial posts at court and kept the throne impotent by making sure that it was usually occupied by little boys, who were invariably the sons of Fujiwara women.

During the early Heian period, then, political power was largely transferred from the throne and the department of state to the Fujiwara regents. Undergirding the Fujiwara position economically were vast holdings in private estates (*shōen*). As early as the eighth century the "equal-field" system of the Taika Reform had begun to break down. The court found it increasingly difficult to make the periodic inspections and reallotments of land necessary to keep the system in working order and inequality in landholding became more and more pronounced. Not only did many small holders, heavily burdened with taxes, abandon their fields; larger holders absorbed these fields and further increased their wealth by opening new lands in the less fully developed areas of the country. By the end of the tenth century much of the public domain had been converted into private estates by aristocratic families, such as the Fujiwara, and also by great Buddhist temples and Shinto shrines. Through the acquisition of documents from the court granting tax exemptions and immunity from interference by central officials, these aristocratic families and religious institutions even secured legal recognition of their estate holdings.

The estate system was expanded further, especially during the tenth century, through the widespread practice of commendation. In order to avoid the various taxes of the central government, the most onerous of which were the labor levies, and to secure greater local protection, peasant families throughout the country commended or transferred their titles to land to estate holders. The peasant family that thus commended its fields continued to work them as before; but now it was part of an estate unit and was obliged to pay only a single harvest rent in kind to the estate holder.

Probably the most fundamental reason for the rise of a military class in the provinces during the middle and late Heian period was the failure of the court to provide effective provincial administration. The growth of private estates was accompanied by a marked decline in the exercise of government at the provincial level. In some regions, such as the central provinces, the estates themselves provided the necessary order. Elsewhere, especially in the Kantō, local families were obliged to take up arms to prevent a lapse into anarchy.

Leadership for the new warrior class of the provinces was provided mainly by descendants of the court aristocracy. The Taira and Minamoto, the most prominent of the warrior clans, were both originally of imperial blood. The leading branch of the Taira (the Ise Taira) became most influential in the region of the Inland Sea, whereas the Minamoto asserted their power chiefly in the Kantō. A third important warrior house emerged from a branch of the Fujiwara family which established its base in the provinces to the north of the Kantō.

The transition to warrior rule in the late Heian and Kamakura periods, therefore, was not so much a matter of revolutionary social upheaval as the first stage in the transfer of power within an aristocratic group of families that had become clearly differentiated by function into civil and military. The civil nobility retained its attachment to the imperial court at Kyoto, while the military, who came to be linked by feudal, lord-vassal relations, increasingly gave allegiance to the warrior regime at Kamakura. The tie between the two was the throne, which remained the unchallenged source of legitimacy for both.

Before turning to court-military relations in the early Kamakura epoch, some final remarks must be made about the decline of the Fujiwara and the rise first of the cloistered emperors (*in*) and then of the Taira clan in the late Heian period. In 1069 Gosanjō (1043–73), who did not have a Fujiwara mother, ascended the throne and became the first emperor in a century or more to challenge the supremacy of the Fujiwara in court politics. Gosanjō died a brief three years later; but his son Shirakawa (1053–1129), who abdicated in 1086 after a reign of fourteen years, assumed leadership in the capital as cloistered emperor. A more detailed discussion of the institution of cloistered emperorship, whereby abdicated emperors

[10]

revived the political and economic fortunes of the imperial family, will be taken up later. Here let us note simply that the rise of the cloistered emperors came about in part because of the decline in Fujiwara leadership and family cohesiveness and in part because of the support that the cloistered emperors came to receive from other houses, such as the Murakami Genji[7] and the Taira.

In the mid-twelfth century two sanguinary struggles, known as the Hōgen (1156) and Heiji (1159) incidents, erupted in the capital. The animosities that brought on the Hōgen incident were complex and caused division within all the great families involved: the imperial family (with the emperor Goshirakawa, r. 1155–58, opposing the ex-emperor Sutoku, r. 1123–41), the Fujiwara, the Taira, and the Minamoto. Perhaps the most significant feature of this brief conflict was the participation in what was essentially a court dispute of armed men for the first time in more than three and a half centuries.

The most powerful figure to emerge from the Hōgen incident was Taira Kiyomori (1118–81). In 1159 he and his clansmen decisively defeated the Minamoto in the Heiji struggle and inaugurated a period of Taira hegemony in the capital that lasted for twenty or more years. The Taira, however, did not undertake to develop new institutions of military rule, but were content to exercise power through the regular channels of administration at court. Kiyomori married Taira women into the imperial family and in 1180 has his own grandson crowned as the Emperor Antoku (1178–85).

Antoku's reign was not a peaceful one. In the very year of his accession several Minamoto chieftains rose in the eastern provinces and began the general struggle that led to the total destruction of the Taira of Kiyomori in 1185 and to the establishment of the first shogunate by Minamoto Yoritomo at Kamakura.

Yoritomo, in constructing his new military government, was careful to do it on the basis of a delegation of authority from the

[7] This was a courtier family that traced its descent from Emperor Murakami (r. 926–66). It should be clearly distinguished from the warrior family of Seiwa Genji, who are referred to in this study simply as "the Genji," or as the Minamoto (an alternate reading for *gen* in Genji).

throne. In 1192 he obtained the title *seii taishōgun*, or "great general for pacification of the eastern barbarians." The charge to pacify the eastern barbarians was anachronistic, since the barbarian problem in that region had been settled nearly four centuries earlier. Yet Yoritomo apparently hoped that this title, which had been held by great warriors in the past, would lend proper dignity to his commanding position among the military.

Yoritomo's realization of the need to relate his power position to a higher level of legitimacy can be seen not only in his desire to obtain the court-delegated title of shogun and to secure other forms of approval for his assumption of *de facto* power, but also in the manner in which he constructed his military government. By its very nature and location this government was clearly beyond direct control of the court in Kyoto. It was, in fact, a private and distinctly separate power center, controlling land and people no longer within the range of imperial authority. Yoritomo was nevertheless able, even under these conditions, to proceed within certain traditional bounds; for there already existed in the estate system ample theoretical precedent for the type of administration he sought to establish. The Heian courtier families, for example, while discharging public duties as minister of the emperor, had long exercised simultaneous private control over their estate holdings. Their administration of these estates was typically patterned on house lines, through the organization of offices such as *mandokoro* (administrative boards) and *samurai dokoro* (boards of retainers). Yoritomo, in clear imitation of this practice of house administration by the courtier families, selected offices with precisely such designations for the conduct of his military rule in Kamakura.[8] Thus he assumed the roles of both imperial official (shogun) and independent territorial lord.

In Kyoto the final victory of Minamoto armies in 1185 and firm establishment of the Kamakura Shogunate, through the appointment of stewards (*jitō*) and constables or protectors (*shugo*) to various estates and provinces, left the Heian courtiers politically adrift. From an economic standpoint, these members of the old regime were still

[8] Yoritomo also opened an office called *monchūjo* (board of inquiry), which was not used by the courtier families.

largely intact; indeed it was not until some thirty years later[9] that military administration came to penetrate deeply into the central and western provinces, where the court aristocracy had long had its largest and most secure estate holdings. Nevertheless the traditional state as they conceived it had already been permanently altered. At the central, regional, and local levels warriors were arrogating responsibilities formerly assumed to be the rightful domain of the court.

The next two centuries were to transform the court's role from an active to a passive one in Japanese history. Although this transformation seems understandable in the light of trends in landholding, social relations and the exercise of power, the court nobility that was in the process of being politically and economically displaced could scarcely look upon its fate with detachment and resignation. A few of the more articulate courtiers felt impelled to take up their writing brushes to formulate specific proposals for the revitalization of the court. The attitudes of other leading nobles concerning the course the court ought to take can be discerned from the general records and accounts of the early medieval age.

The leaders of the old regime, as we shall see, tended to advocate policies of either reform or reaction. Some believed the court should seek a merger or union with the military (*bumbu kenkō*), which would probably require the courtiers to take on certain military functions; others insisted that the court resolutely oppose the military and strive to bring about an "imperial restoration" (*ōsei fukko*).

By and large, those who proposed a union of civil and military urged adoption of a pragmatic approach to the problem of re-adjusting the court to a new role within the national power structure. The extent to which the courtiers would have to be "militarized" in the process would depend on circumstances. A belief was implicit that former techniques of civil bureaucracy and reliance on the power of moral suasion were no longer sufficient; that some form of compulsion, as practiced by the military, had become mandatory for the administration of Japanese society.

The advocates of a "restoration of imperial rule," on the other hand, espoused reactionary programs that called for a return to the

---

[9] After the Jōkyū incident of 1221, which will be discussed below.

[13]

institutional practices of some earlier period in Japanese history before the rise of the military.[10] They sought to deny or reject militarism and to reassert a more traditional form of civil, imperial rule. Where these restorationists differed among themselves was in their interpretation of the historical meaning of imperial rule in Japan. Emperor Godaigo at the time of the Kemmu Restoration, for example, believed that true imperial rule meant direct or personal rule by the emperor. Godaigo appears to have envisioned himself as a kind of sage king capable of dealing with all matters of government by reliance solely upon his own virtue as legitimate sovereign of the land.

To members of the ministerial families at court imperial rule was likely to mean something quite different. Low-ranking courtiers probably looked back for their model to the Nara period, when the country was governed by a broadly based bureaucracy in the service of the throne, when the ideal of ministerial advancement through merit was at least set forth in the legal codes. High-ranking nobles such as the Fujiwara, on the other hand, were apt to stress as the most important element of imperial rule the "assisting" function of one or more key officials next to the throne in support of an emperor who did not act himself but, rather, sanctified the acts of others.

The idea of an assisting function meant in practice the assumption of political powers by someone or some group other than the emperor. Prince Shōtoku (as crown prince-regent) and the Soga leader Umako (d. 626) had handled political affairs of the late sixth and early seventh centuries for Empress Suiko; and the Soga had retained the actual controls of government until the Taika Reform. Even after the Reform, Prince Naka (as crown prince) had been the real ruler at court for more than a decade and a half while his uncle and mother occupied the throne in succession. The establishment some two centuries later of the Fujiwara regency was accompanied by the gradual decline of the Taika-Taihō (*ritsu-ryō*) bureaucracy

[10] This point will be more fully discussed in later sections. Different individuals tended to select different "golden ages" which they wished to hold as models. Godaigo, for example, cherished especially the early tenth century, a time not only before the rise of the military but before the consolidation of power by the Fujiwara regents and the establishment of the office of cloistered emperor as well.

[14]

and the transfer of political powers to the family councils of the Fujiwara regents. Thus by the Kamakura era the Japanese had already experienced long periods during which sovereigns, while reigning and continuing to legitimatize the conduct of court government, had not ruled.

For all who would propose revitalization of the court, either through reform or reaction, there were several facts to face. The military had displayed such vigor in spreading their control over the land that they could scarcely be dismissed as simply ephemeral or unworthy. Nor could the more thoughtful among the old regime deny that the military had in fact brought about some positive good, including the establishment of peace and stability in the land. Clearly it would be necessary to view the rise of the military in terms of fundamental values before final judgment could be passed. The two most famous works of the early medieval period devoted to analysis and evaluation of the momentous social and political changes taking place during this age are the *Gukanshō* of Jien (1155–1225), a Buddhist priest and member of the Kujō branch of the Fujiwara family, and the *Jinnō Shōtōki* of the fourteenth-century courtier-general Kitabatake Chikafusa (1293–1354). The *Jinnō Shōtōki* will be treated in detail in a later chapter. At this point it is necessary to discuss the views contained in the *Gukanshō* and other works of the thirteenth century for an understanding of their influence on early medieval attitudes toward the court, the military, and restoration.

The waning of an aesthetically brilliant court society, accompanied by warfare, natural disaster, and disruption, gave to the twelfth century a pervading mood of pessimism. This pessimism was accentuated by widespread belief that the age was one of *mappō*, or "the end of the Buddhist law." According to Buddhist tradition, history would progress through three stages following the death of the historical Buddha, Gautama (*ca.* 563–483 B.C.). First, there would be a stage of *shōhō*, or "the flourishing of the law," when the teachings of the Buddha would be thoroughly understood and practiced everywhere. This would be followed by a time of *zōhō*, or "the reflected law," when the Buddhist teachings would still be known, but would not be accepted or practiced with the same vigor as before. Finally, there would come an age of *mappō*, when the Buddhist law would disappear and darkness and ignorance would descend upon the world. Some Buddhists believed that *shōhō* and *zōhō* would last five hundred years each; others that each would endure a thousand years. The Japanese seem to have accepted a curious method of calculation whereby they measured *shōhō* and *zōhō* by thousand-year units beginning some five hundred years before the time when Gautama is usually thought to have lived.[11] Thus they believed that the age of the flourishing of the law began about 1000 B.C.; that the age of the reflected law was half over when Buddhism was officially introduced to Japan in the mid-sixth century A.D.; and that the age of *mappō* commenced shortly after A.D. 1000.

Despite the *mappō* pessimism of the times, it was in fact largely in Buddhist terms that the first positive attempts were made to explain the reasons for the rise of the military and their new role in state affairs. The author or authors of the famous war tale, *Heike Monogatari* (Tale of the Heike), express a pessimistic attitude of resignation and an acceptance of military struggle as a reflection of the impermanence of all things; but in other works, such as *Azuma Kagami* (Mirror of the East), we can find a more positive view of the military as emergent protectors of the state (*kokka shugo*).[12]

This view of the military as national protectors was clearly an extension of a much earlier belief in Buddhism as the "guardian of the state" (*gokoku*). Jien had this aspect of Buddhism in mind when he sought to explain the introduction of Buddhist law (*buppō*) to Japan in the sixth century in terms of the imposition of a higher order for the protection of the imperial law (*ōhō*). In discussing the early years of Buddhist influence, for example, Jien claimed justification for the assassination of Emperor Sushun (r. 587–92) in 592 by Soga Umako (d. 626) on the grounds that Umako was the chief proponent of Buddhism at the time and that the emperor, a man of little merit, was himself plotting the murder of Umako. To Jien the

---

[11] Another method of calculation held *shōhō* to be 500 years and *zōhō* 1,000 years.

[12] For a discussion of this see Maki Kenji, "Buke-hō ni Miyuru Rekishikan," in Fuzanbō, *Hompō Shigaku Shi Ronsō*, I, 646–48. Minoru Shinoda has translated part of *Azuma Kagami* (entries from 1180 to 1185) into English in *The Founding of the Kamakura Shogunate, 1180–1185.*

continued propagation of Buddhism as protector of the imperial state was of far greater importance than the life of a single emperor.[13]

Although the Soga had been the first to champion Buddhism, members of the imperial family had gradually become its chief patrons during the late sixth and seventh centuries. Emperor Temmu, as we have seen, claimed that he enjoyed the special protection of the guardian kings of Buddhism. He also actively encouraged the spread of Buddhism in Japan by directing in 685 that Buddhist images and sutras be kept in every house in the country. Although it is unlikely that this directive was carried out to the letter, its issuance marked the beginning of a movement that lasted for nearly a century to make Buddhism the new state religion. The high point of this movement came during the reign of Emperor Shōmu (r. 724–48), possibly the most devoutly Buddhist of all Japan's sovereigns. In 741 Shōmu ordered the construction of provincial temples (*kokubunji*); and during the years 743–52 he had the massive Tōdaiji (Eastern great temple) built in Nara to serve as its central headquarters.

During the Heian period the priest Saichō (767–822), founder of the Tendai sect of Buddhism, asserted that his temple on Mt. Hiei was the new "Center for Protection of the Nation." Such an assertion was fully in keeping with the comprehensive doctrines of Tendai Buddhism, whose practitioners formulated vast syntheses of religious truth and whose monastic complex on Mt. Hiei, the Enryakuji, became the spawning ground for most of the major Buddhist sects that were established in Japan during later centuries.

That the military leaders at Kamakura consciously sought to justify their assumption of national police powers in Buddhist terms can be surmised from their use of the Buddhist word *shugo* as a designation for the constables, or "protectors," whom Yoritomo appointed to the provinces in 1185. By reestablishing order the military had set themselves clearly apart from the Heian courtiers, who had allowed national administration to become greatly weakened over the centuries. The leaders of Kamakura might indeed be regarded as the new "protectors" of the country.

---

[13] Jien, *Gukanshō*, in Okami Masao and Akamatsu Toshihide, eds., *Gukanshō*, pp. 136–40.

Jien's views on court-military relations during the early Kamakura period are especially important because of his personal background and political commitments. Jien was born in 1155, the son of the imperial regent Fujiwara Tadamichi (1097–1164). At the age of eleven he entered Buddhist orders at the Enryakuji on Mt. Hiei and remained a member of the priesthood there for the remainder of his life. On four separate occasions he served as the head abbot of the Enryakuji.

Jien's elder brother was Kanezane (1149–1207), the first of the Kujō branch of the Fujiwara family and, from 1186 to 1196, holder of the office of imperial regent. Kujō Kanezane's name will reappear later in this narrative, for he played a significant role in affairs of the late twelfth century. In addition to serving as imperial regent, he was also the most prominent Kyoto minister to cooperate with Yoritomo and the Kamakura regime. Upon the death of Goshira-kawa in 1192 Kanezane was instrumental in securing for Yoritomo the title of shogun, which the cloistered emperor had long refused to grant him. But Kanezane's ties with Kamakura were ultimately to cause him grief. During the 1190s a strong antishogunate faction, centered around the cloistered emperor Gotoba (1180–1239), emerged at court and forced Kanezane to spend his final years in eclipse. Jien's own fortunes tended to wax and wane with those of his brother. When, for example, Kanezane was relieved of his regency in 1196, Jien was also obliged to step down from the head-ship of the Enryakuji.

Kanezane and Jien, so far as we can discern from the records, were political opportunists. Both were deeply committed to the revival of the Fujiwara house and were willing to make compromises with the military to achieve this. Jien wrote the *Gukanshō* about 1220 at a time when Gotoba and his clique were plotting to overthrow the Kamakura Shogunate. To Jien, Gotoba's plan was sheer folly and he appears to have written the *Gukanshō* chiefly to dissuade the cloistered emperor from pursuing it. In discussing the *Gukanshō*, then, we must keep in mind that Jien wrote it with a strong political purpose.

Jien was the first of Japan's historians to view history as a process of constant change and to seek to analyze the course of change in terms of cause and effect. His whole outlook was profoundly influenced by *mappō* pessimism and in fact he interpreted Japanese history in the broadest sense as a long, downward movement terminating in his own age, which he regarded as degenerate and debased. He divided Japanese history from the time of Emperor Jimmu into seven periods[14] and traced first the decline of the imperial family and then that of the Fujiwara regents, who had provided invaluable assistance to the throne during what Jien termed the "middle ages"; the rise of the cloistered emperors, whose period of supremacy he viewed as a kind of perversion of imperial rule; and, finally, the ascendancy of the provincial warrior families.

Jien's acute consciousness of change is understandable. The authors of earlier historical records may have looked upon Japanese history as an unvarying continuum from the age of the gods.[15] But by Jien's time it could hardly be held that the state, in its manifest form at least, was unchanged or unchanging. Military society was already in a stage of rapid expansion and was challenging the very foundations of court rule. Desire for the restoration of earlier values and practices became a natural sentiment among those of the aristocracy and entrenched priesthood who, like Jien, stood to lose most by the unchecked expansion of warrior control over the land.

Jien attempted to explain historical change chiefly through use of the term *dōri* (literally, principle), a term which he employed with such frequency and with such imprecision that he badly obscured much of what he apparently wished to say.[16] Scholars either have despaired of fully comprehending Jien's *dōri* or have constructed elaborate explanations to suggest a complexity of meanings that surely never occurred to him. More often than not *dōri* appears in the *Gukanshō* to be equatable with the Buddhist law. Jien believed that the fate of the Buddhist law in Japan was inseparable from that

---

[14] *Ibid.*, pp. 325–26.

[15] See comments on *Kojiki* and *Nihon Shoki* in Bitō Masahide, "Nihon ni okeru Rekishi Ishiki no Hatten," in Iwanami Shoten, *Iwanami Kōza Nihon Rekishi*, XXII, 17.

[16] Tsukamoto Yasuhiko calls Jien's *dōri* a "device" or "technique" for dealing with history, its variations and changes, and especially the rise of the military. "*Gukanshō to Jinnō Shōtōki*," in *Kokugo to Kokubungaku* (September, 1962), p. 16.

of the imperial law. He saw as inevitable the decline of court rule during the age of *mappō* and acknowledged that only fierce warriors could be expected to impose order again. Jien particularly admired the achievements of Minamoto Yoritomo, whom he regarded as the last of the great "noble warriors" (Taira and Minamoto).[17] He was less enthusiastic about the low-ranking Hōjō who succeeded to power in Kamakura shortly after Yoritomo's death.

Although Jien presented an over-all Buddhist view of history, many of his specific observations and interpretations were based on purely Shinto mythology and beliefs. He recounted that the Sun Goddess had dispatched her grandson, Ninigi, from the plain of high heaven with the charge that he establish a line of rulers on earth. On the basis of this charge alone the imperial family had occupied the throne of Japan since the founding of the country. Yet it was inevitable, if a single dynastic line was to be maintained, that excessively young or otherwise incompetent rulers should eventually ascend the throne. To provide for this, the Sun Goddess had at the time of Ninigi's departure also directed Ama-no-koyane, the *kami* forebear of the Fujiwara family, to assist the imperial house in a close ministerial capacity. In this way Amaterasu asserted the centrality of the imperial house and, at the same time, made provision for the support of emperors by qualified officials, a function that would become especially important to the proper conduct of affairs during the middle and later (by Jien's calculations) stages of Japanese history.[18]

Thus the Fujiwara, in Jien's mind, had as much right to "assist" the throne as the imperial family had to occupy it. Jien felt that the kind of government perfected by Michinaga (966–1027), the greatest of the Fujiwara regents, was an excellent polity for Japan. He bitterly lamented, on the other hand, the rise toward the end of the eleventh century of the cloistered emperors, who employed what Jien considered to be upstart and unqualified (as well as non-Fujiwara) ministers.[19] It was little wonder that the affairs of the country had

---

[17] *Gukanshō*, pp. 332–33.
[18] *Ibid.*, pp. 331–32.
[19] *Ibid.*

fallen into such sad disorder and that only the military could straighten them out again.

Despite his belief that the over-all trend of history was inevitably downward, Jien acknowledged that there could occasionally be a partial restoration of things. He saw an opportunity for the restoration of the political fortunes of the Fujiwara in 1219 when his great-grandnephew, Yoritsune (1218–56), was invited by the Hōjō to be shogun at Kamakura. To Jien the appointment of the youthful Yoritsune, whom the Hōjō in fact wanted simply to serve as a figurehead, portended a true union of court and shogunate with a Fujiwara minister serving the emperor in the additional capacity of chief of the military families.[20] Yet it was precisely at this time that the cloistered emperor Gotoba was plotting to overthrow the shogunate. Jien urged Gotoba to place his faith instead in the future of the Kamakura regime under Yoritsune.

The death of Yoritomo in 1199 had removed the central prop of fifteen years of military rule and had exposed his young sons, the shoguns Yoriie (1182–1204) and Sanetomo (1192–1219), to political disorder and finally to destruction. The struggle for power that ensued among the eastern chieftains brought to the fore the family of Hōjō Tokimasa (1138–1215). Tokimasa had acted as Yoritomo's guardian in Izu[21] and had remained a close personal adviser of the Minamoto chieftain during his ascent to military leadership. In 1205, however, Tokimasa fell abruptly from ruling circles as the result of a bizarre attempt to elevate a member of his second wife's family to the office of shogun. This placed Tokimasa's son, Yoshitoki (1163–1224), in a position to seize real control in Kamakura. Yoshitoki inherited from his father the headship of the administrative board, and in 1213 he also assumed leadership of the board of retainers.[22] The first office placed him in a key executive position, while the second gave him authority over the shogun's retainers as well as

[20] *Ibid.*, p. 336.

[21] After defeat of the Minamoto by the Taira in 1159 the young Yoritomo (then only twelve) had been banished to the eastern province of Izu.

[22] The first head of the board of retainers was Wada Yoshimori, an eastern chieftain who was one of Yoritomo's staunchest supporters. In 1213 Yoshitoki drove the Wada into revolt and seized this office for himself.

police control over the city of Kamakura. With this combination of powers Hōjō Yoshitoki assumed the office of shogunal regent (*shikken*), from which he and his successors thenceforth conducted government at Kamakura under figurehead shoguns, the first of which was Fujiwara Yoritsune.

One of the most striking characteristics of the Hōjō family of Kamakura times was their rise from relatively modest warrior origins to the height of military society. The Hōjō were an eastern branch of the Taira house; yet, like many other provincial Taira, they became disenchanted with the rule of Taira Kiyomori in Kyoto during the period 1160 to 1181. Hōjō Tokimasa came, on the contrary, to support the cause of Yoritomo during the Minamoto chieftain's exile in Izu. The tie between the two men was further strengthened by the marriage of Yoritomo to Tokimasa's daughter Masako (1157–1225). It appears, however, that this was Tokimasa's sole basis for political advancement. Unlike Kiyomori and Yoritomo, who were immediate descendants of leading Taira and Minamoto chieftains, Tokimasa had little family backing. As a Taira clansman, Tokimasa was qualified to hold administrative office in his native Izu; but he was by no means a power on the provincial level.

The scarcity of information concerning Tokimasa's background suggests that he and his kinsmen had gained little prominence before the Taira-Minamoto war. All members of the Hōjō house who became distinguished during the Kamakura period were descended directly from Tokimasa.[23] Even the vassal families that came to serve the Hōjō regents—the Bitō, the Nagasaki, the Suwa—did not form ties with the Hōjō until after the founding of the shogunate.[24] From these facts we can conclude that the victory of the Hōjō following Yoritomo's death marked the climax of a remarkable rise to political eminence of an obscure eastern warrior and his offspring. Even more remarkable is the fact that the Hōjō were able to perpetuate this eminence for more than a century. In this sense they were unique in rank-conscious Japan of the medieval period.

[23] Satō Shin'ichi, "Kamakura Bakufu Seiji no Sensei-ka ni tsuite," in Takeuchi Rizō, ed., *Nihon Hōken-sei Seiritsu no Kenkyū* (2d ed.), p. 98.
[24] *Ibid.*

[22]

The assassination of the shogun Sanetomo in 1219 brought to an end the line of Yoritomo and made secure the position of the shogunal regent, Hōjō Yoshitoki. Shortly thereafter Yoshitoki requested that the Kyoto court supply a prince of the blood to act as shogun in Kamakura. But the cloistered emperor Gotoba was in no mood to provide the Hōjō with an imperial figurehead to sanctify their usurpation of shogunal power and Yoshitoki had to settle for the young Fujiwara clansman who was Jien's great-grandnephew.

During the time of Yoritomo, relations between Kyoto and Kamakura had been handled smoothly through the good offices of Jien's brother, Kujō Kanezane. But Yoritomo's death in 1199 and the subsequent decline of Kanezane's influence at court caused a disruption in official communication between the two governments that was to continue for more than twenty years. During this period Gotoba and his supporters received irregular and not always accurate reports on the nature of the power struggle in Kamakura. They tended to interpret this struggle in terms of real deterioration of the shogunate as a ruling institution. Later events were to prove that this interpretation was quite incorrect. The struggle in Kamakura concerned not the existence of the shogunate itself, but who would exercise the highest power within its framework.

It was under these conditions that arrangements were made to install Yoritsune as shogun, and Jien attempted to dissuade Gotoba from acting precipitately against the shogunate. But the cloistered emperor rejected Jien's idealistic theorizations and in 1221 threw down the gauntlet before the Hōjō.[25] His challenge was founded partly on a grave miscalculation of the capacity of the Hōjō to rally support among the eastern families and partly on an exaggerated assessment of the military support he could muster in the central provinces. Within a month after Gotoba issued an edict branding Yoshitoki a rebel, a great army marched from Kamakura and

[25] Tsuda Sōkichi, who believes that the *Gukanshō* was written *after* the Jōkyū incident, suggests that Jien leveled praise and blame after the fact when it was clear who had succeeded and who had failed. "*Gukanshō* oyobi *Jinnō Shōtōki* ni okeru Shina no Shigaku Shisō," in Fuzanbō, *Hompō Shigaku Ronsō*, I, 499.

occupied Kyoto. Yoshitoki seems to have flouted an openly announced and widely publicized imperial order. Yet most shogunate vassals (or housemen, *goke'nin*) apparently regarded their loyalty to Kamakura as taking precedence over the higher, but more vaguely defined, allegiance they owed by tradition to the imperial family. Moreover, so restricted was the backing which Gotoba himself actually received during this struggle, known after the year period as the Jōkyū incident, that his rising cannot be regarded as a true counterrevolutionary threat to warrior rule in Kamakura.[26] The military campaign was brief, but the settlement of the Jōkyū incident was extremely important to the shogunate both economically and politically.

As a result of victory over Gotoba's imperial forces, the shogunate was able to confiscate more than three thousand estate lands belonging to courtiers and others who had joined the cloistered emperor. The appointment of stewards to these estates brought a vast increase in the geographical scope and practical power of the Kamakura government. It also created a new network of officials beholden to the Hōjō regents.

The early Kamakura Shogunate had had no effective control over the city of Kyoto,[27] a fact that contributed to estrangement of the governmental centers and that helped precipitate the Jōkyū incident. To prevent a recurrence of military action against the shogunate and to secure greater control over court affairs, Yoshitoki now founded a system of Kyoto deputies (*tandai*). These deputies (two in number) established their offices in the Rokuhara section of Kyoto and hence became known also as the Rokuhara deputies. They came to hold broad powers and in fact were the real administrators of affairs in those provinces westward from Owari (later, from Mikawa) during the remainder of the Kamakura age.

Yoshitoki set the precedent of assigning only high-ranking members of the Hōjō family as Rokuhara deputies. His first two appointees were his son Yasutoki (1183–1242) and his brother Tokifusa

---

[26] Uwayokote Masataka, "Jōkyū no Ran," in Iwanami Shoten, *Iwanami Kōza Nihon Rekishi*, V, 171.

[27] There was a constable posted to Kyoto, but he exercised no real authority and was quickly destroyed by Gotoba's supporters.

(1175–1240), cocommanders of the shogunate army during the
Jōkyū incident. Here we see the beginning of a process that was to
characterize shogunate rule from mid-Kamakura times: the appointment of an increasing number of Hōjō and their direct family
vassals to key posts both in Kamakura and the provinces. While the
Hōjō may have lacked family prestige and solidarity before Tokimasa, they paid careful attention to the cultivation of these qualities
during the years following their ascendancy. Not only did the Hōjō
build a powerful clan structure within their own bloodline, they
also acquired a number of sturdy vassal families. The result, by the
mid-Kamakura period, was an imposing dynastic system.

The principal factor in the success of this system was the concentra-
tion of authority in the hands of the Hōjō family head, known also
as the Tokusō (from an alternate name of Yoshitoki). During the
height of Hōjō power it became axiomatic that the Tokusō also
occupy the office of shogunal regent. There was to be no division
of interests between the Hōjō as a private family and as holders of
real power within the shogunate. On two occasions in the early
years regents were appointed who were not heads of the family:[28]
but they were clearly caretakers for the Tokusō, Hōjō Tokimune
(1251–84), until he reached his majority and assumed the regency in
1268. The private policies of the Hōjō gave an emphasis to family
solidarity that Minamoto Yoritomo had neglected.

In 1224 Yoshitoki died and was succeeded as Tokusō and shogunal regent by his son, Yasutoki. The following year Yoritomo's
wife Masako and the distinguished statesman Ōe Hiromoto (1148–
1225) also died within a month of each other. They were the last of
the great personalities who had supported Yoritomo during his
rise to power. Their disappearance from shogunate councils placed
Yasutoki, at forty-three, in a unique position of leadership; and
indeed Yasutoki's regency from 1224 until 1242 proved in many
ways a coming-of-age for military government in medieval Japan.

The years from Minamoto Yoritomo to Hōjō Yasutoki must be
regarded as transitional, in both legal and institutional terms, from
courtier to dominantly military government. This is not to suggest

[28] Nagatoki (regent 1256–63) and Masamura (regent 1264–68).

that warrior rule at any time during the Kamakura period extended to all corners of the country. Even through much of the succeeding Muromachi epoch there remained three distinct spheres of jurisdiction in Japan:[29] (1) the court sphere, centered in Kyoto and based on the Chinese-style codes and their supplements; (2) the sphere of autonomous estates; (3) the military sphere of the Kamakura and, later, the Muromachi shogunates. Little is known of precise legal and administrative practice in the estates; but from Kamakura times the military encroached ever more openly on both estate lands and jurisdiction. Disputes that arose between vassals of the shogun and estate holders were commonly decided under military codes. Hence the tendency was for warrior rule gradually to displace the estates.

Formal jurisdictional and legal procedure for the military was first set forth during the time of Yasutoki. It is in this sense that he represents the end of transition from the Heian to the Kamakura periods. From a more theoretical standpoint, it is also possible to contrast, as do many Japanese scholars, the political authoritarianism of Yoritomo with Yasutoki's rule by assembly government.[30] These scholars note that the early Hōjō succeeded in broadening the base of military government to meet the demands of eastern warrior families for a greater voice in affairs at Kamakura. They see completion of this broadening in the establishment of a council of state (hyōjōshū) by Yasutoki in 1225. Yasutoki also created the office of cosigner (rensho) to stand in an advisory capacity with the shogunal regent at the council's head. While appointment as cosigner always went to a high-ranking Hōjō (e.g., Tokifusa was the first appointee), no member of the family sat on the first council of state. By the time of Yasutoki's death in 1242, however, the Hōjō held five of nineteen seats.

Yasutoki, who sought to codify warrior rule and ethics in the Jōei Code of 1232, was a man whose views differed markedly from those of Jien. Rather than speculate on matters such as a merger of court and shogunate, Yasutoki attempted to define warrior government

---

[29] This division is followed by Ueki Shin'ichirō in *Goseibai Shikimoku Kenkyū*, p. 6.

[30] This contrast is, in fact, almost universally made in modern Japanese historical texts.

within the limits of shogunate administration that actually prevailed during his time. One of the most distinctive principles which he incorporated in the Jōei Code was that of auto-limitation or the self-restriction of jurisdiction.[31] The aim of Yasutoki and his advisers was not to deny or to threaten the existence of authority spheres outside their control. On the contrary, they were acutely conscious of the delicate relationships which the shogunate maintained with other groups in the country. They specifically acknowledged court and estate, as well as military, jurisdiction and sought to restrain their warrior followers from exceeding the bounds of their designated authorities.[32]

Like Jien, Yasutoki made frequent use of the term *dōri*, not in the sense of a mystical force or religious law but as a designation for the spirit and practice of warrior society. On the basis of his interpretation of *dōri*, Yasutoki attempted both to articulate the personal ethics of the warrior and to standardize the traditional rules of the society to which he belonged. Personal ethics of the warrior in early Kamakura times seem to have derived mainly from two sources: from the roots of provincial society itself in response to the long-standing need to maintain order by force of arms even at the lowest levels of social organization; and from Buddhism, especially its doctrine of negation, which to the warrior implied merger or negation of self in the service of one's lord.[33]

Yasutoki's interpretation of *dōri* as a principle or guide for standardization of the rules of warrior society reflected the highly conservative, and at the same time pragmatic, attitude which he held toward law and its enforcement. In the provisions of the Jōei Code we find him stressing points such as: (1) the sanctity of precedents, especially those laid down during the time of Yoritomo; (2) the strict imposition of penalties for contravention of the law; and (3) the need to exercise "reasonableness" or "common sense" in judicial cases not governable by precedent. The first two points comprised a legalistic affirmation of the generally accepted rules and

---

[31] Ishii Susumu, *Kamakura Bakufu*, in Chūō Kōron Sha, *Nihon no Rekishi*, VII, 405. Also Watsuji Tetsurō, *Nihon Rinri Shisō Shi*, II, 4.

[32] Ueki, *Goseibai Shikimoku Kenkyū*.

[33] Watsuji, *Nihon Rinri Shisō Shi*, I, 311.

procedures of warrior society and the third called for a rational and flexible approach to be taken in the subsequent expansion of those rules and procedures.

Hōjō Yasutoki can be seen to have instituted a code of personal conduct for the warrior as well as a practical legal system for his governance. In contrast to those of the courtier-priest Jien, Yasutoki's views seem eminently realistic. At the same time it must be remembered that Yasutoki directed his attention exclusively to warrior society, which was still largely confined geographically to the east and numerically to those who had been granted status as shogunate housemen. The ideal of national rule, so important to Jien, was not a matter of particular concern to Yasutoki. A member of the Fujiwara or of the imperial family to serve as shogun was deemed necessary for Hōjō claims to legitimacy; beyond that Yasutoki and his advisers saw no need to appeal for integration of a society that they believed to be divided clearly into several jurisdictions. Only with the passage of time and the further militarization of the land would it become necessary for prospective warrior hegemons to consider the need for a more comprehensive attitude toward the state and the manner in which it should be ruled. Meanwhile the events of the next century—especially the Mongol invasions and the attempted restoration of imperial rule in the midst of a dynastic schism—while reducing further the influence of the court in political affairs, served to stimulate a reinterpretation of the imperial institution itself in both religious and ethical terms and thus in a sense to strengthen its theoretical foundations.

We have seen that Buddhism entered Japan as part of a great process of reform and centralization. Political as well as religious leaders from at least the seventh century repeatedly stressed the importance of Buddhism as the guardian and protector of the new state that was emerging under Chinese influence. They designated as centers of national protection the Tōdaiji during the Nara period and the Enryakuji during the Heian period. The Tendai Buddhism of the Enryakuji, with its comprehensive and syncretic outlook, was especially well-suited to serve as the religious safekeeper of centralized imperial rule. It is significant that one of the most outspoken

proponents during the early Kamakura age of a return to the centralized polity of Nara-Heian times in which the Buddhist and imperial
laws had flourished together was Jien, several times head of the
Enryakuji.

Tendai Buddhism was the source from which all the new sects
of the Kamakura period sprang. The great religious figures of the
age—Hōnen (1133–1212), Shinran (1173–1262), Eisai (1141–1215),
Dōgen (1200–53), Nichiren (1222–82)—without exception received
their original training either at the Enryakuji or at one of the other
Tendai monastic centers. Each of these men came to espouse as the
central doctrine of his sect some aspect of Buddhism or Buddhist
practice that was already part of the Tendai synthesis—e.g., the
nembutsu (invocation of the name of Amida Buddha), meditation,
or the original tenets of the Lotus Sutra. Eisai, who later was
acknowledged as the founder of the Rinzai or "sudden enlightenment" school of Zen Buddhism in Japan, may appear to have been
the most conservative of this group insofar as he curried favor with
the ruling classes at both Kamakura and Kyoto and refused to regard
himself as a separatist from the Tendai church. Yet, in fact, it was
Nichiren who seems to have had the strongest attachment to the
old order.

Nichiren, who alone among these religious leaders rose from
truly humble origins as the son of a fisherman in the eastern provinces of Japan, was a religious fundamentalist. He, like so many of
his contemporaries, believed that the age in which he lived was one
of decline and degeneracy. Yet, unlike the other salvationists, who
held that the times permitted no alternative but utter reliance on the
saving grace of Amida Buddha, Nichiren called for a return to the
fundamental doctrines of the Lotus Sutra which Saichō had made
the basis of Tendai Buddhism. He wanted the restoration of an
imperially centered state with a revitalized Tendai church as its
protector. This state had declined because of the spread of false
Buddhist doctrines, such as the *nembutsu* and Zen, even within the
teachings of Tendai. Nichiren insisted that internal rebellion and
foreign aggression would bring disaster to Japan unless these false
teachings were stamped out. Only after the military leaders at
Kamakura refused to accept his demands did he increasingly come to

[29]

see himself as the savior who, with the aid of the Lotus Sutra, would establish a new and spiritually purer order when the final cataclysm arrived.

Another important development during the early medieval age was the restatement of the idea of state protection in Shinto, rather than Buddhist, terms. The concept of *shinkoku*, which first appeared in the *Nihon Shoki*,[34] held Japan to be the "land of the gods" or the "divine land" and, by extension, implied that the gods who created Japan would continue to act as its guardians. This was precisely the interpretation that evolved in the Kamakura period.

It may seem surprising that primitive Shinto had even been able to survive the inflow of vastly more sophisticated Buddhist doctrines some six to seven centuries earlier. Yet Shinto embraced some of the most basic sentiments and beliefs of the Japanese, and by the Nara period distinct efforts were being made to reconcile or synthesize it with Buddhism. This was done essentially through the process of identifying the divine beings of Buddhism with the more important of the native *kami*. Amaterasu, for example, was equated with the cosmic Buddha of Shingon Buddhism, Dainichi. In its completed form this reconciliation was succinctly expressed as *honji suijaku*, or "the essences (buddhas and bodhisattvas) have left traces (*kami*)"— i.e., the *kami* are secondary manifestations in Japan of the primary figures of Buddhism. Clearly Shinto was here regarded as little more than a derivative of Buddhism, a fact that contributed to the former's general lack of appeal in intellectual circles during succeeding centuries.

This is not to suggest that the vitality of Shinto declined everywhere. The esoteric Buddhist sects of the Heian period enjoyed popularity among the leisured aristocrats of the capital. To most provincial families and to the commoner class in general, worship of clan, agricultural, and local deities of Shinto remained a central part of everyday life. So widespread was *kami* worship (*jingi sūhai*) that, with the formation of private estates during Heian times, estate

[34] Kuroda Toshio, "Chūsei Kokka to Shinkoku Shisō" in Kawasaki, *et al.*, eds., *Nihon Shūkyō Shi Kōza*, I, 68. In the annals for Jingū in the *Nihon Shoki*, the king of the Korean state of Silla says: "I have heard that there is a land of the gods (*shinkoku*) in the east and that it is called Nihon."

holders came to see the advantage of supporting local Shinto shrines as focal points for the administration and control of the peasantry.[35] In this way Shinto assumed an increasingly important role in provincial affairs, a role further enhanced by the rise of the military.

In ruling circles as well Shinto began to take on new importance toward the end of the Heian and the beginning of the Kamakura periods. Although the *Gukanshō* is generally regarded as a study of history in Buddhist terms, we have seen that the thinking of its author Jien was steeped also in the myth and lore of Shinto. One of the most significant of Jien's interpretations was the clear distinction he drew between the age of the gods (*kamiyo*) and the historical period, commencing with Emperor Jimmu, which he made the starting point of his book. Authors of earlier works had tended to merge the affairs of gods and men. Jien, by placing the former beyond the purview of history, gave to the age of the gods an aura of sanctity and awe.[36]

As a further indication of the revival of interest in Shinto, study of the *Nihon Shoki*, with emphasis on the sections dealing with the age of the gods, was especially popular at court during the Kamakura period. A fundamental problem which faced Shinto scholars of this era was the need to overcome the widely held feelings of Buddhistic pessimism and impermanency that pervaded men's minds.[37] Ideas such as the end of the Buddhist law and "a hundred kings"[38] could not, in the final analysis, be reconciled with optimistic Shinto belief in the mandate of the imperial family to rule eternally. Jien had attempted, with questionable success, to blend Buddhist and Shinto concepts concerning the continuity of the imperial family during the final stages of historical decline. Other

---

[35] *Ibid.*, p. 75.

[36] Watsuji, *Nihon Rinri Shisō Shi*, I, 353.

[37] Nagahara Keiji, "Kitabatake Chikafusa," in Satō Shin'ichi, ed., *Nihon Jimbutsu Shi Taikei*, II, 124.

[38] "A hundred kings," like *mappō*, thinking was based on a terminal attitude toward history—that is, that all societies must ultimately and predictably decline and succumb. Since Juntoku, who was on the throne at the time Jien wrote the *Gukanshō*, was the 84th emperor of Japan, this meant that sixteen successors remained. By the time of Godaigo (the 96th emperor), there were only four. Hence Chikafusa found it necessary to attack with especial vigor belief in the legend that only a hundred kings would rule.

scholars made direct attack upon Buddhist doctrine. In the *Shaku Nihongi*, compiled about 1272, there is recorded a conversation between the Shinto teacher Urabe Kanebumi and a group of courtiers, including the imperial regent.[39] The topic of discussion was the apparent contradiction between the promise of Amaterasu that the imperial family would occupy the throne of Japan forever and the prevailing belief that the reigning dynasty would come to an end after a hundred kings. Kanebumi informed his listeners that "a hundred kings" should not be taken literally, but in a figurative sense to mean "a myriad kings." Far from portending the extinction of the imperial family, the concept of a hundred kings was a strong reaffirmation of the permanent nature of the imperial institution in Japan.

A distinctive characteristic of *kami* worship in early Japan was the great variety of deities that were revered throughout the land. This diversity made it difficult to organize worship above the local level, and increasingly Shinto thinkers of the Kamakura and early Muromachi periods sought to give more coherent national direction to *kami* worship. Without attempting to do away with belief in lesser *kami*, these thinkers for the most part stressed the preeminence in the Shinto pantheon of the Sun Goddess, Amaterasu, and encouraged a higher worship of her special shrine at Ise. According to the *Azuma Kagami*, Yoritomo himself acknowledged that, since all the land of the realm belonged ultimately to the Ise Shrine, effective rule could be instituted upon approval of the gods as revealed through the Ise Shrine.[40] We have noted the importance which Jien attached to the "will of the gods" (*shin'i*) in the molding of Japanese history. Even more significant, perhaps, was this reverence paid by a military leader such as Yoritomo to the same authority.

In addition to exalting the centrality of the Ise Shrine and its role in sactifying national rule, Yoritomo also sought to strengthen his personal control over the eastern warriors by directing their reverence toward Hachiman, the tutelary deity of the Minamoto clan. To Yoritomo, Hachiman was *gokoku no kami*, or the *kami* who pro-

[39] Recounted in Sakamoto Tarō, *Nihon no Shūshi to Shigaku*, pp. 123–25.
[40] Nagahara Keiji, "Chūsei no Sekai-kan," in Kawade Shobō, *Nihon Rekishi Kōza*, I, 136.

tects the state. By elevating the Tsurugaoka Hachiman Shrine to a leading position in shogunate ceremonies at Kamakura, the Minamoto chieftain underscored the importance he attached to *kami* worship as a tool of military government.[41]

Although it would be difficult, and quite beyond the scope of this study, to trace in detail the interplay of Buddhism and Shinto during the Kamakura period, some remarks must be made concerning the response of devout Buddhists to the revival of Shinto about this time. In the great popularization of Buddhism during this age the rapid growth of the Amidist sects of Pure Land and True Pure Land Buddhism was particularly striking. Among the first to react to the new competition of the Amidists were the Heian sects of Shingon and Tendai, which had been instrumental in the earlier movement to merge Buddhism and Shinto—Shingon by founding Ryōbu (Dual) Shinto and Tendai through its Sannō Shinto. One of the principal arguments that followers of the older sects used to counter Amidist popularity was that Amidism was simply a phenomenon of a period of the end of the Buddhist law and that its practices, which called upon men to place absolute faith in the saving grace of Amida during a time when all other so-called methods for betterment or salvation had failed, could not be reconciled with Shinto.[42]

Although the great founders of Amidism in Japan, Hōnen and Shinran, showed little inclination to compromise with Shinto, later leaders of the new sects, such as Ippen (1239–89), not only accepted *kami* worship but even affirmed the tradition of identifying buddhas and bodhisattvas with the Shinto gods. Thus, despite the enormous success of the Amidist sects in propagating their simple formula for salvation, Amidist preachers were forced to recognize the practical need to accommodate or to reconcile their beliefs with the deep-rooted devotion of the Japanese people to *kami* worship.[43]

The most important phase in the reorganization of Shinto during the early medieval period was the formulation of so-called Ise Shinto. Ise Shinto was closely associated with the movement about this time to assert the primacy of Shinto over Buddhism, as reflected

[41] *Ibid.*
[42] Yomiuri Shimbun Sha, *Nihon no Rekishi*, V, 251.
[43] *Ibid.*, p. 252.

in the slogan *shimpon butsujaku*: the Shinto *kami* are the "essences" and the Buddhist divinities are the "traces." [44] It also came to exert a strong influence on the writings of men like Kitabatake Chikafusa and thus to bear directly on the larger questions of dynastic succession and imperial rule, which were central to the Kemmu Restoration and to the events that surrounded it. In its origins, however, Ise Shinto was less the product of purely doctrinal inspiration than of economic and factional pressures within the organization of the Ise Shrine.

The Shinto establishment at Ise consisted of two main parts: an inner shrine (*naikū*) and an outer shrine (*gekū*). The inner shrine was constructed to house the spirit of the Sun Goddess, Amaterasu, while the outer shrine was dedicated to a god of the harvest, Toyouke-no-kami. Both these component shrines were served on a hereditary basis by special priestly families, the Arakida in the inner shrine and the Watarai in the outer. Since the inner shrine was older and unquestionably enjoyed greater prestige than the outer shrine, it became customary for successive generations of the Watarai family to seek to improve their position either by calling for a closer merger of the shrines or by claiming the superiority of the outer over the inner shrine. Special circumstances gave the Watarai their best opportunity after the establishment of military government at Kamakura.

In earlier centuries the imperial court had maintained responsibility for the upkeep of the Ise Shrine. With the decline of the court's financial structure about mid-Heian times, however, government funds paid to Ise began to dwindle. Officials of the shrine were forced to seek additional income and soon entered into competition with the other major institutional and familial entities of the age for the acquisition of landed estates. The holdings they gathered for the Ise Shrine came to be known by the special term *mikuriya*, and revenue derived therefrom provided amply for the upkeep and activities of the shrine until the Kamakura period, when stewards and other representatives of the military began to appropriate or to withhold increasing portions of the rice income normally payable to Ise. Again shrine officials were forced to seek new sources of revenue. This time they directed their efforts into intensive campaigns to

[44] See discussion in Nakamura Naokatsu, *Yoshino-chō Shi*, pp. 24–28.

encourage people to journey as pilgrims to Ise and to make votive offerings to the shrine. Because tradition decreed that only the imperial family could have direct access to the precincts of the Ise Shrine, it was necessary to appoint intermediaries, known as *oshi*, to deal with the pilgrims and to receive their offerings. It was as a result of competition between *oshi* of the inner and outer shrines that the earliest form of Ise Shinto developed.

Ise Shinto ultimately became a strong reaffirmation both of the supreme holiness of Amaterasu and, by extension, of the primacy of the imperial family as her direct descendants on earth. Through Ise Shinto, worship of many *kami* was channeled upward to become a higher worship of Amaterasu. It is ironic, therefore, that the first statements of Ise Shinto should be made not in exaltation of Amaterasu, but as a challenge to her position.

The Watarai family and their *oshi* were very aggressive in their campaigns to promote "Ise visiting (*Ise-mairi*)." Yet they found themselves constantly at a disadvantage in seeking to obtain offerings for their patron deity when people had the alternative of donating their money to Amaterasu and the inner shrine. Accordingly, the Watarai sought to demonstrate, by whatever means possible, that the outer shrine was either equal to or the superior of the inner shrine. Their most important claim was that the harvest god of the outer shrine was in reality Kunitoko-tachi-no-mikoto, the first deity to appear in Shinto mythology and therefore a personage quite senior to the later-born Amaterasu.[45] They cited as their source of authority the *Shintō Gobusho*, a collection of texts supposedly of great antiquity but proven by later scholars to be a product of the Kamakura period, possibly compiled under the auspices of the Watarai themselves.[46]

The texts of the *Shintō Gobusho* were not carefully written or logically constructed, but were collections of random borrowing from a number of systems: Confucianism, Taoism, *yin-yang*, five elements, etc.[47] It can scarcely be imagined that they attracted many

---

[45] Yomiuri Shimbun Sha, *Nihon no Rekishi*, p. 254.
[46] Kuroda Toshio, *Mōko Shūrai*, in Chūō Kōron Sha, *Nihon no Rekishi*, VIII, 154.
[47] *Ibid.*, p. 155.

readers during the Kamakura period. Yet the *Shintō Gobusho*, as a scriptural basis for Ise Shinto, did underscore two important tendencies of the day: Shinto thinkers were turning more and more away from Buddhism; and Shinto itself was being invested with ethical qualities, however rudimentary they might be at this early stage.

When Kitabatake Chikafusa returned to Ise in 1336 to prepare for the removal of Godaigo's court to that region, he was met by both Watarai Ieyuki, then eighty-one years of age, and Arakida Okitoki. The Kitabatake were a great family of Ise Province and Chikafusa's interest in the scholars of the Ise Shrine is well known. Later generations were to consider the *Jinnō Shōtōki* a classic of Ise Shinto thought. This is probably an exaggeration, since Chikafusa's interests extended to matters far beyond the purview of Shinto. Nevertheless, we can see even in his opening lines the strong influence of the Ise school: "Great Japan is the divine land. Its foundations were first laid by Kunitokotachi-no-mikoto and it has been ruled since time immemorial by the descendants of Amaterasu Ōmikami. This is true only of our country; there are no examples among foreign lands. It is for this reason that we call our land the divine land."

The next important stage in the development of Shinto thought during the Kamakura era was the period of the Mongol invasions of 1274 and 1281. I shall discuss in the next chapter the effects of the invasions on Hōjō rule. Suffice it to note here that the Kamakura regime had become overextended. The continuing deterioration of the estate system of landholding, upon which shogunate leaders relied for the maintenance of control in distant provinces, and the appearance of warrior groups not beholden to Kamakura were simply two factors that contributed to the decentralizing tendencies of the late thirteenth and fourteenth centuries. The need to deal with the threat of foreign attack at coastal points distant from Kamakura further increased the problems of provincial administration already besetting the Hōjō.

Never before in recorded history had a foreign country attempted to invade the Japanese isles. Because of the uniqueness of these occurrences during the early medieval period, later Japanese tended to exaggerate and even to distort the circumstances surrounding the Mongol invasions. It was not difficult for subsequent generations to imagine the people of the thirteenth century rising spontaneously to repulse a foreign aggressor, or to envision the galvanization of a spirit of Japanese nationalism in the face of continuing outside threat. In fact, the burden of repulsing the foreign aggressor fell almost entirely on a limited group of warrior families in Kyushu, with the vast majority of the Japanese people having no contact whatsoever with the invasions.

Even so, there can be little doubt that the psychological impact of the Mongol invasions on the literate or informed sectors of Japanese society was profound. At the very least the invasions gave the Japanese a new sense of awareness of their national existence apart from other countries. When *kamikaze*, or "divine winds," arose on both occasions to destroy the Mongol fleets, this awareness was transformed into a distinct feeling of Japanese uniqueness and superiority. The warriors of Kyushu had fought desperately and at great sacrifice against the Mongol intruders; yet popular sentiment held that the key to victory was not Japanese arms, but the efficacy of Japanese prayers to the *kami* protectors of their land.

At the height of the second invasion attempt in 1281 the priests of the Iwashimizu Hachiman Shrine had gathered to beseech the gods to prevent the devastation of Japan by the Mongols. As they prayed the priests were astonished to see that, although there was no wind at all that night, the emblems at the entrance to the shrine were fluttering briskly. A short while later, when word arrived from Kyushu that a second great *kamikaze* had blown the Mongols out to sea, the Hachiman priests gave thanks to the gods for answering their prayers so speedily.

In this chapter I have attempted, as a prelude to examining in greater detail the origins of the Kemmu Restoration, to trace the development of several interrelated strains of thought during the Kamakura period concerning matters such as the rise of the military, the idea of state protection, and the revival of Shinto. The Restoration itself was ostensibly an attempt by the imperial court to resume power after destruction of the Kamakura Shogunate. But it would be a mistake to regard this attempt as simply a naked play for political power. The main participants in the Restoration and its aftermath were variously motivated—some as much religiously as politically or economically—to act as they did. Even though the real power of the court and its direct supporters declined steadily throughout the Kamakura period, concepts such as *shinkoku* ("land of the gods" or "divine land") had come to inject a new intellectual vigor into court society by the time of the Kemmu Restoration. We have noted that the idea of state protection in Japan originated with Buddhism but that during the twelfth and thirteenth centuries it came to be seen also as the function of the Shinto gods and, on a more practical level, of the military. The experience of the Mongol invasions and the *kamikaze* confirmed in a strongly religious sense that the most powerful of these sources of protection were the *kami*, and that Japan alone enjoyed its divine benefits. The potentiality for such a claim to uniqueness was, of course, inherent in Shinto from earliest times. But it was not until the events and intellectual developments of the Kamakura period that *shinkoku*, with the meaning of "divinely protected land," came to be widely recognized as a special quality of the Japanese state. It remained for the events of the Kemmu Restoration to impel Chikafusa to translate *shinkoku* from a general concept of divine protection into a positive reaffirmation of faith in the imperial family and its line of legitimate sovereigns.

II

Decline of the Kamakura Shogunate and Dispute over Imperial Succession

IT IS POSSIBLE to analyze much of Japan's early political history in terms of competition for power among the families that constituted its ruling aristocracy. The position of the imperial family was of course unique, since access to the throne was the principal goal in all interfamily competition. In another sense the imperial family was much like the others, insofar as it too was obliged at times to contend openly for power. This was especially true from the eleventh century when cloistered emperors, as ranking members of the imperial family, began to challenge the long-standing dominance of the Fujiwara at Kyoto. Warrior families of the twelfth century, by adding the element of military coercion, opened a new dimension of family competition. At the same time they also operated to a great extent within the traditional political framework set by the older houses.

Since the history of the final years of the Kamakura period was centered on the affairs of two families—the Hōjō and the imperial family—further comment should be made on the nature of the aristocratic family and how it functioned as a political unit.

One of the first aims of the family was to perpetuate itself economically, an aim that could best be achieved through the acquisition of private, heritable holdings in land. During the Nara and Heian periods the elite court families, headed by the Fujiwara, accumulated vast income-producing estates in contravention of the principle of public domain set forth in the Taika Reform. Later the imperial family (after establishment of the office of cloistered emperor) and the provincial warrior families followed similar processes of estate acquisition.

The family also stressed hierarchical solidarity, both from the obvious need for self-defense and in order to compete as effectively as possible with the other family units for political power. It became customary for the family to concentrate authority in a head and to empower him to hold concurrently the highest public position to which the family was entitled. The Fujiwara family head (*uji no chōja*) was ideally the imperial regent, and the chief of the Minamoto, under normal circumstances, was preeminently entitled to assume the office of shogun. There were of course times when this concurrence of private and public leadership did not hold true. Such departures from normal practice usually implied internal family discord, a weakening of public authority, or a combination of both.

The case of the Hōjō during the early Kamakura period is an excellent example of the importance attached to family backing and solidarity by contenders for political power in the early medieval age. Although of modest origins, the Hōjō, once in power, strove to strengthen themselves as a politically functioning family unit. The principle by which the office of shogunal regent was reserved exclusively for the Hōjō family head (Tokusō) was the cornerstone of continued Hōjō success. There could be no question where highest authority lay, either in private family matters or in public decision-making. Moreover, the greatest potential threat to any house—the succession dispute—was minimized by the Hōjō.

The passage of time and altered political and economic conditions, especially after the Mongol invasions, brought pressures to bear on both the Hōjō and the imperial family. The manner in which these families reacted set the stage for the decline of the Kamakura Shogunate and inauguration of the Kemmu Restoration. Comparison of the two houses is particularly interesting: while one sought to sustain its position by tightening private family controls, the other, long deprived of real power, fell to quarreling over public succession and finally split into two distinct branches.

The manner in which the Hōjō functioned as a political unit can best be understood by making clear certain aspects of legal and institutional development during this early period of military rule. First, there was at this time no absolute distinction between the legislative and judicial functions of government. Yasutoki provided a foundation of law based on military precedent and custom in the

Jōei Code. From then on it became the highest responsibility of the Kamakura Shogunate to issue judicio-legislative decrees in response to suits brought before it. The majority of these suits concerned disputes over land. This is hardly surprising in view of the exclusively agrarian base upon which the shogunate stood. It was vital to the success of military government that problems involving holdings in land be speedily and equitably settled. Minamoto Yoritomo had exercised this power directly and personally. His judicial arm, the board of inquiry, was authorized only to hear testimony and to compile evidence; final judgement rested solely with Yoritomo.

Under the Hōjō, on the other hand, this judicio-legislative power came to rest with the council of state. The council in turn used both the board of inquiry and the administrative board to prepare suits and to aid in legal processing. These boards did not compete with each other, but operated within separate and specially defined areas of responsibility. They received suits on the basis not of the nature of the suits themselves, but on their geographic places of origin. Thus the administrative board handled petitions originating within the city of Kamakura, while the board of inquiry processed those submitted by people living outside the military capital.[1] This sense of geographic division within the judicial structure is a significant commentary on the development of the shogunate itself. It does not, as we shall see, imply that the administrative board, in dealing exclusively with cases that emanated from Kamakura, was somehow superior to the board of inquiry. Rather it appears to reflect the piecemeal growth of the shogunate. That is, the shogunate was essentially an eastern power and only gradually was able to extend its control to other sections of the country. Even at the end of the Kamakura period, great tracts of land still remained outside its effective jurisdiction. Shogunate leaders tended to think constantly in geographic terms—e.g., to distinguish between the shogunate seat in Kamakura and the rest of the country, or between the eastern provinces and those in the west.

In addition to being classified by the geographic place of origin,

---

[1] Satō Shin'ichi, *Kamakura Bakufu Soshō Seido no Kenkyū*, p. 35.

legal suits of the military sphere during the Kamakura period were also distinguished according to the social status of the parties involved. For this purpose the shogunate recognized three broad social groups: shogunal housemen (*goke'nin*), nonhousemen (*higoke'nin*) and commoners (*zatsunin*). It is difficult to determine precisely how this separation of suits according to litigant status was applied during the early years of Hōjō rule. References from various sources indicate that nonhousemen and commoner suits from Kamakura went through the administrative board, while those originating outside the city were processed by the board of inquiry. Unfortunately the important question of which body handled houseman suits at this time has not been fully answered, although one authority believes they may have gone through the board of inquiry regardless of their places of origin.[2]

This type of judicial procedure determined by place of origin and social status, then, was a natural outgrowth of the shogunate's early development as an eastern military power seeking to extend its jurisdiction to other parts of the land. Toward the end of the Kamakura period these determinants gave way to a division of suits at law based on the nature of the actions or disputes from which they arose. Thus distinction came to be made between petitions resulting from criminal behavior and those arising from disputes over property, and, further, between those relating to fixed property and to movable property.[3] But let us turn to certain other developments within the judicio-legislative sphere of the shogunate at mid-Kamakura that were to have an important influence on the nature of Hōjō rule during its final years.

The Hōjō were ever anxious to maintain and improve the efficiency of their judicial machinery. When in the year 1243 they observed that poor attendance and general neglect of duty were beginning to affect proper functioning of the council of state, they divided the council (which then consisted of thirteen members) into three sections, each to convene five days per month. Their hope was that smaller groups would be able to adjudge more rapidly and

---

[2] *Ibid.*, p. 36.
[3] *Ibid.*, pp. 59–62.

equitably the mounting number of claims entering the judicial channels of the shogunate.[4]

In 1246 the regent Tsunetoki (1214–46) died and was succeeded by his younger brother, Tokiyori (1227–63), who was then only nineteen years of age. A group of eastern chieftains, with the former Fujiwara shogun Yoritsune—the great grandnephew (now an adult) in whom Jien had placed so much hope for a union of court and military—at their head, chose this occasion to plot against the Hōjō. The incident was speedily settled when Tokiyori discovered their plans in advance and hustled Yoritsune back to Kyoto. Nevertheless, the new regent feared that further discontent among the shogunal housemen might lead to more serious rebellion. He therefore decided to seek, as an antidote for this discontent, even greater efficiency in the handling of legal claims, especially those involving housemen. An additional body attached to the council of state and devoted primarily to the processing of houseman suits would, he felt, bring renewed confidence in the worthiness of the shogunate.

Accordingly Tokiyori established in 1249 the board of coadjutors (*hikitsukeshū*) to join the administrative board and the board of inquiry as a judicial adjunct to the council of state. From its inception the board of coadjutors came to occupy a position superior to its sister bodies. Not only did the coadjutors hold sole responsibility for houseman claims, they also possessed authority to review cases that the other boards were unable to process efficiently.[5] And in subsequent years, when it became customary for warriors qualified by birth for membership on the council of state to serve first with the coadjutors, this board gained further prominence as a training ground for many of the highest ranking officers in Kamakura.

In its early years at least, the board of coadjutors fulfilled admirably Tokiyori's aim of expanding and strengthening the judicio-legislative process of the shogunate. But after the Mongol invasions, as we shall see, it also became one of the avenues by which the Hōjō were able to establish a family monopoly within the council of state and to destroy the council's usefulness as an impartial deliberative assembly.

[4] *Ibid.*, p. 46.
[5] *Ibid.*, p. 54.

There can be no question that the Mongol invasions marked a turning point in the fortunes of the Kamakura Shogunate. Yet it is not sufficient to say simply that the burden of repulsing the Mongol expeditionary forces and of maintaining a defense perimeter in Kyushu for several decades thereafter so weakened the shogunate that it was no longer able to continue as an effective national government. The Mongol threat was in fact a catalyst that served to accelerate more fundamental economic and social processes that would have resulted in the collapse of the Kamakura Shogunate sooner or later.

The foundation of this first shogunate lay chiefly in its houseman structure, its network of retainers located in estates and provinces throughout the land. But the passage of time inevitably brought a weakening of this structure. Growth of commerce, for example, caused distress and the loss of holdings among many housemen, especially the stewards, who found their fixed and seasonal incomes from land insufficient to meet the ever-rising costs of a period of extended peace. The alienation of steward holdings was further hastened by the custom of divided inheritance, which often resulted in the fragmentation of family lands upon the passing of each generation. Finally, blood and other personal ties, which had originally linked distant housemen closely to Kamakura, came ultimately to be replaced by local commitments and loyalties. In this way a broad process of decentralization was set in motion that Kamakura found impossible to control.

Hōjō leaders were well aware of the financial difficulties that beset the shogunal housemen from about the mid-thirteenth century. After several preliminary attempts to prevent the alienation of houseman lands and holdings, the Hōjō finally sought solution to this problem through the issuance of "virtuous administration" (*tokusei*) decrees —decrees that were in effect little more than outright demands for debt-cancellation.[6] Far from achieving the desired purpose of placing the houseman structure once more on a sound financial footing, these decrees seem to have had the long-range effect (after a temporary disruption of credit relations) of driving the stewards

---

[6] The first *tokusei* was issued in 1297.

and others to increasingly greater reliance on the merchant and the money-lender.[7]

Of more immediate danger to the Hōjō after mid-century was the emergence in the central and western provinces of a new group of warriors (*kokujin*) outside the control of the shogunate's regional administration. The appearance of these warriors at this time was, in large part, a natural result of the continuing breakdown of the estate system. Failure of estate orderliness forced large- and middle-scale peasants not only to take up arms in defense of their own lands, but also to group with others for mutual protection. The Hōjō unflatteringly labeled such groups *akutō*, or "rowdy bands," but they greatly feared their inherent threat to shogunate rule. Left alone, these bands would undoubtedly continue to disrupt provincial administration.

Hence, when the Hōjō found themselves faced with the need in the 1270s to provide for the defense of Kyushu against invasion by Mongol forces from the mainland, they turned for military support not only to their shogunal housemen, but also to these *akutō* warriors.[8] This seemed an excellent way to reduce lawlessness in the west and at the same time to channel the energies of these non-housemen into a worthwhile effort. But in thus engaging outsiders to join in the defense of Kyushu, the Hōjō jeopardized the entire theoretical foundation of the Kamakura Shogunate. For the principal bond that tied the houseman warrior to the shogunate (or, more specifically, to the shogun, even though he was by this time a puppet of the Hōjō regents) was his willingness to render devoted military service in the event of war and to perform symbolic guard duty in time of peace. This responsibility for military service and guard duty was assumed by the houseman as part of a personal vow of loyalty to his military lord (the shogun). It was the houseman's *exclusive right* to undertake such responsibility. Once the lord or his deputy began to grant this right indiscriminately to others,

---

[7] Many warriors were so dependent on the services of the moneylender that they could not afford to accept debt-cancellation and thereby incur his future displeasure. Furthermore, moneylenders frequently included clauses in subsequent contracts stating that *tokusei* decrees would not apply.

[8] For a discussion of *akutō*, see Yasuda Motohisa, *Nihon Zenshi*, IV, 200–2.

they violated a relationship of sacred trust and encouraged a confusion of loyalties that could only lead to the ultimate dissolution of the Kamakura vassalage system itself.

To the further distress of the Hōjō, the Mongol invasions, unlike the typical civil struggles of medieval Japan, provided no plunder for distribution among the victorious. It was customary for military leaders of this period to reward not only their active followers but also the great religious institutions which prayed vigorously for victory. In the final decades of the thirteenth century the Hōjō were so besieged for reward from both warriors and religious institutions that their judicial system became dangerously overtaxed.

Thus the later Hōjō regents found their power position in the shogunate increasingly threatened, both from within and from without, by growing discontent and disorder. They reacted by drawing to themselves ever greater powers of government: (1) by accelerating the appointment of Hōjō clan members and vassals to high offices at Kamakura and in the provinces; (2) by gradually transferring the decision-making process of the council of state and its adjuncts to their own private family meetings (*yoriai*).

We have seen that the early Hōjō, even while laying the foundation for assembly rule within the shogunate, were careful to place ranking members of their family in key administrative posts. Apart from the office of shogunal regent itself, these included the two deputyships at Kyoto and the associative position of cosigner at Kamakura. The Hōjō were especially anxious, in this manner, to strengthen their family as a unit. By decreeing that the private powers of the Hōjō family head (Tokusō) and the public duties of the shogunal regent be exercised at all times by the same Hōjō chieftain, they made careful provision to minimize discord within their own ranks.

We have already observed that, while no Hōjō sat on the first council of state, by the time of Yasutoki's death in 1242 the family held five of nineteen positions. Some twenty-five to thirty years later they had increased their holdings in seats to nearly half of the council's total.[9] The principal means that the Hōjō used to secure this near-monopoly after the mid-century was by assignment of

[9] Satō, "Kamakura Bakufu Seiji no Sensei-ka ni tsuite," pp. 100–2.

family members to the board of coadjutors. This board, it will be recalled, served not only as the main organ for the processing of houseman claims, but also as a training ground for prospective appointees to the council of state.

The aim of the Hōjō in thus seeking to monopolize seats on the council of state was not simply to secure a dominant voice in the decision-making process of that body. While this may have been behind some of the early Hōjō appointments to the council, it became clear toward the end of the century that the real intention of the Hōjō leaders was, on the contrary, to deprive the council of effective power. This can be observed most strikingly by examination of the age distribution of council members at various intervals during the thirteenth and early fourteenth centuries.

Toward the end of the Kamakura period the average age of new appointees to the council of state declined steadily.[10] During the early years of the council (following its establishment in 1225), approximately one third of its members were over fifty, and of the remainder none was under twenty-five. By the period from 1302 until the fall of the shogunate in 1333, however, three of eight new appointees were in their thirties, while two were in their early twenties and three were nineteen or under.

Thus the council of state came increasingly to be occupied by young and inexperienced people, many of whom were members of the Hōjō family itself. As the council's effectiveness as a deliberative assembly declined proportionately, Hōjō leaders began to transfer its decision-making powers to their own family meetings held at the private home of the Hōjō regent. Although the origin of these meetings can be traced to an earlier period, it was really from the time of Tokimune (regent, 1268–84) that they became politically important.[11] Those who attended included, at first, not only members of the Hōjō family, but also their private vassals (*miuchi*), certain prominent figures from the council of state, and chieftains like Adachi Yasumori (1231–85), who had special relations with the Hōjō.[12] Later the number of outside participants declined and

---

[10] Satō Shin'ichi provides a chart showing this decline, *ibid.*, p. 111.

[11] Yasuda, *Nihon Zenshi*, p. 221.

[12] He was, in fact, the maternal grandfather of the future regent Sadatoki.

these meetings came to be dominated by the Hōjō and their vassals.

It is important to understand the special status of the personal vassals of the Hōjō during the Kamakura period. The office of shogunal regent, it will be recalled, was originally formed by combining the headships of the administrative board and the board of retainers. For practical purposes the Hōjō regents usually appointed their leading vassals as successive vice-heads of the board of retainers[13] and gave them authority to conduct the affairs of that body. This meant that the direct vassals of the Hōjō were allowed to participate in high-level government at Kamakura and, as acting heads of the board of retainers, to exercise leadership over the shogunal housemen of the land. But the transfer of power from the council of state to the private family meetings of the Hōjō toward the end of the century brought change not only to the office of regent itself, but also to the status of these Hōjō vassals.

From the beginning the leader of the Hōjō occupied a position as both public official and private family head, as was typical of leaders of premodern aristocratic houses. During the period of normal functioning of the council of state, his public role as shogunal regent at the head of the council was the more important. But with the growing formalization of Hōjō family meetings after mid-century, the Hōjō leader's position as Tokusō, or private family head, became crucial, for it was chiefly in this capacity that he sought to direct affairs at Kamakura.[14] From a theoretical as well as a practical standpoint this shift in function from public regent to private Tokusō was highly significant, characterizing as it did the broad change from assembly rule to Hōjō authoritarianism. In this process of change the Hōjō came to rely more and more on their personal vassals. This in turn made sharper the difference between these vassals, who owed

---

[13] The head of the board of retainers was titled *bettō* and the vice-head *shoshi*.

[14] In the final years of Hōjō rule the principle that Tokusō and regent should be the same person was completely abandoned. For example the last Tokusō, Hōjō Takatoki, withdrew from the regency in 1325. For the last eight years of the Kamakura period Hōjō vassals, Kanazawa Sadaaki and Akabashi Moritoki, served as regents.

allegiance to the Hōjō, and the shogunal housemen, who theo-retically paid direct homage to the shogun.

After the death of Tokimune in 1284, his young son Sadatoki (1271–1311) became regent and Tokusō. A great rivalry arose at this time between Adachi Yasumori, as a leading shogunal houseman and eastern chieftain, and Taira Yoritsuna (d. 1294), then the most influential of the Hōjō vassals. In 1285 Yoritsuna charged the Adachi family with planning rebellion and persuaded the regent to take military action against them. The resulting struggle, known as the Shimotsuki (Eleventh Month) incident, brought destruction to the house of Adachi. But its repercussions extended far beyond this single eastern family, for those who supported the Adachi carried the fighting even to the northern provinces of Kyushu.[15] It became clear that houseman discontent over the growing trend toward Hōjō authoritarianism was more widespread than had been suspected. At the same time, removal of the Adachi from Hōjō family councils served only to increase this trend and to strengthen the position of the Hōjō vassals *vis-à-vis* the shogunal housemen.

After the Eleventh Month incident, Taira Yoritsuna wielded great power within the new Hōjō structure of rule. But so glaring was his abuse of this power and so corrupt were his ways that in 1293 the adult Sadatoki, in order to protect his own position, attacked and destroyed Yoritsuna, his kin, and his closest followers. This new incident did not signal a decline in the influence of the Hōjō vassals as a group, for the fall of the Taira simply brought to the fore the family of the Nagasaki. Nevertheless it did impel Sadatoki to seek governmental reform. Then, as from the outset of Hōjō rule, the most important function of military government lay in the handling of legal claims. Yet misuse of the board of coadjutors and emasculation of the council of state had greatly impaired Kama-kura's judicio-legislative process. In the same year (1293) Sadatoki abolished the board of coadjutors and appointed special agents (*shissō*) to transmit legal claims directly to him. For all practical purposes this transfer of judicio-legislative power from the regular institutions of the Kamakura Shogunate to the hands of Sadatoki as

[15] For a detailed discussion of this subject see Taga Munehaya, "Hōjō Shikken Seiji no Igi," in *Kamakura Jidai no Shisō to Bunka*, pp. 288–320.

private head of the Hōjō family marked completion of the trend toward political authoritarianism of the Hōjō at Kamakura. Before the end of the year Sadatoki did, in fact, reinstitute the board of coadjutors, but it never regained its former position of authority.

In addition to assuming authoritarian political powers in the military capital, the Hōjō also sought to strengthen their position in the provinces by appointing an increasing number of family members and personal vassals to constableships throughout the land.[16] As in the case of their early efforts to place clansmen in high administrative posts at Kamakura and Kyoto, the Hōjō from the beginning took each opportunity to assign their people to constable vacancies. Two special opportunities did arise after the Jōkyū incident of 1221 and after destruction of the Miura family in 1247.[17] But the trend toward monopolization of these posts became especially significant from the time of the Mongol invasions, which the Hōjō used as an excuse to appoint their people as constables to the provinces of the San'yōdō, San'indō, and Kyushu. By the end of the Kamakura period the Hōjō held or controlled through their vassals no less than thirty constable positions, or nearly one half the national total.

Family solidarity and efficient administration of warrior society based on just laws and assembly government were the principal ingredients of early Hōjō success. In the face of mounting difficulties from the mid-century on, as we have seen, the Hōjō sought to draw greater power to themselves by transferring the decision-making process from public organs of the shogunate to private family councils. In this way they were able to avoid disputes over succession, so frequent a concomitant of declining family influence in the premodern period. Through the institution of the Tokusō, the Hōjō may even have extended their period of rule at Kamakura beyond its normal life expectancy.

Disputes over succession represented a complex phenomenon in medieval Japan, and generalizations are difficult. Even so, we can

---

[16] For statistics on this process see Satō Shin'ichi, *Kamakura Bakufu Shugo Seido no Kenkyū*, pp. 181–86.

[17] The Miura had plotted with the former Fujiwara shogun, Yoritsune.

note certain characteristics of earlier disputes that should be helpful in analyzing the conflict which arose within the imperial family toward the end of the thirteenth century.

Imperial succession disputes had erupted between Temmu and Kōbun (r. 671–72) in 672 and between Saga (r. 809–23) and Heizei (r. 806–9) in 810. In both cases the issue was the throne and was speedily settled (in favor of Temmu and Saga) by the use of arms. The next prominent dispute was between the ex-emperor Sutoku and Emperor Goshirakawa during the Hōgen incident of 1156. This time the prize was headship of the imperial family following the death of the cloistered emperor Toba. Again it was decided (in Goshirakawa's favor) by military force. Had Sutoku been victorious, he would presumably have assumed the office of cloistered emperor immediately. Goshirakawa, however, remained emperor and did not open his cloistered office until 1158. Intertwined with the imperial struggle at this time was dispute over succession to the headship of the Fujiwara. Decline in the fortunes of the Fujiwara from the eleventh century brought internal quarreling and division.[18] Family leaders aligned themselves on both sides during the Hōgen incident and again during the Heiji incident of 1159, but achieved no lasting settlement. By the early Kamakura period the Fujiwara clan had fragmented into five distinct branch families.[19]

One fact emerged from the experiences of the imperial and Fujiwara families. As the military continued to consolidate power in their hands, it was they who increasingly became the real arbiters in court succession disputes. Goshirakawa won over Sutoku simply because the Taira and Minamoto who backed him were victorious in combat with Sutoku's supporters. Various Fujiwara leaders rose and fell during these years according to the fortunes of their warrior allies. After the founding of the Kamakura Shogunate, the most successful Fujiwara contenders for public position were those who were willing to serve the shogunate at court—for example, Kujō Kanezane, Kujō Michiie (1193–1252), and the heads of the Saionji branch from the time of Kintsune (1171–1244).

---

[18] Fujiwara Yorinaga was made family head even though this older brother, Tadamichi, held the position of imperial regent (*kampaku*).
[19] Ichijō, Nijō, Kujō, Konoe, and Takatsukasa.

Following Gotoba's abortive attempt to overthrow the Hōjō, the order of imperial succession came to be decided solely by Kamakura. In 1221 the Hōjō placed Gotoba's nephew, Gohorikawa (r. 1221–32), on the throne. Gohorikawa was succeeded by his son, Shijō (r. 1232–42), who died suddenly in 1242 (aged eleven) without a successor. The two leading ministers at that time in Kyoto— Saionji Kintsune and Kujō Michiie—proposed a son of Juntoku (r. 1210–21) as successor. But the shogunate rejected this proposal on the grounds that Juntoku, who was still alive and in exile, had actively supported his father Gotoba during the Jōkyū conflict. Instead, the shogunate gave its benediction to a child of Tsuchimikado (r. 1198–1210), another of Gotoba's sons but one who had opposed military action against the Hōjō. The new emperor, Gosaga (r. 1242–46), from the first felt indebted to the Hōjō for his position. During his reign cordial relations were established once again between Kyoto and Kamakura.

Gosaga's enthronement demonstrated clearly that the court had lost all initiative in matters of imperial succession. Moreover, as later events were to prove, failure of the shogunate to act decisively on subsequent succession questions did not automatically mean that the imperial family or the court as a body could resume that initiative. In fact it soon became apparent that the imperial and other court families no longer had means of effectively deciding disputes without the intervention of the military. Gosaga's immediate descendants encountered only frustration in their efforts to settle the order of succession when the shogunate failed to take a firm position. Ultimately the imperial family split into two branches. Although Godaigo temporarily reasserted the supremacy of one branch, the failure of his restoration brought a major dynastic schism that was not settled for more than half a century. Meanwhile succession disputes became endemic throughout court society. Nearly all the great court families, as well as certain families closely associated with leading religious institutions, began about this time to quarrel over succession. These included the Konoe, Nijō, Ichijō, Saionji, Tōin, and Yoshida.[20] In many cases the contenders for family headship

[20] Murata Masashi has given summaries of these disputes in *Namboku-chō Shi Ron*, pp. 78–86.

used the confrontation between the northern court in Kyoto and the southern court at Yoshino to the south as a basis for arguing their own causes. If one contender remained with the northern court after 1336, the other was likely to join the southern forces.

Further comment on the special nature of imperial succession and the headship of the imperial family is necessary to clarify the specific issues that were involved in the dispute after Gosaga's death in 1272. Inasmuch as succession to the throne was crucial to the functioning of the entire body politic, all families were intimately concerned with the manner in which it was handled. Interestingly, apart from the inviolable principle that the emperor must always be a member by birth of the imperial family, there appear to have been no fixed rules governing succession. As late as the sixth century, succession, which tended at that time to be transmitted from brother to brother, was handled in a very informal fashion: that is, a successor was not actually designated until after the death of the reigning sovereign. The practice of appointing a crown prince (*kōtaishi*) or heir apparent to the throne began about the mid-sixth century under Chinese influence and as part of the process toward the formalization of governing procedures at court.

A number of women occupied the throne during the seventh and eighth centuries, but after the scandalous affair between Empress Kōken (r. 749–58) and the priest Dōkyō (d. 772) in the 760s women were by general consent excluded from the line of imperial succession. There was a growing inclination thereafter to apply the principle of primogeniture to prospective male candidates, although this principle was also frequently ignored and many brothers, younger sons, and nephews, as well as uncles, succeeded to the throne. The emperor's polygamous marital relations made primogeniture, in any event, difficult to apply strictly, since the court invariably regarded a second son by a high-born consort more worthy of the imperial position than a first son by a lowly concubine.

A practice which served to increase the frequency of succession within the imperial family was that of abdication, both voluntary and forced. The first emperor to abdicate was Keitai, who the records say reigned from 507 until 531. By the Nara and Heian periods abdication had become common practice. Voluntary abdication occurred for a variety of reasons, including illness and the desire to transfer the ritual burdens of state to another. Forced abdication, on the other hand, became one of the principal means by which ministerial houses such as the Soga and the Fujiwara sought to control the imperial family.

Empress Jitō (r. 690–97), who abdicated voluntarily in 697, was the first to assume the formal title of retired sovereign—*dajō tennō*, or simply *jōkō*. Later a second title, that of priestly retired sovereign (*dajō hōō* or *hōō*), was adopted by those ex-emperors who took holy Buddhist vows. The first *hōō* was Uda, who abdicated in 897.

The retired empress Jitō continued to assist her grandson and successor, Monmu (r. 697–707), in his imperial duties until her death in 707, and a number of other sovereigns during the next few centuries also participated, to a greater or lesser degree, in the decision-making process at court after their abdications. Thus, by the mid-Heian period, there was a tradition dating from Jitō's reign of retired sovereigns "assisting" the throne (as earlier there had been a tradition of crown princes, such as Prince Shōtoku and Prince Naka, assisting the throne). During the time of Fujiwara supremacy, of course, neither emperors or retired emperors counted for much. From 967 until 1068 the Fujiwara thoroughly dominated the imperial family, marrying their daughters to emperors and frequently forcing early abdication. It was not at all unusual during this age for several retired or priestly retired sovereigns to be living in Kyoto at the same time. Not until the decline of Fujiwara power toward the end of the eleventh century did the opportunity arise for the imperial family to reassert itself politically. It was then that the system of the cloistered emperors was inaugurated.

The term for cloistered emperor is *in*, a word that was originally used to designate various buildings such as the dwellings of courtiers, certain structures in the imperial palace compound, and the like. Later, *in* came to refer specifically to the palaces of retired emperors and, by extension, to the retired emperors themselves. The first retired emperor to open an administrative office (*inchō*) of his own was En'yū (r. 969–84). In theory, then, En'yū might be called the first "cloistered emperor," but in fact his administrative office and those of subsequent retired emperors were of little importance, since real power was held by the Fujiwara for nearly another century. The term "cloistered emperor" is usually reserved for the line of politically significant senior retired emperors beginning with Shirakawa (r. 1072–86), who opened his *inchō* in 1086. In most cases the cloistered emperors eventually took Buddhist vows and became also priestly retired sovereigns, but it was in no sense necessary to enter the priesthood to be a proper cloistered emperor.

The system of the cloistered emperor opened a dynamic new phase in the history of the imperial family. Not only was the imperial family able to compete once again in court politics; through the cloistered emperors it was also able to build an extensive economic base in private estate holdings. The system was unique in that edicts issued from the cloistered emperor's office became a new source of authority which rivaled the throne itself. At the same time the accumulation of estates and the need to establish firm family control over these estates caused the cloistered emperor to assume a role quite similar to that held by the heads of other aristocratic houses. He became undisputed leader of the imperial family, acting both as private family head and as holder of the highest public position to which the family was entitled. (There could be no question that in prestige as well as authority the cloistered emperors of the twelfth and thirteenth centuries far exceeded the emperors of the same period).

On those occasions when, owing to circumstances, there was no cloistered emperor, the emperor assumed headship of the family. Goshirakawa, Gotoba, Gohorikawa, and Gosaga all reigned as emperor for brief periods without cloistered emperors. But in each case these men soon abdicated and became cloistered emperors themselves. Only Shijō, who was both emperor and family head after the death of Gohorikawa in 1234, failed to open a cloistered office. Since Shijō, as we have seen, died at the age of eleven in 1242, obviously he did not live long enough to take this step.

At the height of their power the cloistered emperors singlehandedly (and often quite arbitrarily) dictated succession to the throne. Toba, Goshirakawa, and Gotoba are examples of cloistered emperors who seem to have appointed and dismissed emperors at will. In one instance, as we shall note later, the decree of a cloistered emperor was used in place of transference of the regalia—the traditional symbols of imperial authority—as a means for changing occupancy of the throne. After the Jōkyū affair, of course, the shogunate assumed full responsibility for imperial appointments. In 1221 the shogunate even broke precedent by placing Gotakakura, who had never been emperor himself, in the office of cloistered emperor. Although the public offices of the imperial family were once again greatly reduced in power, private family headship, including control over most of the family holdings, was an authority which the cloistered emperors (and, in their absence, the emperors) continued to enjoy. To a certain extent this paralleled the later situation in Kamakura, when the office of shogunal regent was reduced in importance and Hōjō family power came to be concentrated in the hands of the Tokusō.

The imperial family held two principal blocs of private income-paying estates: the so-called Chōkōdōryō and Hachijōinryō. It is difficult to gauge the combined value of these blocs, but it must have been considerable. The Hachijōinryō, which was formed by the cloistered emperor Toba, consisted of more than 110 component holdings and the Chōkōdōryō, the creation of the cloistered emperor Goshirakawa, of some 180. After the deaths of Toba and Goshirakawa these blocs were transmitted as part of the corporate wealth of the imperial family. In order to minimize the danger of their being fragmented or lost through political vicissitudes, these and other parcels of landed holdings were frequently placed in the names of princesses or religious institutions closely associated with the imperial family. Thus the Chōkōdōryō was nominally held by Goshirakawa's daughter, Sen'yōmon'in, for sixty years, from his death in 1192 until her own in 1252. During this time the various family heads, whether emperors or cloistered emperors, retained residual control over the bloc.

Gosaga, as we have observed, had ascended the throne in 1242 through the good offices of the Hōjō. Since there was at the time no cloistered emperor, he assumed the position of head of the imperial family as well as that of emperor. But Gosaga remained emperor for only four years. In 1246 he abdicated the throne in favor of his son

Gofukakusa (r. 1246–59) and opened his own office of the cloistered emperor. Gofukakusa in turn abdicated in 1259 to make way for a younger brother, Kameyama (r. 1259–74). When the cloistered emperor Gosaga died in 1272, Kameyama was still on the throne and Gofukakusa was the sole retired sovereign.

Gosaga left explicit written instructions about the disposition of certain personal holdings and estates, but made no comment in his will about the matter of imperial succession. The consensus among present scholars is that Gosaga avoided mentioning succession simply because it had become customery since the Jōkyū incident for the shogunate to determine how it should be handled.[21] In other words Gosaga deferred to the Kamakura government in the matter of deciding whether succession should go to the line of Gofukakusa or to that of Kameyama.

After the Jōkyū incident the shogunate had dealt with succession questions decisively. Gosaga's own appointment to the throne had been made against the wishes of certain leading ministers at court. Yet now, as the supporters of both Gofukakusa and Kameyama pressed for a decision, shogunate leaders appeared to vacillate. They were absorbed at the time with the Mongol invasion threat and perhaps wished only to avoid embarrassing complications in their relations with the court. At any rate they decided to ask Gosaga's consort, Ōmiya-no-in (1225–92), the mother of both Gofukakusa and Kameyama, to indicate her husband's personal wishes concerning the succession. Ōmiya-no-in replied that the former cloistered emperor had long favored his younger son, Kameyama, and that he would have preferred the succession to go to his line. The shogunate immediately confirmed the emperor Kameyama as head of the imperial family and rejected Gofukakusa's request that he be made cloistered emperor.

The succession question was at this point seemingly settled in favor of the Kameyama line. In 1274 Kameyama placed his son Gouda (r. 1274–87) on the throne and elevated himself to the position of cloistered emperor. But the settlement which had enabled Kameyama to act in this fashion did not go unchallenged. Gofuka-

[21] For example, see *ibid.*, p. 50, and Kuroda, *Mōko Shūrai*, p. 327.

kusa's supporters were most disgruntled and claimed that succession should have gone to the line of the retired sovereign, since he was the elder son of Gosaga. As we have noted, neither primogeniture nor seniority among brothers had ever been a fixed rule for deciding the order of imperial succession. Hence claims based on Gofuka-kusa's seniority were not in themselves likely to induce the sho-gunate to reverse its position. More important was the fact that Gofukakusa had the support of influential ministers who urged that succession be transferred to his line. Chief among these was Saionji Sanekane (1249–1322). Since the Jōkyū incident, members of the Saionji family had acted as the principal liaison officials (*mōshitsugi*, or "mouthpieces") between the court and Kamakura. Now Sane-kane in his advice to the shogunate on court affairs began to espouse the cause of the senior (Gofukakusa) line in opposition to that of the junior (Kameyama) line.

There is no need here to trace in detail the complexities of the succession dispute during the next few decades.[22] Suffice it to say that the shogunate allowed a member of the senior line to succeed Gouda in 1288 and that by the turn of the century it had agreed to the proposal that succession alternate between the two lines. It has been suggested that the Hōjō may even have deliberately encouraged division within the imperial family to prevent reemergence of the court as a power factor at a time when their own authority was on the wane. For the purposes of our discussion the important question is how these decisions concerning succession, whatever their moti-vation, affected the structure and functioning of the imperial family.

A rivalry similar to that of Gofukakusa and Kameyama had emerged in the tenth century between Reizei (r. 967–69) and En'yū (r. 969–84), sons and successors of the emperor Murakami (r. 946–67). Until well into the following century succession alternated between the Reizei and En'yū lines. But this was the age when the Fujiwara were at the summit of their power, and reconciliation was finally achieved through the intermarriage of Fujiwara women with both lines. In the case of Gofukakusa versus Kameyama, there was

----

[22] For a detailed narrative of the succession dispute, see George Sansom, *A History of Japan to 1334*, Appendix IV, pp. 476–84.

little hope that this means of reconciliation could be successfully employed. In fact all normal contact between the two lines was rapidly diminishing and it soon became apparent that they stood on the verge of permanent division.

Division of a family meant division not only of its headship, but of its principal economic resources as well. The imperial family, as we have seen, derived its income mainly from two blocs of estate holdings—the Chōkōdōryō and the Hachijōinryo. When the imperial princess San'yōmon'in, holder of the Chōkōdōryō, died in 1252, this bloc was placed in the name of Gofukakusa. Hence Gosaga's elder son already held nominal claim to the Chōkōdōryō at the time of his father's death, although confirmation of Kameyama as family head meant that he in theory could exercise a higher jurisdictional control over this and other family holdings. The Hachijōinryō, meanwhile, was still registered as the property of another princess, Ankamon'in. When this princess died in 1282, about the time when the shogunate was yielding to demands that the senior line be allowed to participate in the order of succession, Kameyama immediately requested and obtained permission from Kamakura to have the Hachijōinryō placed in his name. Thus, while Gofukakusa retained title to one of the principal estate blocs of the imperial family, Kameyama assumed nominal possession of the other. In fact the concept of nominal possession was itself soon ignored, and both parties came to regard their respective titles to these holdings as permanent. For all practical purposes the imperial family had split into two separate branches with separate branch heads. From the locations of their priestly retreats, these branches were distinguished in the literature of the period as the Jimyōin-tō (senior branch) and the Daikakuji-tō (junior branch).[23]

Discontent with shogunate rule appears to have become widespread by the early years of the fourteenth century. Many housemen had clearly lost confidence in the integrity of their overlords, and charges of shogunate injustice and corruption were increasingly

---

[23] Fushimi was the first to use the Jimyōin as a retreat and Gouda the first to retire to the Daikakuji.

heard throughout the land. The mounting authoritarianism of the Hōjō and their direct vassals (*miuchi*) served only to intensify feelings of dissatisfaction. Yet it is difficult to judge precisely from the available chronicles how far the shogunate's administration of affairs had deteriorated. Hōjō Takatoki (1303–33), the last Tokusō, is usually pictured in stereotyped terms as the "bad last ruler" of a dynasty in full decline: he listened to the advice of evil ministers, ignored the people's suffering, and spent his days in perpetual revelry.[24] Such conventional stylization, presumably intended to glorify by comparison the subsequent restoration of the imperial family to power, makes difficult evaluation of the actions and policies of Takatoki and other shogunate leaders in their final years.

In the midst of more fundamental problems the continuing dispute over succession to the throne may for a time have seemed to these leaders a matter for little real concern. But after division of the imperial family into two distinct branches, they were forced to acknowledge the degree of discord that was wracking not only the imperial family but all of court society. Settlement could no longer be achieved by shogunate directive alone. Indeed the shogunate's capacity simply to referee the succession dispute had by this time been greatly reduced. This was made clear in 1300 when it became necessary to decide on the disposition of still another bloc of estate lands—the Muromachi'inryō, consisting of some seventy to eighty holdings—which had been held in the name of a third princess, Muromachi'in, until her death that year. The shogunate tried to avoid a clash between the junior and senior branches by assigning the Muromachi'inryō to a niece of Gofukakusa and Kameyama, a nonentity well outside the family quarrel. But within a year the former emperor Gouda attempted to gain control of this bloc of lands by granting the lady in question honorary title within the junior branch. In the face of outraged protests by supporters of the senior branch, the shogunate was obliged to reverse its decision and to allow the Muromachi'inryō to be divided equally between the Jimyōin-tō and the Daikakuji-tō.

To further complicate the dispute over succession, it appeared

---

[24] Gotō and Kamada, eds., *Taiheiki*, I, 36–37.

within a few years that both branches, but especially the junior, might split again. The shogunate sought to prevent this by bringing the branches together in 1317 in an agreement, known as the Bumpō compromise, which was designed: (1) to maintain the principle of alternate succession between the main lines of each branch; and (2) to fix at a maximum of ten years the period that candidates from either branch might occupy the throne. The Bumpō compromise also allowed for one exception to the alternate succession rule in order to correct the line of descent within the junior branch. The Daikakuji-tō emperor Gonijō (r. 1301–8) had died suddenly in 1308 and had been replaced by an emperor of the Jimyōin-tō. By rights Gonijō's son, Prince Kuninaga (1300–26), should have been made crown prince in preparation for the next transfer of succession. But the boy was young and sickly and it was decided instead to install Gonijō's brother, the future emperor Godaigo, as crown prince. Soon the junior branch found itself embroiled in competition between the Gonijō line, represented by the supporters of prince Kuninaga, and the line of Godaigo. By the terms of the Bumpō compromise Godaigo was made emperor in 1318 and Kuninaga was designated his crown prince. Godaigo was to serve his term and then to relinquish forever all claims to the throne to Kuninaga and the Gonijō line.

The senior branch, although it had reluctantly accepted the compromise, did not like the idea that two junior emperors would reign in succession. The person most dissatisfied with the Bumpō compromise, however, was Godaigo. Unlike most of his immediate predecessors, who had been young boys, Godaigo was at the time of his accession a man of thirty. He abhorred the practice of alternate succession and wished to bequeath the throne to one of his own sons. An opportunity to fulfill the latter wish appeared to present itself in 1326 when Prince Kuninaga died; but the shogunate insisted at that time that Godaigo accept a crown prince from the senior branch.

Meanwhile, in 1321, Godaigo's father, Gouda, had abolished the office of cloistered emperor which he had held by virtue of his son's occupancy of the throne. It is not clear precisely why Gouda took this step. The net effect was certainly to strengthen Godaigo's position, since he thereby became head of the junior branch and, as emperor, holder of what was once again the highest public position of the imperial family. Gouda had until this time been a restraining influence on Godaigo and seems to have been especially anxious to prevent division of the junior branch into two lines. In fact, Gouda had been most insistent on the provision in the Bumpō compromise that Kuninaga be made crown prince under Godaigo. Gouda wanted his second son to act merely as a caretaker until the descendants of Gonijō could be firmly reestablished as the main line of the junior branch.

With the withdrawal of the cloistered emperor Gouda from active politics, Godaigo reopened the records office (*kirokujo*) as a channel for his conduct of imperial administration. The records office had originally been created by the emperor Gosanjō in 1069. Gosanjō's purpose at that time was to assert general regulatory control over the estate system and to obtain a means for exercising ruling powers in competition with the Fujiwara regents. When Gosanjō's successor, Shirakawa, opened his office of cloistered emperor in 1086, this body in a sense superseded the records office. But on those occasions during the next three centuries when there was no cloistered emperor, emperors tended to use the records office as their personal administrative arm.[25] Godaigo in particular made a display of reviving this office as a central organ of imperial rule. Implicit in his action was a challenge to government by regents and cloistered emperors as well as by the military.

Shogunate leaders were undoubtedly apprehensive about the attitude and behavior of the emperor Godaigo; yet they took no steps to curb his activities or the activities of his supporters until 1324, when an antishogunate plot was discovered at court. Military officials in the capital made a series of arrests and sent the ringleaders, two lower-ranking ministers named Hino Suketomo and Hino Toshimoto (who had the same surname but were not related), to Kamakura for interrogation. The two Hino had apparently been at the head of a group known as the "free-and-easy" society (*bureikō*), which met under informal circumstances to dine together and to hear

---

[25] Kuroda, *Mōko Shūrai*, p. 424.

learned scholars, but also to plot secretly against the "eastern barbarians." Although the *Taiheiki* implies that the emperor had privately encouraged the Hino, Godaigo at this time sent a personal message to Kamakura disclaiming all knowledge of their conspiracy. Perhaps shogunate leaders were anxious to prevent the affair (known after the year-period as the Shōchū incident) from causing further unrest between court and military. In any event they accepted Godaigo's word and dealt in surprisingly lenient fashion with the conspirators, releasing Toshimoto outright and banishing Suketomo to the island of Sado.

The shogunate's policy of leniency seems only to have encouraged the antishogunate activists at court. Whether or not he had actually been privy to the 1324 plot, Godaigo now took the lead among these activists and spent the next few years covertly seeking support among warriors and great temples of the central provinces. Before he could put his plans into operation, however, they were revealed to the shogunate in 1331 by Yoshida Sadafusa, a court minister who had until this time been one of Godaigo's closest advisers.[26] Threatened with arrest, Godaigo fled the capital and took refuge on Mt. Kasagi with Kusunoki Masashige (d. 1336), a loyalist supporter from the province of Kawachi who had risen in his behalf. But before the end of the year the emperor was captured and Kusunoki, under heavy attack by shogunate armies, was forced to abandon his positions at Kasagi and later at Akasaka fortress in Kawachi. This brief struggle is known as the Genkō incident. Among its victims were Hino Toshimoto, executed in 1332, and Hino Suketomo, executed during the same year on Sado.

The shogunate likened Godaigo's role in the Genkō incident to that of the cloistered emperor Gotoba during the Jōkyū struggle a century earlier and decided that, like Gotoba, he too should be sent into exile. Before carrying out this sentence, however, shogunate officials attempted to clarify the matter of imperial succession. They

---

[26] Sadafusa had previously admonished the emperor about his military preparations. It has been suggested that his disclosure to the shogunate at this time was really for the purpose of saving Godaigo. Sadafusa was convinced that the anti-Hōjō plot could not succeed and hoped to minimize Kamakura's displeasure toward Godaigo by placing the blame on others. See Murata, *Namboku-chō Shi Ron*, p. 28.

had taken the most unusual step, even before Godaigo's capture, of designating the crown prince as emperor. The accession of the new emperor (Kōgon of the senior branch) was conducted in the absence of any act of abdication by Godaigo and without the regalia, part of which at least was still in Godaigo's possession. The only authority for the accession ceremony was an edict from Kōgon's father, the former emperor Gofushimi (r. 1298–1301), who was now patriarch of the senior branch.[27] There was, nevertheless, precedent for this procedure. When the Taira, under attack by Minamoto armies in 1188, had fled westward from the capital with the child emperor Antoku (r. 1180–83) and the regalia, the cloistered emperor Go-shirakawa had decreed that Antoku's brother, Gotoba, be placed on the throne in his stead. The ceremonies of investiture were carried out on this basis alone. Since Antoku was drowned at the battle of Dannoura in 1188, he had no opportunity to challenge the legiti-macy of his successor. Godaigo, on the other hand, steadfastly refused to abdicate and went into exile in the Oki Islands with the firm conviction that he was still rightful sovereign of the land.

Removal of Godaigo from Kyoto in the third month of 1332 did not provide the shogunate with a lasting solution to the Genkō rising. Although shogunate forces were able to bring the capital once more under control, they could not deal effectively with mounting guerrilla activities in the surrounding provinces. The principal loyalist leaders at this time were Kusunoki Masashige, who was still at large, and Godaigo's son, Prince Morinaga (1308–35).

Morinaga is an interesting product of this age: a combination of court noble and military commander. Godaigo had attempted to make him crown prince in 1326; but when the shogunate insisted on a member of the senior branch (the later emperor Kōgon), he directed Morinaga to take Buddhist vows and appointed him head priest of the Enryakuji on Mt. Hiei. In view of Godaigo's desire to obtain military commitments from religious institutions of the home provinces, it is likely that Morinaga's appointment to the En-ryakuji was for the express purpose of establishing liaison with this

[27] Although the accession ceremony (*senso*) was carried out, enthronement (*sokui*) was postponed until the regalia could be obtained from Godaigo.

important Buddhist center. During the Genkō incident Morinaga returned to lay life and took an active part in the fighting. By the time of final reckoning with the Hōjō in 1333, he had amassed a following sufficient to make him an important factor in any balance of military power in and around the capital.

Alarmed by the success of loyalist arms in the central and western provinces, the shogunate dispatched an army westward from Kamakura in the first month of 1333. Divisions of this army brought certain regions near the capital under control, but they could not reduce the key position which Kusunoki had assumed at Chihaya fortress in Kawachi.

In the early spring it was learned that Godaigo had escaped from the Oki Islands and was under the protection of a warrior named Nawa Nagatoshi (d. 1336) in Hōki Province. As more and more supporters rallied to the loyalist cause, the shogunate felt obliged to send additional reinforcements from Kamakura. One of the generals in charge of its new contingent was Ashikaga Takauji, an eastern chieftain and a ranking member of the Minamoto clan. Upon reaching the central district in the fourth month, Takauji suddenly announced support of the imperial cause and, joined by other loyalists, attacked and destroyed the shogunate installations in Kyoto. The following month Nitta Yoshisada (1301–38), another Minamoto chieftain, rose in the Kantō and struck down the Hōjō at Kamakura. The system founded by Yoritomo a century and a half earlier lay in ruins.

Godaigo returned to Kyoto in the sixth month of 1333 much in the manner of a traveler completing a long journey. Since he had never willingly abdicated, he saw no need now to go through the formalities of reascending the throne. Rather, he took the position that Kōgon had never been a legitimate emperor. While treating him with civility and confirming the holdings of the senior branch, Godaigo nullified all court appointments made during his absence from the capital and replaced Kōgon's year-period, Shōkei, with his own earlier designation of Genkō. To Godaigo the restoration of his branch of the imperial family to real power was an accomplished fact.

[65]

III

The Kemmu Restoration*
1333–1336

The Court in Power

⬡ THE ESTABLISHMENT of a military government at Kamakura had served to institutionalize the fundamental division of Japan's ruling aristocracy into court families (*kuge*), including closely related temples and shrines, and military families (*buke*). In terms of real power the military were unquestionably in the ascendancy during the Kamakura period. Yet even after the Jōkyū incident of 1221 the court families were able to retain sufficient administrative and jurisdictional rights, including the appointment of provincial officials and the management of estate lands, to sustain hopes of one day recovering national leadership. Jien had been among the first to assess the alternatives open to the court in its competition with the military. Although unwavering in his conviction that the highest levels of rulership should by inherently divine right be the sole prerogative of the court aristocracy, Jien was realistic enough to see that the court could not, at the time he wrote, directly challenge warrior hegemony. Hence he advocated a union of court and military through the appointment of a member of his branch of the Fujiwara to be shogun at Kamakura.

Although Jien's plan for union reflected both family opportunism and personal naïveté,[1] he touched upon an important point in stressing the need for some type of reform through alliance (e.g., a Fujiwara to assume at least titular military leadership of the land) that would enable the *kuge* to challenge *buke* supremacy. This reformist line of thinking came to be shared by others of the early medieval age,

---

* See Appendix 4 for a discussion of the term "imperial restoration."

[1] Jien, for example, called for a "moratorium" on strife until the infant shogun Yoritsune could grow up and take personal charge of affairs at Kamakura.

[66]

including Prince Morinaga and Kitabatake Chikafusa who, if they did not urge an actual merger of court and shogunate, at least called for the assumption of certain military functions by members of the court nobility. This should not suggest that either of these aristocrats became reformists to the exclusion of all reactionary sentiment. Chikafusa, for example, was insistent that the court be made once again the center of national administration and that strict hierarchical principles be followed in the appointment of imperial ministers. At the same time he, as a courtier-general, came to symbolize in his own person the ideal of merger between courtiers and the military.

In contrast to those who acknowledged the need for reform along military lines, others of the court nobility persisted in their demands for an unconditional restoration of the court to power. Chief among these was the emperor Godaigo himself. Godaigo was especially encouraged in his restorationist convictions by the seemingly overwhelming mandate he received from those courtiers and warriors who backed him in his struggle against the Hōjō. In fact, many of these backers were motivated more by a desire to oppose the Hōjō than by any compelling urge to advance Godaigo's personal cause. It soon became apparent that the emperor, despite his temporary elation at power regained, presided over an essentially unstable coalition, which would remain intact only so long as he could meet the demands of all who comprised it.

Godaigo's consciousness of his role as a restorer can be seen in his choice of the year-name Kemmu[2] in imitation of the Chien-wu period (A.D. 25–56) of the emperor Kuang-wu, restorer of the Han dynasty in China. The era which Godaigo most esteemed as a model for imperial rule in Japanese history was the Engi period (901–23) of the early Heian emperor Daigo. To demonstate his personal admiration for Daigo he even took the unusual step of selecting as his own posthumous name Godaigo, or the "Later Daigo."[3] Godaigo was attracted to the Engi period as a time, ostensibly at least, of direct imperial administration before the consolidation of power in the hands of Fujiwara regents, before the interference in

[2] The first year of Kemmu was 1334.
[3] It was customary for such names to be selected by others after the emperor's death.

court affairs by cloistered emperors, and before the rise of the provincial military. These three groups—regents, cloistered emperors, and the military—were, in Godaigo's mind, the parties chiefly responsible for the deterioration of government during the centuries preceding his succession to the throne. Only by denying all three future access to power would it be possible to restore the throne to its rightful position of eminence and to correct the evils that had come to beset society.

The system of cloistered emperors had, as we have seen, been discontinued (at least so far as the junior branch of the imperial family was concerned)[4] by Godaigo's father, Gouda, in 1321. Upon his triumphal return to the capital in 1333, Godaigo sought to thwart the aspirations of regents and the military as well by declining to make appointments to either the office of imperial regent or that of shogun. Although he subsequently granted shogunal commissions to certain of his sons, including Prince Morinaga, Godaigo steadfastly refused to bestow the title of shogun on a military chieftain or to condone the establishment of a new shogunate. Indeed he seems to have viewed the military as simply a tool to make possible his own return to power. Though later forced to make significant concessions in the appointment of warriors to lesser central and regional posts, Godaigo never accepted the contention of the reformists at court that the times demanded adoption of coercion as a basic technique of rule.

At the same time it is clear that, despite his fascination with ideals in the past, Godaigo was more directly concerned with the problem of gathering authoritarian powers to himself in the present. The *Teiheiki*, while praising him for his scholarship and virtue, notes also that he was headstrong and overly assertive in his efforts to gain control of the land. For this reason he was unable to hold power for more than a few years.[5] However this may be, events were to prove that Godaigo was not sufficiently enamored with time-honored precedents to abstain from violating those which did not suit his immediate purposes. Another source, the *Baishōron*, quotes him as saying, "My new measures will become the precedents of the

[4] The senior branch continued the practice.
[5] *Taiheiki*, I, 38.

future."[6] If in fact he did make such a statement, it must be interpreted at least in part as a reply to his critics. Medieval society was, for both court and military, a society based on precedent, and those who undertook "new measures" (*shingi*) were viewed as intruders upon the established rights of others.

Godaigo's early reputation as a man of wisdom and scholarship has been drawn also from the diary of his predecessor, the former emperor Hanazono (r. 1308–18) of the senior branch, who was surprisingly impartial in his comments on contemporaries and their affairs. In the second month of 1322, shortly after discontinuance of the office of cloistered emperor, Hanazono observed: "His Majesty studies with special care the way of the *Doctrine of the Mean*. It would be an excellent thing if this should bring a return to pure and simple governing practices. In the present age scholarship has long been abandoned. Perhaps now there will be a restoration (*chūkō*)."[7] To Godaigo, restoration implied a radical alteration in existing political institutions. Hanazono, on the other hand, presumably intended in this context to convey the idea of something closer to a renaissance or a revitalization of cultural and moral attitudes in government. Ten months later he added: "In recent days pure and simple governing practices have been restored. His Majesty has already shown himself to be a ruler of wisdom."[8] We have no way of knowing how widely Hanazono's sentiments were shared at court. Nevertheless, it would appear that in the early years of his reign the emperor Godaigo did indeed give rise to expectations, at least among certain highly placed observers, of a new and more worthy phase of imperial administration.

An area of scholarship to which Godaigo was particularly attracted was Sung Neo-Confucianism. The principle of *taigi-meibun* (literally, "supreme duty and name-position"), which defined the

---

[6] *Baishōron* in Hanawa Hokiichi, ed., *Gunsho Ruijū*, XX, 163. The *Baishōron*, although a far shorter work and lacking the literary embellishments of the *Taiheiki*, covers much the same ground up to the death of Nitta Yoshisada in 1338. It was written about 1349, probably by a retainer or follower of the Ashikaga. Biased in favor of the latter, it contrasts interestingly with the *Taiheiki*, which is generally sympathetic to the southern court.

[7] *Hanazono Tennō Shinki*, 1322:2:12.

[8] *Ibid.*, 1322:12:25.

relationship between sovereign and subject in terms of absolute loyalty on the part of the latter toward the former, accorded nicely with Godaigo's own ideas of the ties that should bind ruler and ruled. Yet the type of loyalty that actually prevailed in provincial warrior society at this time was only indirectly related to the sovereign, insofar as all warrior groups had to maintain at least the fiction of ultimate allegiance to the throne. This was not difficult during a period when the "throne" could be represented by several persons, including contending emperors and former or cloistered emperors. When Ashikaga Takauji, for example, later turned against Godaigo, it was a relatively simple matter for him to transfer allegiance to a member of the senior branch of the imperial family and thereby to maintain the façade of legitimacy.

For most members of military society the real focus of loyalty was the direct overlord. Moreover, the loyalty which warriors rendered to their overlords was not absolute, but was based on reciprocity. The warrior expected reward for his services, not so much for himself as for his family and its perpetuation. He gave his life in battle in anticipation of the benefit that this sacrifice would bring to his family.[9] The frequent shifting of sides by individuals during this period was also based to a great extent on family considerations. Many families, especially during the subsequent war between the courts, tried to take both sides in the hope of salvaging something no matter which side won.

Among the learned men to whom Godaigo granted special favor at his court were the martyred ministers Hino Suketomo and Hino Toshimoto. The two Hino are examples of ministers selected and promoted by Godaigo on the basis of merit rather than birth. The favor they received was, needless to say, deeply resented by members of the more prestigious ministerial houses, such as the Fujiwara and the Murakami Genji (including the Kitabatake branch), who maintained that rank should be apportioned on a basis chiefly determined by family standing; and who believed that only a small group of the highest ranking officials should be allowed to assist the emperor directly in rule.[10]

[9] Watsuji, *Nihon Rinri Shisō Shi*, I, 305.
[10] Jien suggests in the *Gukanshō* that a committee of four or five be appointed to select this small group.

The problem of inherited status versus merit had, without question, become a perplexing and pressing one for the court nobility. The success of the Fujiwara in earlier centuries had demonstrated that there could be relatively effective central administration in premedieval Japan despite the restriction of ministerial recruitment to only a few privileged families. By the end of the Heian period, however, with the weakening of court rule and the growth of military power bases in the provinces, the monopolization of governing rights by a handful of bureaucratic families at the center was shown to be an increasingly difficult (and, after the founding of the Kamakura Shogunate, impossible) principle to maintain. Continued insistence on strict family ranking and hierarchy simply deprived the court nobles of needed flexibility in their efforts to compete with the military. Among the latter, on the other hand, hierarchy, although still important, had come to be much less crucial. The case of the Hōjō was ample proof that ability and performance by members of a warrior family could make up for deficiencies in lineage in a way that was still inconceivable at court.

Chikafusa was one among the court nobles who felt especially the need to seek reconciliation of the birth and merit principles. He was not prepared to relinquish to any appreciable extent the traditional privileges of the upper echelon of the aristocracy, but, as we shall see, wished to retain all the old prerogatives of birth, while cultivating and maintaining a high level of competence and morality among governing officials.

The imperial family tended to look upon inherited status somewhat differently from the courtier families. Emperors and cloistered emperors were undisputed holders of the highest, most sacred positions at court. Their concern was not with protecting status per se, but with preventing others from usurping the powers that were supposed to accompany that status. Within court society the greatest danger to the imperial family lay in domination by one or more ranking ministerial houses. In order to compete with these houses the imperial family tended, when opportunity arose, to encourage the advancement of competent ministers from lesser families—that is, to stress merit over birth. Thus the ninth-century emperor Uda, father of the illustrious Daigo, had attempted to check the rise of the Fujiwara by placing in key positions men of modest if not obscure lineage, including the scholar Sugawara Michizane (845–903). In the eleventh and twelfth centuries cloistered emperors, as a means of regaining power for the imperial family, even sought the support of officials who had served in the provinces. Whereas Jien and Chikafusa, as Fujiwara and Murakami Genji respectively, idealized imperial rule as rule by a small group of ranking ministers next to the throne, Uda and the early cloistered emperors believed that true rule by the imperial family was impossible so long as such oligarchic groups enjoyed a disproportionate share of rights and privileges at court.

It is therefore not surprising that Godaigo, in his urge to reassert the political authority of the throne, was also wary and suspicious of those with powerful family connections and claims by birthright to high position. In the early years he had been well served by men such as Yoshida Sadafusa (1274–1338) and Madenokōji Nobufusa (b. 1258), older ministers who had been appointed by his father and who represented continuity in administration by the upper echelon of the courtier class.[11] Increasingly, however, Godaigo came to seek the support not only of lower ranking court officials, but also of warriors from less prominent military families, such as the Kusunoki and the Nawa, who, he apparently hoped, would serve to check the ambitions of the Ashikaga and other leading chieftains of the land.

Perhaps the most telling indication of Godaigo's desire to exercise personal rule can be found in the manner in which he chose to issue his imperial commands. We have already noted his eclecticism in the selection of models from the past. While esteeming most highly the Engi period of Daigo, he also attached great significance to revival of the records office, which the eleventh-century emperor Gosanjō had created to challenge the monopolization of power by Fujiwara regents. Instead of using the channels of the records office to express his own wishes in government, however, Godaigo turned to yet another model or ideal in the past, this time from the period of the former emperor Saga, who had reigned from 809 until 823. It was during Saga's time that the first extracodal offices were instituted to streamline the cumbrous T'ang-style administrative system set forth in the Taihō code of 701. By means of the *kurōdo dokoro*

[11] Murata Masashi, *Namboku-chō Ron*, p. 38.

(sovereign's private office), Saga and his immediate successors were able to issue direct edicts, known as *rinji*, in place of the former type of imperial decree which had required time-consuming polishing, revision, and approval by various offices and bureaus before actual promulgation. Godaigo not only employed the *rinji* as his personal mode of administrative expression, he even eschewed the use of scribes from the *kurōdo-dokoro* in their preparation, preferring to write these edicts in his own distinctive brush style.[12] Impractical as it may seem, Godaigo does indeed appear to have planned, at least in the early stages of his Restoration, to deal virtually by fiat with every matter of government through the issuance of personally composed and transcribed edicts.

Shortly after his return to the capital, Godaigo issued a series of edicts calling, among other things, for the confiscation of "enemy holdings," for the return of holdings "wrongfully seized" during the recent years of fighting, and for the review of "improper judicial decisions" by former shogunate officials.[13] His aim, apparently, was to take what he deemed the first steps necessary to assert court jurisdiction in the critical area of disputes over land. Yet in the process he also sought to place himself in the position of sole arbiter of such disputes by decreeing that his personal decisions were to override any and all defenses set forth on the basis of existing statutes or legal custom.

The vagueness in wording of these early edicts (which lands were to be considered enemy holdings? wrongfully seized holdings? holdings obtained through improper judicial decisions?) and Godaigo's arbitrary manner of implementing them portended an unavoidable increase in the number of land disputes. Until this time there had been at least one principle which had served to set an outer limit to these disputes and which had come to be regarded as immutable in judicial proceedings of the court and the estates as well as of the military: that occupancy for twenty or more years should constitute an incontestable right to the proprietorship of any holding.

---

[12] Godaigo even sent *rinji* to people formerly regarded as too low in rank to be recipients. See Satō Shin'ichi, *Namboku-chō no Dōran*, in Chūō Kōron Sha, *Nihon no Rekishi*, IX, 18.

[13] *Ibid.*, p. 17.

Under Godaigo's new measures, it soon became clear, no holding could be regarded as fully secure in the eyes of the court without a document from the emperor himself either rewarding or confirming its title. The result was a virtual deluge of claims and counterclaims, which the emperor could scarcely have handled alone however great his diligence.[14] Before long he was obliged to open several new offices to assist in these and other administrative matters. But before discussing them let us turn first to the growing danger of a renewal of armed conflict, this time among his own supporters, which Godaigo was also forced to face in the very first days of his assumption of power.

There could have been little doubt of Godaigo's intent, even before his return to the capital, to revive the court politically. Yet the question had still remained how far he would seek to administer national affairs on a strictly personal basis. His leading supporters were men of ambition and were not likely to surrender willingly all their rights and powers. Their common goal of destroying the old shogunate once achieved, they could be expected in the ensuing period of reconstruction to seek the political settlement most advantageous to themselves, in relation to each other as well as to the throne.

A brief glance at Godaigo's principal commanders—Ashikaga Takauji, Nitta Yoshisada, Prince Morinaga—will reveal some of the personal aims and animosities that lay behind the façade of alliance against the shogunate. Takauji and Yoshisada, as heads of Minamoto branch families and leading Kantō warriors, were natural contenders for the power position recently occupied by the Hōjō.[15] Both were keenly aware that victory over their former overlords could open the way to establishment of a new military hegemony in the east. From the standpoint of deployment, Yoshisada, who had led the main assault on Kamakura, was temporarily in a more favorable position; otherwise, the Nitta were ill-equipped to contend directly with the Ashikaga. The Nitta had originally been senior in rank among the Minamoto, but during the Kamakura period their fortunes and

---

[14] *Ibid.*, p. 19.
[15] For further comment on the differences between Ashikaga Takauji and Nitta Yoshisada see H. Paul Varley, *The Ōnin War*, p. 23.

prestige had waned while those of the Ashikaga had waxed. When the Ashikaga, after Yoshisada's occupation of Kamakura, set up a rival camp in the city environs under Takauji's infant son, Yoshiakira (1330–67), the Kantō warriors soon began to flock to their standard. The *Baishōron*, reflecting its own bias in favor of the Ashikaga, states: "How auspicious it is that the various commanders are all aligning themselves with the four-year-old lord [Yoshiakira]. People say that this is surely a sign that [the Ashikaga] are to serve eternally as shoguns."[16] In any event, the Ashikaga were apparently successful in eliminating the brief tactical advantage of the Nitta at Kamakura. Before long Yoshisada felt obliged to move his base of operations to Kyoto where, by associating himself more directly with the policies of the throne, he hoped to check the rising power of Takauji.

Prince Morinaga had joined Takauji in the assault on the shogunate's deputy system at Rokuhara, destruction of which had for the time being rendered Kyoto an "open city." To the alarm of Morinaga, who was awaiting the return of his father, Takauji began to form a new military control system of his own in the capital, recruiting to his personal service not only former functionaries of Rokuhara but other housemen from nearby provinces as well. Morinaga now saw Takauji as the principal threat to peace and the reestablishment of court rule. Hence, even after the emperor's return, Morinaga continued to maintain in the provinces outside Kyoto a posture of military preparedness as a challenge to the ambitions of the Ashikaga.

We cannot be certain what Morinaga's true attitudes and motives were, for the records are incomplete and in places contradictory. He was obviously quite pragmatic in his view of the warrior families and understood the need for a strong military arm in government. This can be seen clearly in an exchange of notes with Godaigo (recorded in the *Taiheiki*) in which the emperor upon his own arrival in the capital attempted to persuade Morinaga to lay down his arms and to return in peace to the court:

[From the emperor to Prince Morinaga] The realm has already been pacified. The remaining power of the military has been put down and virtuous

<hr>

[16] *Baishōron*, p. 162.

rule is being administered. Why, then, are you still acting in a warlike fashion and assembling troops? At the time of the great disturbance of Genkō you returned temporarily to lay life to deal with the enemy. But now, since peace has once again been restored, you should immediately cut your hair, don your priestly robes, and return to your duties at the Enryakuji.

[From Prince Morinaga to the emperor] The land has now been ordered and the people rejoice in tranquility. This is partly the result of your wonderful virtue and partly owing to the success of my plans. Yet Ashikaga Takauji, who earned merit in only one battle, wishes to impose his will over all men. If we do not strike while his forces are still few, he will come to add his might to the treachery of Takatoki. Since it is for this reason that I am recruiting troops and preparing for war, I am by no means committing an offense. As for the matter of my returning to the priesthood, people who cannot discern things until they occur before their eyes will undoubtedly wag their tongues. Yet the fact is that, even though the rebels have been unexpectedly defeated and the country has once again been pacified, there is no doubt that many rebels still remain in hiding, that they are watching developments and are awaiting their opportunity. In these times if those above do not possess majesty, those below will surely have insolent hearts. We live in an age when civil and military ways (*bumbu no nidō*) must be combined for the purpose of rule. If I should return to the priesthood, casting aside the power I command as a great general, who would defend the court militarily? There are two methods by which the Buddhas and Bodhisattvas seek to aid living beings: through force and through persuasion. Persuasion takes the form of gentleness and forbearance and places compassion first; force appears as great power and wrath and has as its aim punishment. There are many instances in the histories of both Japan and China when, during times that demanded wise council and military leadership, men who have taken Buddhist vows have returned to lay life and sovereigns who have abdicated have reascended the throne. Thus the so-called Hermit of the Waves, Chia Tao, left his priestly retreat and became a minister at court. And in our country the sovereigns Temmu and Kōken renounced their vows and resumed imperial rank. Which course on my part would be better for the country—to live in obscurity on Mt. Hiei guarding but one temple, or as a great general to pacify the country to its farthest extent. . .[17]

The remarks attributed here to Prince Morinaga constitute one of the most forthright statements in the literature of the early medieval

[17] *Taiheiki*, I, 392, 393.

period of the need for the court to adopt military techniques of rule. Morinaga sought mainly in Buddhist terms to justify his demands for the use of coercion at this point in Japanese history.[18] To implement coercion and to deal with the dangers that he saw threatening the court, he called upon the emperor to grant him both the title of *seii taishōgun* and a direct commission to chastise Takauji. Although Godaigo refused the latter request on the grounds that the Ashikaga chieftain had been guilty of no overt wrongdoing, he did appoint Morinaga shogun as a concession to secure his return to the capital.

During the earlier period of guerrilla warfare against the Hōjō, while Godaigo was still in exile in the Oki Islands, Prince Morinaga had taken certain steps to establish his own sphere of administrative as well as military control in the central provinces. He had, for example, issued a series of directives (*shirei*) dealing with the assignment of lands acquired as booty during the fighting in this region. To Godaigo the issuance of such directives constituted an unauthorized assumption of governing prerogatives, not justifiable even under emergency conditions. Hence Morinaga's subsequent request for the title of shogun to add to the considerable *de facto* powers he had accumulated by the summer of 1333 served only to increase the doubts which Godaigo already harbored about the prince's ultimate ambitions. It was perhaps characteristic of Godaigo that he should respond so instinctively to what he regarded as a threat, even from his own son, to the exercise of direct imperial rule. While granting the shogunal title, Godaigo sought from this time to reduce the range of Morinaga's real authority. The edict he issued calling for the return of "wrongfully seized" holdings was undoubtedly intended at least in part to reverse Morinaga's earlier directives and to affirm the throne as the sole source of such decrees dealing with the disposition of land.[19]

As later events were to demonstrate, Morinaga's agreement to return to the capital was from his standpoint a tactical error, both in his confrontation with Takauji and in his relations with Godaigo.

---

[18] Professor Yoshito Hakeda suggests that the kind of force or coercion attributed to the Buddhas and Bodhisattvas in this passage from the *Taiheiki* is actually another form of love, since its ultimate aim is to benefit living beings.

[19] Satō, *Namboku-chō no Dōran*, p. 22.

Cut off from his forces in the provinces, the prince found himself unable to establish a competitive political base in Kyoto. In an earlier age Minamoto Yoritomo had taken the title of shogun to grace his established position at the head of a functioning military government. Without such a government, the office carried no specific powers, and in the end it proved of little worth to Morinaga.

We know almost nothing of Morinaga's actions during the next year, a fact which in itself suggests that his role in central affairs was on the decline. The *Taiheiki* accuses him of being a man of excess and violence, who would not accept the return of peace to the land and whose warlike behavior simply attracted other men of violence. Because of his presence in the city, there was constant apprehension and decent people were afraid to walk the streets at night.[20] Then suddenly, in the tenth month of 1334, Morinaga was accused of plotting against the Ashikaga and, with imperial acquiescence, was placed in their custody.[21] The details of his arrest are not entirely clear, but we do learn that he was subsequently transported to Kamakura and in 1335 was murdered there by Takauji's brother, Tadayoshi (1306–52).

Owing to the scarcity of records, it is impossible to document fully the establishment of the various offices and boards that came to comprise Godaigo's administration or to determine precisely how these bodies functioned. We do have sufficient information, however, to draw a general picture of the governing structure that evolved during the Restoration period and to comment on its over-all effectiveness.

Two of the earliest administrative bodies were the records office, which Godaigo had once before opened to symbolize his assumption of the management of court affairs, and the board of rewards (*onshōkata*), which he now formed to begin work on the settlement of claims for reward by those who had participated in the overthrow of the Hōjō. The records office, it appears, was

---

[20] *Taiheiki*, I, 425.

[21] The *Baishōron* states that Morinaga was actually directed in his anti-Takauji plot by Godaigo, while the *Taiheiki* maintains that the prince acted alone.

intended simply to assist the throne in the details of day-to-day administration. It was composed of middle-ranking courtiers and lesser military leaders, such as Kusunoki Masashige and Nawa Nagatoshi, who were least likely to challenge the emperor's exercise of personal rule. The board of rewards, on the other hand, was staffed chiefly by higher ranking courtiers (with no warrior participation in the beginning), headed first by Tōin Saneyo and then by Madenokōji Fujifusa (1295–1380?). These men tried to discharge their duties conscientiously and impartially; but the difficulties they faced were overwhelming, and in the final analysis it was probably in the area of claims settlement that the new government failed most grievously.

The *Taiheiki*, while saluting the efforts of Saneyo and Fujifusa, is devastatingly critical of court practice in regard to claims. As with all matters during the Restoration period, the ultimate blame for such mishandling must, it would appear, be placed on Godaigo, since he delegated administrative powers only grudgingly. It was the emperor himself who authorized generous grants not only to the principal participants in the struggle against the Hōjō, but also to court favorites such as Lady Renshi and the Shingon priest Monkan (1278–1357). Inclusion of the latter as the recipients of major rewards was itself a seemingly unnecessary gesture of extravagance in view of the more pressing need to satisfy those who had actually joined in the fighting. Thereafter, if we are to believe the *Taiheiki*, the process of claims settlement degenerated to the lowest levels of inefficiency, favoritism, and corruption. Warriors from the various provinces streamed into Kyoto to present their petitions. Yet so ill-equipped were the courtiers to handle this multitude of petitioners that even "after the passage of several months no more than twenty or so persons had been granted rewards, and these were not based on equity." [22] The meritorious were reportedly virtually ignored and only those skillful at flattery and cajolery could hope for ultimate satisfaction. Although Madenokōji Fujifusa in particular sought to set aright the settlement process, at every turn he found himself either overruled or outmaneuvered by confidants and

[22] *Taiheiki*, I, 396.

cronies of the emperor who were able to arrange seemingly at will the transfer of holdings both to themselves and to their own intimates. Before long "not a bit of land remained in all the sixty-six provinces of Japan to distribute among warriors of the various regions."[23]

Added to the general uncertainty concerning the disposition of holdings created by the imperial edicts (discussed above) which Godaigo issued shortly after his return to the capital, the failure at this time to deal speedily and equitably with claims for reward cast serious and perhaps irreparable doubt on the capacity of the court to perform the essential judicio-legislative function of medieval government. Even after discounting the obvious hyperbole of the *Taiheiki* account, one is forced to conclude that the new government's policies in regard to land and rewards were disastrous. The Hōjō had set the standard for legalistic excellence. Godaigo's failure to recognize that social order in his age was dependent upon the maintenance of a complex of jurisdictional rights and laws, both statutory and customary, was a principal factor in his inability to retain popular support.

From the facts presented thus far it seems clear that Godaigo began his rule with a general disregard for legalism and a belief in the capacity of the virtuous ruler to deal with all matters of government directly and simply—that is, with a minimum of ministerial assistance and with little if any delegation of real authority. The obviously adverse results of his initial administrative measures, however, soon forced the emperor both to broaden the scope of participation in government and to relinquish some of the decision-making powers he had hoped to monopolize in his own person. In an edict issued toward the end of the seventh month of 1333 he decreed:

Even after the fighting [against the Hōjō] warriors and common people were not free from anxiety. Therefore we issued edicts to save them from losing their holdings. But it is bothersome [to attempt] to handle in detail all matters that arise. This is especially so when it causes men from the various provinces, both far and near, to come to the capital. They are

[23] *Ibid.*, p. 397.

interfering unnecessarily with the work of farming and in fact are causing discomfort among the people. Henceforth these edicts (which we issued after the fighting) are to be disregarded. We now order that the confirmation of lands, with the exception of those belonging to the family of [Hōjō] Takatoki and his anti-court confederates, be handled justly by [the governors of] the various provinces of the land. There is to be no violation of this order. However, in the case of emergency decrees, what is stated here shall not be considered binding.[24]

Thus, in the face of mounting judicial confusion and the clogging of the capital by petitioners seeking confirmation of their holdings or the return of those already confiscated, the emperor directed the provincial governors to assume responsibility for the ordering of titles to land. In addition he now defined the term "enemies of the court" to apply only to relatives of the former Hōjō leader, Takatoki, and to those who had directly supported him. This definition was presumably intended to allay the anxieties of those who had failed to respond to the call to arms against the shogunate or who had remained in sympathy with its policies. Finally, it is revealing of the character of Godaigo to note that even as he granted new authority to others he added a final clause reserving the right to withdraw it in any situation he regarded as constituting an "emergency."

Nevertheless, the relinquishment of authority to provincial officials contained in the above edict was quite clearly a concession on Godaigo's part occasioned by the urgent need for a more practical approach to the administration of national affairs. It does not appear, however, that the scope of this newly delegated authority was to extend much beyond an inquiry into existing titles to holdings and an assertion of the court's right to conduct such inquiry. Far more important from the standpoint of the delegation of imperial authority was the establishment about this time of a special settlements board (*zasso ketsudanjo*) to function as the principal judicial arm of administration at Kyoto. Formation of this board was by far the most significant step taken by Godaigo to adapt his rule to the proven methods for governing medieval society evolved by the military during the Kamakura period.

[24] Tōkyō Teikoku Daigaku, *Dai Nihon Shiryō*, 6¹, 145.

The settlements board came to function much in the manner of the old board of coadjutors, which had heard suits and had prepared cases for presentation to the council of state under the Hōjō. In composition it had representatives from many groups, including ranking courtiers and warriors as well as former functionaries of the board of coadjutors at Kamakura. This diversity of membership tended in time to reduce the board's efficiency, as the various factions vied for control. Both courtiers and the military attempted to recruit as many of their supporters as possible, and by the following year the ranks of the settlements board had swelled to more than a hundred. Its overstaffing even became the target of an anonymous satirist of the period, who referred to it as the board from which "no one was excluded." [25]

Two other central governing bodies which Godaigo instituted, but about which we know very little, were the *kubosho* and the *mushadokoro*. The former seems to have been patterned on the earlier board of retainers of the Kamakura Shogunate, while the *mushadokoro* was apparently designed to provide police control in the capital. [26] Nitta Yoshisada, as head of the *mushadokoro*, may have tried to use this office to strengthen his own political position at court.

In regard to regional administration Godaigo seems to have had two general aims: (1) to abolish estate-holding and to return to the Taika ideal of universal public domain and a system of threefold taxation; and (2) to strengthen the position of the provincial governors vis-à-vis the military constables. The emperor's anti-estate measures met with little appreciable success. To set a proper example, however, he relinquished title to many of the holdings of his own junior branch of the imperial family and thus dealt a blow to the branch's economic fortunes from which it never fully recovered.

The fact that Godaigo was either unable or unwilling to cancel the various constableships of the land suggests that from the outset, despite his attempts to implement authoritarian rule at the capital, he held little real hope of reversing the course of military control in

[25] Contained in the Nijō-Kawara Lampoons.
[26] Yomiuri Shimbun Sha, *Nihon no Rekishi*, p. 77.

provincial administration. Throughout the Kamakura period constables had functioned side by side with court-appointed governors, their very existence symbolic of displacement of the court's regional system by the military. At first the duties of the constables were restricted by law (the Jōei Code) to certain constabulary functions and to the drawing up of guard rosters for shogunal housemen in their respective provinces. But inevitably these military representatives came to assume administrative responsibilities that intruded upon the spheres of authority long held by the provincial governors.

During the early Kamakura period the continued existence of well-ordered estates in the central and western provinces had reduced the shogunate's need for strong regional control and had tended to inhibit, at least in this region, the growth of constable power. It was not until the further breakdown of the estate system and the growing trend toward regionalism about the time of the Restoration and shortly thereafter that the constable emerged as the key figure in a new balance of central and provincial forces in the land. One scholar has suggested that the dual structure of governors and constables, as it was retained during the Restoration period, provided an institutional bridge, so to speak, between the regional systems of the Kamakura and Muromachi shogunates.[27] In fact, there is little to show that the court was especially constructive or consistent in its policies toward these regional officials. Apparently the best Godaigo felt he could do was to restate the traditional civil responsibilities of the provincial governors in an effort to enable them to compete more effectively with the constables. Yet he immeasurably weakened the collective position of the former by failing to restrict appointment to members of the court nobility alone. Not only did he agree to the assignment of military men to these posts; in certain cases, such as that of Nitta Yoshisada in Echigo, he allowed a warrior to become governor as well as constable in the same province.

In his desire to stress the material as well as the jurisdictional revitalization of the court, Godaigo decided in the first month of

[27] Shimizu Mitsuo, *Nihon Chūsei no Sonraku*, pp. 340–41.

[83]

1334 to undertake extensive and costly repairs to the imperial palace. He has been criticized (e.g., in the *Taiheiki*) for commencing such repairs at the very moment, so to speak, when the court was demonstrating its incapacity to handle properly claims for rewards that were pouring into its administrative channels. According to the *Taiheiki*, the cost of repairs was to be met through diversion of the revenue from two provinces—Aki and Suō—and through a five percent assessment of the income of "stewards and warriors" of the land.[28] Far from seeking to mollify the military, who were already distressed by the laxity and inequities of claims settlement, Godaigo appears here simply to have given them additional cause for grievance. It is not surprising that the *Baishōron* speaks of the mounting resentment about this time of warrior families toward courtier government and of the increasing sentiment among the former for return to some type of "Yoritomo-like" rule.[29]

In one sense Godaigo had a good reason for his decision to repair, indeed to reconstruct, the imperial palace. From the latter part of the tenth century—that is, from precisely the time when the Fujiwara began to exert complete mastery over the imperial family—the palace had on several occasions been ravaged by fire and had been allowed to fall into general disrepair and disuse. Emperors were thereafter obliged to move frequently, often living in the homes of Fujiwara or other ministers of state. The temporary residence of the emperor at any particular time was called the *sato daira* (literally, "country" palace), a term which served as a constant reminder of the uncertainty that had come to surround the material existence of the sovereign during these centuries. To Godaigo this aura of uncertainty, with its implications of waning influence and prestige, must have been intolerable. We could scarcely expect him to have rested content until the throne and its surroundings were restored materially to a level in keeping with his conception of the emperor's new role in political affairs.

About the time that the decision was reached to repair the palace, the court also issued the rather surprising announcement that it would soon commence the production of money. Coins had first

[28] *Taiheiki*, I, 398.
[29] *Baishōron*, p. 163.

been minted in Japan during the Nara period, partly to facilitate the collection of tax revenues needed for construction and development of the new capital city. Although some minting had been continued into the early Heian era, from the ninth century the practice was gradually abandoned by the imperial court. Apart from this attempt to produce money at the time of the Kemmu Restoration, the Japanese for some six hundred years appear to have contented themselves with the use of imported Chinese copper cash as their principal medium of exchange. Not until the time of Toyotomi Hideyoshi (1536–98) at the end of the sixteenth century did a central regime finally undertake the issuance of a new national currency. The failure of successive Japanese governments, both court and military, to seek the establishment of a central monetary system reflects at least in part the fact that no government from mid-Heian times had sufficient control or commanded sufficient confidence to back such a system. Regrettably, we know almost nothing of the results of the court's decision in 1334 to issue coins (to be known as *kenkon tsūhō*) and paper money, although such a decision was certainly in line with Godaigo's centralist ideas.

Failure of the Restoration

Marxist historians in Japan view the early years of the fourteenth century, including the brief interlude of the Kemmu Restoration, as a highly significant period in their country's history. According to their general analysis, it was at this time that Japan made the transition from a slave to a feudal society.[30] The focus of their interpretation is on changes in peasant relations: they see the final disappearance of the practice of slavery and the widespread adoption of landlord-peasant ties based on serfdom. There can be little doubt that momentous changes in landholding and in the pattern of agricultural production were taking place during this epoch which witnessed the continued growth of a provincial warrior class and the steady deterioration of the estate system of land tenure. The

[30] The most representative proponent of this thesis is Matsumoto Shimpachirō. See "Namboku-chō Nairan no Sho-zentei," in *Chūsei Shakai no Kenkyū*.

present study is concerned with what the Marxists call the "super-structure" of the state and deals mainly with institutional and intellectual developments at the upper level of Japanese society during the early medieval period. Yet it would be misleading if this discussion of the emperor Godaigo's efforts to reinstitute central imperial rule should suggest that decision-making in governing circles was alone responsible for the course of events during the Restoration. Japanese society was in a phase of dynamic develop-ment, reflected most dramatically in the struggle for land and power among the provincial military. It is unrealistic to suppose that, even at the time of Godaigo's triumphal return to the capital in the fifth month of 1333, the country had settled into a state of general peace. Within a few months, in fact, sporadic outbursts of fighting were being recorded in various parts of the land. And by the following year conflict in the provinces had become virtually uninterrupted.

The mismanagement of affairs at the capital and the lack of understanding on the part of Godaigo and his courtier advisers of the problems of the military served simply to increase feelings of unrest in the provinces. Works such as the *Taiheiki*, the *Baishōron*, and the *Hōryaku Kanki* [31] are uniform in their criticism of the court's administrative policies and practices. This criticism is well sum-marized in a passage from the *Taiheiki* in which Madenokōji Fuji-fusa, former head of the board of rewards, expresses his dismay over the course of events under the Restoration government:

Although the great struggle is over, the people remain impoverished and continue to suffer. Moreover, the country is still not at peace. It is a time when those in office should spit out their food to listen to grievances;[32] when remonstrating ministers should present petitions and correct their lord's errors. Yet the hundred officials only immerse themselves in pleasure and pay no heed to whether the country is being well governed or not. They cater to His Majesty's every whim and say nothing about the welfare of the realm. In consequence the number of petitioners gathered at the records and settlements offices decreases daily, as the allegations of claimants and defendants alike are aimlessly disposed of. Suits are no longer submitted

[31] The *Hōryaku Kanki* covers the period from the Hōgen incident of 1156 to the death of Godaigo in the first year of Ryakuō (1338).
[32] That is, they should be prepared to hear grievances at all times.

[86]

and no one strikes the admonitory drum. Seeing this, the courtiers believe that the virtue of rule by nonaction prevails throughout the land and that the people all revel in the splendid changes that have come about. How lamentable it is that things have reached this illusory state. At the beginning of the great struggle of Genkō the warriors of the land all flocked to the imperial side, thinking that with victory in this battle they would be rewarded for their meritorious service. And indeed after the reestablishment of peace there were unknown tens of thousands of fellows who had served loyally and who wished rewards. But the only ones who have thus far received them are courtiers and their underlings. This is the reason why petitions have been abandoned and why suits are no longer submitted; others, resentful over their failure to receive rewards for loyal service and dissatisfied over unjust governing practices, have returned home to their provinces... Although the court should be seeking to dispel the resentment of the warriors, it has decided first to undertake repairs to the palace. For this purpose stewards of the various provinces are being levied one twentieth of their incomes. How grievous it is that the burden should be placed on these men when they are still suffering from the ravages of war.

Moreover in the provinces the constables are losing their authority and only the power of the governors is being enhanced. Lower class, non-ranking deputies of the latter are confiscating estates that have been established since the Jōō period [1222–24]. And other provincial functionaries, police officials, and middle- and lower-grade soldiers are gaining a disproportionately large share of influence. That is not all. The designation "shogunal houseman," which has been used for many years (since the time of Lord Yoritomo himself) as a designation for warriors of the provinces, has in this generation at length been abolished. As a result, daimyos and other members of great houses are now no better than common people. It is impossible to gauge how many tens of thousands bear resentment because of this.

Although the enemies of the court might in the natural course of things have come to ruin, those who have in fact pacified the land and who have set His Majesty's mind at ease are Ashikaga Takauji, Nitta Yoshisada, Kusunoki Masashige, Akamatsu Enshin, and Nawa Nagatoshi.... When men act in the highest manner, with outstanding gallantry and loyalty, what sense does it make to attempt to rank them one before the other? Their rewards and appointments should be equal. Yet Enshin alone has received confirmation of but one holding and has even had his constableship rescinded. What was his offense?

Alas, in today's government selection for reward is not based on merit, and slander is the rule. What is more there is the fear that the emperor's decisions may soon be changed. Should a person appear who has the qualifications to be a leader of the military houses and should he challenge the court, warriors of the land who are filled with resentment and dissatisfied with the way of government would undoubtedly flock to him of their own accord.[33]

Fujifusa voices concern here for what he considers the needless disruption of hierarchical relations among the military. He also sounds an ominous note in predicting the rise of a new military hegemon to rally those among the provincial warriors whose traditional rights and privileges had been directly threatened or usurped by the court. Perhaps the most disgruntled of these warriors was Akamatsu Norimura (Enshin, 1277–1350), a chieftain of Harima who had been in the forefront of the fighting in the central provinces and who had played a leading role in the final assault on the shogunate's installations at Rokuhara. Inexplicably the court granted Norimura only one holding as reward; moreover it canceled his constableship in Harima.[34] When the break later occurred between Godaigo and Ashikaga Takauji, Norimura was among the first to throw in his lot with the Ashikaga. In so doing he launched the Akamatsu on a course that was to lead to their emergence before the end of the century as one of the leading constable-daimyo families under the new shogunate founded by Takauji.

Ashikaga Takauji does not appear to have participated actively in the work of reestablishing central control after destruction of the Hōjō in 1333. He was, if anything, conspicuous in his absence from administrative circles throughout the Restoration period. It may be that he sought deliberately to dissociate himself from court policies, especially as these policies came to clash with his own interests and ambitions. According to the *Baishōron*, people at this time were quick to comment on the fact that government was being con-

[33] *Taiheiki*, II, 16–17.

[34] The seeming neglect of Norimura is often contrasted with the excessive rewards given to Chigusa Tadaaki, who also participated in the assault on Rokuhara. For example see George Sansom, *A History of Japan, 1334–1615*, p. 36.

ducted "without Takauji" (Takauji *nashi*).[35] Certainly the non-participation of the Ashikaga chieftain, for whatever reason, proved in the end unbalancing to the coalition of courtiers and warriors over which the court presided. Yet it would not be correct to charge the Ashikaga alone with responsibility for the ultimate collapse of this coalition. Rather, it was a product of the whole complex of relations among its leading members, including Prince Morinaga and Nitta Yoshisada, as well as the Ashikaga brothers, Takauji and Tadayoshi.

Even as the emperor proclaimed a new era of civil rule under the court, these courtier and warrior leaders had begun to contend openly for tactical advantage and personal power. In the central provinces, as we have seen, Prince Morinaga had attempted to check the growing influence of Takauji, while in the Kantō Nitta Yoshisada had sought to oppose the supporters of the Ashikaga, who had gathered at Kamakura under the nominal command of Takauji's young son, Yoshiakira. Nitta's subsequent withdrawal from the Kantō was the same as recognition, at least on his part, of the paramount position of the Ashikaga in that region. The court seems also to have acknowledged this paramountcy, for it soon rewarded Takauji and Tadayoshi with the governorships of Musashi and Sagami, posts which had been held through most of the Kamakura period by leaders of the Hōjō and which had long been symbolic of the eastern overlordship of that family. In the twelfth month of 1333, moreover, Godaigo directed Ashikaga Tadayoshi to proceed to Kamakura with Prince Naringa (1326-44) for the purpose of establishing a regional headquarters there to oversee the administration of the Kantō. There could be little doubt that the affairs of the eastern provinces were now securely in the hands of the Ashikaga.

Apart from Nitta Yoshisada, those at court most alarmed by the consolidation of Ashikaga power in the east were Prince Morinaga and Kitabatake Chikafusa. These two appear to have joined in a plan, actually implemented before the assignment of Tadayoshi to Kamakura, to set up a rival power center in the north.[36] In the

[35] *Baishōron*, p. 163.
[36] Satō, *Nambokuchō no Dōran*, p. 41.

eighth month of 1333 Chikafusa's young son Akiie (1318–38) had been appointed governor of Mutsu and had proceeded there in the tenth month in the company of his father and Prince Norinaga. The administrative office which he opened in Mutsu was outwardly organized on civilian lines, but in fact became a recruiting center for warriors of the region.[37] Before long Akiie had a military force in the northern provinces of sufficient size to play a deciding role in later engagements between the court and the followers of Takauji.

In the sixth month of 1335 the court received a severe shock when a plot to assassinate the emperor was uncovered in Kyoto. The ringleaders were Saionji Kimmune (1310–35), a ranking courtier, and Hōjō Tokioki, younger brother of the former Tokusō, Takatoki. Tokioki, despite reports of his death after the fall of Kamakura two years earlier, had in fact fled secretly to Mutsu in the north. He later made his way disguised as a priest to the capital, where he called upon Kimmune to join him in plans to overthrow the Kemmu regime and to reinstate military rule under the Hōjō. Tokioki had good reason for seeking out Kimmune. During the Kamakura period, the Saionji family had enjoyed great prominence, owing largely to their close ties with the Hōjō, whom they had served as liaison officers (Kantō *mōshitsugi*) in Kyoto after the Jōkyū incident. At court they had held many of the highest positions (in the words of the *Taiheiki*, "half the officials of the land were selected from this house alone"),[38] while Saionji women had frequently married into the imperial family.

The Saionji had tended, during the succession dispute within the imperial family, to align themselves with the Gofukakusa, or senior, branch. The victory of Godaigo and the junior branch, therefore, was not politically favorable for them. According to the *Taiheiki*, Kimmune agreed to join in Tokioki's plot for the following reasons: (1) to return imperial authority to the Jimyōin-tō; (2) to improve the fortunes of his own house; and (3) to repay in part the long-standing debt of gratitude which the Saionji felt for the Hōjō.

---

[37] Akiie seems to have opened a type of shogunate, with offices such as council of state, board of coadjutors, and board of retainers.
[38] *Taiheiki*, II, 21.

Upon discovery of the assassination plot, Kimmune was seized and put to death. Tokioki and his personal cohorts, however, managed to escape to the eastern and northeastern provinces. Reports filtering back to Kyoto revealed that the scheme against Godaigo had not been simply an attempt at political coup in the capital, but was part of a much wider plan for rebellion by other surviving members of the Hōjō and their still-loyal supporters thoughout the land. Obviously the earlier effort to destroy the Hōjō at Kamakura had not been completely successful. In addition to Tokioki, Takatoki's son Tokiyuki (1323–53) was also still at large and was now at the head of a considerable force in Shinano.

Backed by leaders of the Suwa and Shigeno families of Shinano, Tokiyuki launched a campaign against the headquarters of Prince Narinaga and Ashikaga Tadayoshi at Kamakura in the seventh month of 1335. Tadayoshi, unable to hold firm the defenses of the former military capital, was forced to flee westward with Narinaga to the province of Mikawa. It was at the time of his departure from Kamakura that Tadayoshi ordered the execution of Prince Morinaga, who had been held captive there under pitiful circumstances for nearly a year. In Mikawa, long one of the base provinces of the Ashikaga,[39] Tadayoshi paused to regroup his forces and to appeal for help to the capital.

When word of the fall of Kamakura reached Kyoto, Takauji began immediate preparations to go to the aid of his brother. He made two requests of the court: first, that he be granted the titles of *seii taishōgun* and *sōtsuibushi*;[40] and, secondly, that he be given certain administrative powers over the Kantō, including the right to reward, personally and without reference to Kyoto, those warriors of the eastern provinces who should support him in his coming campaign against the Hōjō. Godaigo had thwarted Takauji's desire to become *seii taishōgun* in 1333 by allowing Prince Morinaga to assume this title and by restricting Takauji to the lesser

[39] For a discussion of the Ashikaga position in Mikawa see Varley, *The Ōnin War*, p. 23.

[40] Satō Shin'ichi suggests that the title of *sōtsuibushi* implied territorial authority, while that of *seii taishōgun* signified the personal overlordship of a military hegemon (*Namboku-chō no Dōran*, p. 108).

rank of *chinjufu shōgun* (general of the pacification office of the north). Once again he sought to deny the Ashikaga chieftain the title he coveted by bestowing it on Prince Naringa, who was still with Tadayoshi in flight from Kamakura.[41] Godaigo also hesitated to grant outright the administrative powers requested by Takauji. While commenting that "there should be no difficulty" in allowing Takauji to reward his troops personally,[42] he took no steps to issue a formal authorization to this effect.

Takauji, meanwhile, decided to wait no longer and on the second day of the eighth month he departed from the capital, without an imperial commission, to join his brother in Mikawa. Together they entered the Kantō where, in a brief series of encounters, they thoroughly defeated Tokiyuki and his followers and recaptured Kamakura on the eighteenth day. The Hōjō had held this city for less than a month.

Once in Kamakura, Takauji gave every indication that he intended to remain. Despite directives from the court calling upon him to return to Kyoto, he set about erecting a headquarters on the site of the old shogunate and began independently to exercise those powers which he had requested from the court before his departure to the Kantō.

In the process of conferring rewards for victory in battle Takauji confiscated the holdings of Nitta Yoshisada in Kōzuke Province and assigned them to one of his leading followers in the east. The enmity between Nitta and Ashikaga which led to this act by Takauji had, of course, been long in the making. Takauji charged that Yoshisada had slandered him before the emperor by calling into question his loyalty to the throne. In all likelihood the charge was correct, since the Nitta chieftain had by this time few if any alternative means by which to compete with the Ashikaga other than to seek a reduction of their political influence at court. After some

---

[41] When Tadayoshi halted in Mikawa, he sent Naringa on to Kyoto.

[42] *Taiheiki*, II, 37. It was at this time, according to the *Taiheiki*, that the emperor granted the character *taka* (meaning "revered") from his own personal name (Takaharu) to Takauji to be used henceforth to represent the *taka* (meaning "high") in the latter's name. Other sources, however, state that it was granted in the early days of the Restoration. Interestingly, Chikafusa, when writing about Takauji, invariably refrained from using the newer form.

deliberation the court decided that Takauji, in the light of his present actions, did indeed constitute a threat to imperial rule; and in the eleventh month of 1335 the emperor commissioned Nitta Yoshisada to lead an expeditionary force to chastise him in the east.

The military activities of the next few months may be summarized briefly. Yoshisada, after some initial successes in the Kantō, was gradually driven back to the region of the central provinces by Takauji and Tadayoshi. In the second month of 1336 the Ashikaga and their supporters, scattering the loyalist troops before them, entered the capital and forced the emperor to flee to refuge on Mt. Hiei. But their occupation of the city was to be short-lived. A powerful army under Kitabatake Akiie was already on the march at great speed from the north and soon arrived to dislodge the Ashikaga from their newly established positions. With surprising suddenness Takauji and Tadayoshi found themselves not only expelled from the capital but in great danger throughout the central provinces. In council they decided to withdraw to the west, where they already had allies in Suō and Nagato Provinces and where they hoped to gain additional support from the chieftains of Kyushu. Before leaving, Takauji secured an edict from the former emperor Kōgon of the Jimyōin-tō directing him to chastise Nitta Yoshisada and other "rebels." The Ashikaga now had their own claim to legitimacy and the conflict had become, at the highest level, a contest between the two branches of the imperial family.

Takauji remained in Kyushu from the second to the fourth month of 1336, during which time he brought most of that island under his sway. With his strength renewed he departed from Kyushu in the fifth month to return to the central provinces. On the way he and Tadayoshi, in a coordinated action on sea and land, engaged the enemy under Nitta Yoshisada and Kusunoki Masashige at Minatogawa in Settsu Province. The victory of the Ashikaga in this battle was decisive. Masashige was killed and Yoshisada was able to withdraw only with the greatest difficulty. Takauji and his commanders soon reoccupied the capital and once again forced the emperor to seek sanctuary on Mt. Hiei. Godaigo remained under the protection of the mountain monks for nearly six months. When he finally returned to the capital toward the end of the year, he was obliged by Takauji to relinquish the regalia to the new emperor Kōmyō (r. 1336–48) of the senior branch, who in the meantime had been installed as his successor. Godaigo never acknowledged the validity of this succession and later claimed that the regalia he had given to Kōmyō were false. He made this claim after his own escape in the twelfth month of 1336 to Yoshino, where he and his followers established a rival court and inaugurated the dynastic schism that was to last for more than half a century.

IV

Kitabatake Chikafusa
and the Cause of the Southern Court

IN PURELY LEGAL AND INSTITUTIONAL terms the Kemmu Restoration appears to have been a highly reactionary political movement. At a time in Japanese history when the centrifugal pull of regional and local forces was making increasingly difficult the maintenance of an effective system of governmental control by either *kuge* or *buke*, the emperor Godaigo sought to assert his right, which he saw as divinely granted, to exercise extraordinarily authoritarian powers of central rule. Godaigo believed that the imperial office should be more than simply a position from which to perform the sacerdotal rituals of state necessary to sanctify or legitimize the governing acts of others. In general, emperors had themselves performed these very acts until the usurpation of their powers in the Heian period. Even after that virtually all elements of society had continued to accept without challenge the principle that ultimate political legitimacy did indeed derive solely from the throne, and that all who would exercise public authority must do so on the basis of a delegation from this source. In practice, of course, acceptance of this principle simply provided a point of departure for competition among courtier and military families for real governing powers. The throne itself, as Godaigo clearly saw, had for centuries been deprived of all but the smallest portion of these powers, although the imperial house had been able to reenter family competition through the system of the cloistered emperor.

Godaigo, in his effort to "restore" direct imperial rule, sought nothing less than to reverse the course of nearly five centuries of institutional growth under both court and the military. His Restoration became, it is clear in retrospect, a final bid by the court nobility to assert its claim to the right of rulership of the land. The strains of a century and a half of military dominance had brought about grave divisions within court society. Succession disputes and the incapacity of the imperial and courtier families to resolve them successfully were the inevitable results of declining economic and political fortunes. Special circumstances gave Godaigo the opportunity to assume temporarily the role of active, and not simply titular, head of state. Yet there is little to show that he was able in any appreciable degree to meet the demands of either of the major sectors of aristocratic society. On the contrary he alienated many among the courtiers as well as among the military.

Godaigo's last years were spent in comparative obscurity. Although he continued to live at Yoshino until his death in 1339, we know little of his personal activities following the failure of the Restoration three years earlier. His final words before death, in the account of the *Taiheiki*, provide a terminal note of melancholy to a life that was essentially tragic. At the same time they contain a characteristic challenge to all who might abandon the principles for which he had so stubbornly fought: "Even though my bones be buried beneath the moss of these southern mountains, my spirit will always yearn for the heavens above the northern palace. Should there be those who lightly betray my instructions, they will not, if lords, be true lords or, if subjects, be truly loyal subjects." [1]

The most important figure to rise to prominence among the *kuge* during the period of war between the courts was Kitabatake Chikafusa. Chikafusa emerged not only as the chief commander of the southern forces but also as the most articulate commentator on the principal issues of concern to the courtier families. His was the last voice of any significance to speak out for *kuge* supremacy. He became, indeed, the final spokesman for a former ruling elite whose capacity to influence the major course of events in Japanese history was at length exhausted. In his writings, especially the *Jinnō Shōtōki*, Chikafusa set forth the views and attitudes of a leading courtier during the last stage of transition to a fully warrior-oriented society. No study of the Kemmu Restoration would be complete without an analysis of his interpretation of the turbulent times in which he

[1] *Taiheiki*, II, 342–43.

lived. Chikafusa was deeply committed to the cause of the southern court, although not necessarily to the goals of the Restoration government that had preceded its founding. His commitment was based partly on the narrow interests of his upper echelon of the court nobility. It arose also from a profoundly religious belief in the unique quality of Japan and its imperial institution.

The Kitabatake were a branch family of the Murakami Genji, a great clan which traced its ancestry back to the tenth-century emperor Murakami (r. 946–67). Unlike members of the Seiwa Genji, who had become leading warrior chieftains in the provinces, the Murakami Genji had remained largely in the capital to serve as civil ministers at court. At first they enjoyed little prominence, since this was the heyday of the Fujiwara regents. But from the late eleventh century the Murakami Genji, mainly through the employ of successive cloistered emperors, were able gradually to challenge the power monopoly of the Fujiwara in ministerial circles. Tsuchi-mikado Michichika (1149–1202), a member of the clan, earned special distinction at the court of Gotoba during the early years of the Kamakura period. It was he, in fact, who took the lead in orga-nizing the antishogunate movement that led to the downfall in 1196 of Jien's brother, Kujō Kanezane, who had until that time been the principal liaison official between Kyoto and Kamakura. Even before this event Michichika's daughter, as one of Gotoba's consorts, had given birth to the future emperor Tsuchimikado (r. 1198–1210). With Tsuchimikado's accession to the throne in 1198, Michichika became unchallengeably the most powerful figure at court and remained so until his death in 1202. The Kitabatake branch of the Murakami Genji stemmed from one of Michichika's grandsons.

Chikafusa's birth in 1293, therefore, was into a family of con-siderable standing at court and his rise in rank was rapid, especially after he received the favor of the emperor Godaigo upon the latter's succession to the throne in 1318. In such high regard did Godaigo hold the young Kitabatake leader that he entrusted him with the care and upbringing of his second son, Prince Yonaga. The prince's premature death in 1330 caused Chikafusa, then only thirty-seven, to retire from public life and to take Buddhist vows. In consequence

[97]

he appears to have taken no part in the turmoil and upheaval that resulted first in the exile of Godaigo in 1331 and then in his return to the capital upon the overthrow of the Kamakura Shogunate in 1333.

We first encounter Chikafusa during the Restoration period in the announcement that he would accompany his son Akiie, who had been appointed governor of Mutsu, and Prince Norinaga to the northern provinces in the tenth month of 1333. Since Akiie was at the time only a youth of fifteen, we may suppose that his activities as governor of Mutsu were closely supervised by his father. It is surprising, however, that a high-ranking minister such as Chikafusa, who had been close to the emperor in earlier years, should have left the capital shortly after the Restoration was inaugurated and have remained in virtual obscurity in a distant region for the next two years. We have noted that Chikafusa—probably in conjunction with Prince Morinaga—became convinced of the need to open a military base in the north to counterbalance the dominant position of the Ashikaga in the Kantō. This may explain in part his lengthy absence from Kyoto; yet it is also possible that Chikafusa remained away because, as we shall see in our examination of the *Jinnō Shōtōki*, he was in fundamental disagreement with the major policies of the Restoration government.

Chikafusa finally returned with the army of Akiie when the latter sped down from the north in the early months of 1336 to drive the Ashikaga from the capital and force their temporary retreat to Kyushu. Although Akiie returned shortly thereafter to his post in Mutsu, Chikafusa went down to Ise where the Kitabatake had their principal family holdings. The province of Ise is situated adjacent to the Yoshino region of southern Yamato and no doubt Chikafusa's return to the family at this time was to prepare for the removal of Godaigo and his court to sanctuary in Yoshino before the end of the year.

In Kyoto, Kōmyō (r. 1336–48) of the senior branch of the imperial family had already been installed as the "northern emperor." Kōmyō owed his position entirely to the pleasure of the Ashikaga. Indeed, until unification in 1392 he and his successors lived in constant fear that the Ashikaga, in proposals to the southern court, might negotiate them out of existence. From all appearances

Takauji had agreed only with the greatest reluctance to take those final steps which had forced creation of the southern court. Godaigo had adamantly refused to acknowledge a new shogunate or military establishment outside the central framework of the Kemmu government. If the Ashikaga were to seize the opportunity to assume leadership of the warrior class, they had no alternative other than to dissociate themselves from his rule. Yet the fact that they were almost invariably the ones to initiate peace overtures during the first decades of the war between the courts[2] suggests that the Ashikaga remained sensitive to the tenuousness of their claim to legitimacy. The northern court was too obviously the product of highly irregular political maneuvering.

Takauji had hoped to model his shogunate on the lines of the former military regime at Kamakura. Circumstances, however, made difficult his plans to create a permanent institutional structure at this time, since nearly all effort had of necessity to be concentrated on dealing with the offensive threat of the southern court. For several years there was widespread fighting, extending from Kyushu in the west to Mutsu in the north. But the southern court could not long match the military potential of the Ashikaga and their allies. By the end of 1338 many of its leading commanders were dead—including Kitabatake Akiie, Nawa Nagatoshi, and Nitta Yoshisada—and its strength was on the wane.

Chikafusa sought to revive the southern war effort by making a bid to muster new support in the eastern provinces. In the ninth month of 1338 he set forth from Ise with a fleet of ships bearing Prince Norinaga and other leaders. En route they encountered a violent storm and Norinaga's ship was blown back to Ise. Chikafusa, who managed to reach the coast of Hitachi, later interpreted this as a divine occurrence, since it enabled the prince to be present at Yoshino upon the death of his father, Godaigo, the following year.[3] Shortly before his death Godaigo transferred the regalia to Norinaga, who ascended the throne as the second southern emperor, Gomurakami (r. 1339–68).

---

[2] Observed by Murata Masashi in *Namboku-chō Shi Ron*, p. 98.
[3] Kitabatake Chikafusa, *Jinnō Shōtōki*, in Iwasa Masashi, *et al.*, eds., *Jinnō Shōtōki, Masu Kagami*, pp. 190–91.

It was during his stay of more than four years in the Kantō that Chikafusa wrote the *Jinnō Shōtōki*. Apparently his only aid in composition of the first draft in the autumn of 1339 was an imperial genealogy. The work as it now stands includes revisions made in 1343.

In the opening lines of the *Jinnō Shōtōki* Chikafusa stated that, since "great Japan is the divine land (*shinkoku*) . . . and . . . it has been ruled since time immemorial by the descendants of Amaterasu Ōmikami," it is therefore unique among the countries of the world. We have seen that the concept of a divine land, interpreted specifically as a "divinely protected land," came to be widely held during the first century of the medieval period, especially at the time of the Mongol invasions. With Chikafusa, *shinkoku* thinking shifts its emphasis from divine protection to divine descent (i.e., of the Japanese imperial family). At the same time it acquires a new dimension of national consciousness and a new sense of Japanese uniqueness and superiority. Whereas in other countries, such as India and China, order had frequently been disrupted and rule had often changed hands, in Japan alone there had been no departure from the exercise of highest authority by successive sovereigns of a single imperial line from the founding of the state until the present time.[4] This extraordinary continuity of rule gave to Japan a special national entity or essence (*kokutai*), of which all subjects of the land should be constantly aware.

In fact, the course of events in Chikafusa's own age had given rise to doubts about the extent to which subjects were aware of the foundations of the Japanese state and of the manner in which its throne had been transmitted from earliest times. Chikafusa stated as his reason for writing the *Jinnō Shōtōki* a desire to dispel such doubts by informing the people anew of the details of these matters.[5]

The *Jinnō Shōtōki* is divided into six parts, the first of which is devoted largely to a discussion of the origins of Japan and the age of the gods, and the remaining five to a chronological treatment of the imperial reigns from Jimmu to Gomurakami. Since his stated

[4] *Ibid.*, pp. 48–49.
[5] "The way of the gods is not readily revealed; and ignorance of the origins of things can lead to disorder." *Ibid.*, p. 49.

purpose was to provide "a record of the legitimate [or direct] line of descent of the divine sovereigns," Chikafusa made no attempt to be exhaustive in his presentation. He dealt chiefly with those facts which he deemed necessary to explain the manner in which imperial succession had progressed through the ages. His digressions were aimed not so much at giving a fuller and more balanced treatment of Japanese history as they were at setting forth personal views and attitudes toward developments with which he was especially concerned. As a result, the *Jinnō Shōtōki* is not simply a record of imperial succession, but a highly slanted political tract as well.

Chikafusa's view of history was basically Shintoistic. He attacked with vigor what he considered the false beliefs of *mappō* and "a hundred kings," which had produced widespread historical pessimism since the end of the Heian epoch. There was, to his mind, no trend in history that moved inevitably or unalterably downward. Although there might be temporary reversals or declines, these would invariably be rectified with the passage of time.[6] History was fundamentally constant, its aberrations correctable. Chikafusa's thinking, like that of all medieval Shintoists, was strongly influenced by Buddhist and Confucian ideas; but at base his optimism stemmed from an unshakable faith in the eternal order of state and society in Japan as set forth by the founding gods. The stability of this order lay in its ordained social hierarchy. Chikafusa held that men were born with differing *kami*-natures, that some were intended to be emperors, others to be ministers of state, and still others to be farmers. It was natural that there should be some mobility within the various classes, but it was contrary to the divine order that individuals strive for ranks and positions to which they were not entitled by birth. This was perhaps the most characteristic tenet of Chikafusa's sociopolitical creed and one to which he returned time and again in his writings. Jien had expressed similar aristocratic views of society and had attributed the actual changes which occurred among both classes and individuals to the operation of a mysterious principle which he termed *dōri*. Chikafusa, on the other hand, denied that

---

[6] "It is as true now as it has always been: the wicked will not last long but will perish, and the disordered world will be set aright." *Ibid.*, p. 180. See also Nagahara, "Kitabatake Chikafusa," p. 124.

change was anything but temporary and held to his belief in ultimate correctability.

Chikafusa applied the principles of overall historical constancy and correctability to his analysis of imperial succession. To understand how he did this it is necessary first to examine his usage of the word *shōtō* in the title *Jinnō Shōtōki*. *Shōtō* may be interpreted variously, depending on the precise meaning one ascribes to the first character, *shō*. This character, as it is used in political terminology, ordinarily means "legitimate"—i.e., widely accepted as or sincerely believed to be "rightful" (in either a moral or legal sense). Hence *shōtō* may properly be rendered as "legitimate line." Chikafusa, however, preferred to interpret *shō* as something closer to "direct" or "straight" (in the sense of not being crooked) and *shōtō* as "direct line." He believed that within the progress of legitimate succession there was a special direct line, from which there might be deviations but to which there would always be returns (*shōtō e kaeru*).[7] It was precisely the capacity of the Japanese imperial succession to return invariably to its direct course or line that ensured its eternal continuance and that set Japan apart politically from countries like India and China: "In our country alone has the imperial succession been unbroken from the beginning of heaven and earth until the present. Although, as is inevitable within a single family, the succession has occasionally been transmitted collaterally, it has always returned to the direct line."[8] Before examining further this idea of the direct line, however, let us first note Chikafusa's approach to the broader question of legitimate succession.

Legitimacy and constancy were closely related concepts to Chikafusa. The basis for imperial legitimacy, as universally accepted by

---

[7] I have decided to render *shōtō* as "direct line" to distinguish it from "branch line." But it is clear that Chikafusa also intended the former to have ethical connotations, since on occasion he replaced it with the term *seiri* (correct principles): that is, he spoke of a return to "correct principles" as part of the periodic return to the direct line of imperial succession. Tsuda Sōkichi points out that Chikafusa sometimes tried to equate "direct line" with "line of the eldest son" but that he could not carry this interpretation too far because it would have weakened his argument in support of Godaigo's junior branch of the imperial family. See "*Gukanshō oyobi Jinnō Shōtōki ni okeru Shina no Shigaku Shisō*," in Fuzanbō, *Hompō Shigaku Ronsō*, I, 506–8.

[8] *Jinnō Shōtōki*, pp. 48–49.

the Japanese, was the pledge of Amaterasu to her grandson Ninigi that his line of descendants would rule Japan eternally. The sole absolute qualification for an individual's right to succeed to the throne was birth into the imperial family, and the symbol of his occupancy of the throne was possession of the regalia. With the single exception of Gotoba, all sovereigns up to and including Godaigo were understood to have commenced their reigns upon transference to them of the regalia. Working from these facts, Chikafusa had little difficulty in compiling a list of legitimate sovereigns through the accession of Godaigo which few, if any, of his contemporaries would have found necessary to challenge.[9] He had, then, nothing of importance to add to the question of imperial legitimacy before the issue which arose in 1331, when the Hōjō exiled Godaigo and elevated a prince of the senior branch, Kōgon, to the throne. Although Chikafusa did not believe that the senior branch of the imperial family should have been allowed to partici- pate in the line of succession after the death of Gosaga, he in no sense denied the legitimacy of those senior branch emperors who had in fact exercised imperial authority before Godaigo.

Where Chikafusa innovated in his analysis of pre-Godaigo suc- cession was in his attempt to identify a special "direct line" of imperial descent within the broader stream of legitimate sovereigns (ninety-five through Godaigo) who had occupied the throne of Japan from the time of Jimmu. There is much that is contrived about Chikafusa's efforts to trace this direct line and in fact the idea, as he defined it, was not really essential to his principal claim—for which the *Jinnō Shōtōki* is best known—of the legitimacy of the southern court. Yet he undertook to present it, I believe, from a desire to solve a fundamental dilemma in his own attitude toward the throne and its role in Japanese history: how to reconcile the principle of unbroken hereditary succession with a personal belief in the need for ethical kingship.[10] After Chikafusa's time the real power of the throne

[9] He listed the empress Jingū (traditional dates as regent 201–69), but excluded Kōbun (r. 671–72) and Chūkyō (r. 1221).

[10] Bitō Masahide observes that Chikafusa, in his use of the terms "direct line" and "correct principles," attempted to restrict the application of Con- fucian political ideals to a single family line. "Nihon ni okeru Rekishi Ishiki no Hatten," in Iwanami Shoten, *Iwanami Kōza Nihon Rekishi*, XXII, 45.

declined so precipitously that, by the Tokugawa era, scholars could describe the political role of the emperor almost entirely in abstract terms. Ideals could be imputed to him with no fear that this remote personage, guarded from the view of all but a small coterie of court officials, would violate them by his personal conduct. To Chikafusa, however, the emperor had always been and was, either actually or potentially, a very real participant in the exercise of political power. And, as a historian, he was obliged to note that certain sovereigns had not acted in an ethically appropriate fashion. The explanation for this, he believed, lay in the doctrine of the direct line.

Chikafusa postulated, probably under the influence of Chinese thinking, that the gods had originally intended imperial succession to proceed in strict generational order from father to son. He observed that this ideal manner of succession had maintained through the reigns of the first twelve sovereigns (from Jimmu to Keikō; the dates of rule, whether traditional or historical, of these and other sovereigns in the ensuing discussion may be found in Appendix I).[11] The next emperor should have been Keikō's son, the fabulous warrior Yamato-takeru; but, because of the latter's untimely death, the succession went to a younger brother, Seimu. Seimu later designated Yamato-takeru's son to follow him on the throne and in so doing revealed his own reign, in retrospect, to have been the first deviation from the direct line of generational succession. Chikafusa asserted the need from Seimu's time to distinguish between legitimate reigns (which he designated as *dai*) and generations of direct descent (*sei*).[12] Seimu's reign, by this definition, was the thirteenth *dai* but was not a *sei*, since the direct line was seen to have gone instead through Yamato-takeru and his descendants (see Appendix 2).

Although the direct line was supposed to be "straight," Chikafusa acknowledged a certain inscrutability about its course. The point is that it could be discerned as straight only in long-term perspective. When, for example, one of two or more brothers

[11] Inoue Mitsusada hypothesizes that in the seventh century the Japanese came to admire the Chinese principle of imperial succession from father to son. They thereupon asserted that their earlier sovereigns had succeeded in this ordered fashion from generation to generation. *Shinwa Kara Rekishi E*, in Chūō Kōron Sha, *Nihon no Rekishi*, I, 270.

[12] *Jinnō Shōtōki*, p. 77.

ascended the throne, it might not become clear for several generations whether he was truly of the direct line. This point is illustrated by the fate of Nintoku, a son of Ōjin, and his lineal descendants. Nintoku, who has traditionally been regarded as one of the most virtuous of Japanese sovereigns, initiated a line that continued for ten reigns until the emperor Buretsu. According to the records the latter was an exceedingly evil man, who engaged in such cruelties as the disembowelment of pregnant women. When he was assassinated at the age of eighteen without a direct heir, the ministers of state selected Keitai, a descendant in the fifth generation from another son of Ōjin, to be Buretsu's successor. To Chikafusa it was Buretsu's evilness that caused extinguishment of the line of Nintoku. He noted that "no matter how great the virtue of the ancestor, if the descendants are lacking in virtue their conduct of imperial affairs will inevitably be terminated,"[13]

Thus a line of descent within the imperial family which began auspiciously with a "good first" ruler (Nintoku) came to an ignominious end with a "bad last" ruler (Buretsu). Chikafusa saw the restoration of imperial virtue in the elevation of Keitai as pleasing to the gods. But he took care to stress that ethical considerations should never cause the ministers of state to violate the natural order of succession. Although Nintoku's line had lost virtue by the time of Buretsu and thus would "inevitably be terminated," it was only because Buretsu was childless that these ministers could rightfully take this opportunity to select Keitai as his successor: "So long as there is a candidate in the natural line of succession [i.e., a son of the emperor], the other princes, no matter how great their wisdom, cannot hope to succeed to the throne. Only when a line has come to an end is it in accord with heaven to select someone of wisdom from another branch of the imperial family."[14]

Chikafusa pointed to the branch lines of Temmu and Montoku as two other major deviations from the direct line of imperial descent. The emperor Tenji's death in 671 had brought on a struggle for the throne between his son, Prince Ōtomo, and his brother

[13] *Ibid.*, p. 89.
[14] *Ibid.*, p. 90.

Temmu.[15] Temmu emerged victorious and founded a line that was to continue for nearly a century, ending with the empress Shōtoku, whose reputed affair with the notorious priest Dōkyō qualified her to a place among the "bad last" rulers of Japanese history. When Shōtoku died without children in 770, the ministers selected Kōnin, a grandson of Tenji, as her successor. Chikafusa viewed Kōnin's succession not only as a return to the direct line of Tenji, but also as a restoration (*chūkō*) of imperial virtue similar to that which had resulted from the appointment of Keitai to the throne in the sixth century.[16]

Montoku's line was a brief one and was terminated when his grandson, Emperor Yōzei, was deposed by the imperial regent Fujiwara Mototsune (836–91) in 884. Yōzei appears to have been criminally insane and no doubt Mototsune acted wisely in removing him from office. Yet Chikafusa, in praising Mototsune's action, seemed to contradict his earlier assertion that the ministers of state should not interfere with the normal progress of a reign nor with the natural order of succession. A century later the Fujiwara at their zenith were able to appoint or dismiss emperors at will. But by then they could set forth the fiction that each abdication was in accord with the wish of the emperor concerned. Yōzei's abdication at this earlier date, on the other hand, was obviously forced. Nevertheless, it had, in Chikafusa's eyes, the gratifying effect of bringing to the throne the elderly Kōkō, whose immediate descendants included Uda, Daigo, and Murakami, the inspirational precursors of the Kemmu Restoration.

As hypothesized earlier, Chikafusa seems to have evolved his theory of a direct line of imperial succession (within the larger continuum of legitimate succession) in an attempt to reconcile, at least partially, the inviolable principle of hereditary transmission of the Japanese throne with the need for virtuous rule. He was, in any case, able to use the direct line theory as a means to explain why certain Japanese sovereigns had possessed virtue and others had not. In a famous passage in the opening chapter of the *Jinnō Shōtōki*, Chikafusa asserted that the essential qualities of ethical rulership in Japan,

[15] This struggle is known, after the year-period, as the Jinshin incident.
[16] *Jinnō Shōtōki*, p. 99.

even when absent in individual sovereigns, were eternally symbolized by the three regalia. The mirror, he believed, stood for uprightness (*seichaku*), the jewel for compassion (*jihi*), and the sword for decision or resolve (*ketsudan*). The rightful possessor of the regalia ought to base his rule on uprightness and compassion and implement it with resolve.[17] Chikafusa gave as part of the instructions of Amaterasu to Ninigi at the time of bestowal of the regalia: "Illuminate the world with the brightness of this mirror; rule it with the excellence of this jewel; and by brandishing this sword quell all those who do not submit to you."[18]

In another passage Chikafusa spoke more specifically of what the sovereign should do: (1) he should distinguish between good and evil and appoint worthy ministers; (2) he should allot lands properly; (3) he should reward the meritorious and punish transgressors. Of these various principles of virtuous rule, Chikafusa placed greatest stress on the first. He believed that once the sovereign has appointed worthy ministers (whose worthiness shall be judged by birth as well as by merit), he need not personally concern himself further with administrative matters. Chikafusa's view was typical of that traditionally held by the high-ranking courtier: that the emperor's function was essentially one of ministerial sanctification.

Chikafusa clearly admired the type of oligarchic government that Jien had idealized in the *Gukanshō*. Like Jien, he praised the great Fujiwara ministers of the past, who held their mandate to serve the throne from Ama-no-koyane, the "assisting" *kami*. He also spoke eloquently of the scholarship and loyalty of the Murakami Genji, who alone among the Genji had performed uninterrupted service at court from the time of their origins in the tenth century.

Although it was through the office of cloistered emperor that the Murakami Genji had first gained their opportunity to compete with the Fujiwara, Chikafusa was generally critical of the historical role

---

[17] *Ibid.*, p. 177.

[18] *Ibid.*, p. 60. This quotation is based on a passage from the annals of the emperor Chūai in the *Nihon Shoki*. When Chūai went to Kyushu to subdue Kumaso tribesmen, a local chieftain greeted him with objects similar to the regalia and urged him to use them to pacify and govern the world. During Kamakura times the words of this chieftain came to be regarded as those that had originally been spoken by Amaterasu in her instructions to Ninigi.

of the cloistered emperors. It was fundamental to him that government in Japan, whatever its outward form or forms, should always have the throne at its center: that is, ultimate governing authority should always be traceable back to the throne. By this criterion, both the Fujiwara regency and the later Kamakura Shogunate were properly instituted branches of a unitary government under the emperor. Only in the case of the cloistered emperorship did Chikafusa see a type of government with administrative channels entirely separate from the throne.[19] The cloistered emperors were themselves usually former sovereigns and always high-ranking members of the imperial family; yet their system of rule was contrary to the intent of the founding gods that government in Japan be eternally under the aegis of an unbroken line of legitimate sovereigns.

It is difficult to summarize Chikafusa's attitude toward the military. He acknowledged the need for coercion in government; yet he seems to have been uncertain as to whether the coercive function should be the sole prerogative of a special group of warrior families. At one point in the *Jinnō Shōtōki* he stated emphatically that the minsterial class in Japanese society was by nature divided into civil and military, and that

It would be impossible to dispense for even a moment with either the civil or the military functions of government. It is said that "when the country is disturbed, the warrior receives preference over the civil official; but in time of peace it is the civil official who enjoys first rank." In this way the various methods of government are made the basis for allaying the apprehensions of the people and for preventing strife.[20]

Elsewhere, however, Chikafusa stressed with equal vigor that the warrior should never be regarded as equal to the court official. He observed that in an earlier age courtiers had been the ones to lead the emperors' armies. Only with the turmoil which arose toward the end of the Heian period did it become necessary to engage specialists

[19] "The old form [of government] changed . . . edicts from the office of the cloistered emperor came to be highly regarded . . . and the emperor became little more than a figurehead." *Ibid.*, p. 142.
[20] *Ibid.*, p. 116. The quotation is from the *Huai-nan-tzu*.

in the arts of war to restore order to the country. The principal causes of turmoil at that time were the improper allocation of lands, which enabled men to accumulate huge private estate holdings, and the imprudent distribution of ranks and positions. Chikafusa remained forever the formalist in regard to the latter point: ranks and positions should be granted only in strict accordance with traditional qualifications first of birth and then merit.

This formalism can be seen in his view of the twelfth-century founder of military government, Minamoto Yoritomo. Like most chroniclers of the early medieval period, from Jien to the authors of the *Taiheiki*, Chikafusa lauded Yoritomo for his work in bringing stability and order to the land. At the same time he criticized the Minamoto chieftain for coveting and accepting excessively high rank, and asserted that it was for this reason that his line had come to an end in the second generation.[21]

To Chikafusa the ideal military man was Hōjō Yasutoki. Unlike Yoritomo, Yasutoki was content to administer shogunate affairs from the appropriately modest post of shogunal regent, to which he had succeeded upon the death of his father Yoshitoki in 1224. But whereas Yoshitoki, in Chikafusa's opinion, had simply had the good fortune to rise to power in Kamakura as the authority of the Minamoto declined, Yasutoki was a ruler of rare wisdom who was considerate toward the imperial court and solicitous of the people's welfare. Indeed, it was owing principally to Yasutoki's merit that the Hōjō were able to remain in power for another century.[22]

Under the early Kamakura Shogunate the court, although it had lost political power, had at least enjoyed tranquillity and the people had been spared the anguish of further disorder. In view of this, Chikafusa held, the provocations of the cloistered emperor Gotoba that led to the Jōkyū struggle (in which Yasutoki played a prominent role as a cocommander of the shogunate's expeditionary force) were entirely unwarranted. Since the Hōjō had done no wrong at the time, the cloistered emperor should not have attempted their overthrow. His actions were premature: only when the court could

[21] *Ibid.*, p. 177.
[22] *Ibid.*, pp. 162–63.

provide government on a higher level of excellence would it be justified in moving against the shogunate.[23]

We can see in the early medieval period a growing tendency toward this sort of open criticism of imperial policy, by courtiers as well as warriors. Such criticism had a much stronger political content than that directed toward "bad" rulers in the remote past, such as Buretsu and Yōzei. Chikafusa, as we have noted, even used the examples of Buretsu and Yōzei to show how the inherent virtuousness of the imperial line was periodically reaffirmed or reenforced by the selection of especially worthy successors, like Keitai and Kōkō.[24] The precipitate and ill-conceived actions of the cloistered emperor Gotoba, on the other hand, caused feelings of resentment and bitterness that were to persist for more than a century. Loyalist sentiments did not prevent Chikafusa, for example, from leveling some of his sternest censure at Gotoba. And to leaders of the military the Jōkyū incident was nothing less than a "rebellion (go-muhon)." Years later warriors of the east, still deeply suspicious

[23] "It is quite likely that later generations, in considering this disturbance of Jōkyū, will be troubled in their hearts; and this could well cause those below to defy those above. It is important, therefore, to have the details of this event clearly understood. Yoritomo's meritorious exploits were unprecedented; yet, because he took charge of affairs in the country so completely, it is not surprising that the cloistered emperor felt uneasy. Moreover, when Yoritomo's line came to an end [shortly] after his death, the conduct of affairs was assumed by the nun Masako and the rear vassal Hōjō Yoshitoki. It was to be expected that the cloistered emperor should wish to reduce the power of the military and to resume personal control of government. But the ancient form of government had been on the wane from the time of Shirakawa and Toba. During Goshirakawa's period military uprisings occurred, treacherous subjects disrupted the land, and the people fell into a state of almost complete misery. Yoritomo quelled these disorders himself. And, although the imperial family was not restored to its former status, the capital was once again at peace and the people were given respite. All people, both high and low, were made secure and from the four directions they submitted to Yoritomo's virtue. Thus, even when his son Sanetomo died, there were none who went against his successors. How could the court expect to overthrow the military leaders unless it had virtue sufficient to exceed theirs?" *Ibid.*, pp. 159–60.

[24] It was one thing for Chikafusa to use an idea such as that of the direct line to explain the unethical behavior of sovereigns in a former age; it was quite another, as we shall see in a moment, for him to attack specific policies of more recent or even contemporary rulers and still to maintain the inviolable sanctity of their imperial positions.

of the court, were to apply the same term to the intrigues of Godaigo against the Kamakura Shogunate.[25]

Chikafusa was keenly aware that the authoritarian and largely unsuccessful measures of Godaigo during the Restoration period served only to increase the opportunity for criticism of imperial politics. One of his aims in writing the *Jinnō Shōtōki* was to make clear the distinction he saw between the imperial line as a transcendent source of virtue in government, which was above criticism, and the behavior of individual sovereigns, which was not. Undoubtedly he would have preferred to remove the sovereign entirely from the arena of political competition and to entrust to the ministerial class sole responsibility for national administration.

Chikafusa had previously distinguished between two types of ministers or officials: civil and military. The former had held sway through the Heian period and the latter had maintained order during Kamakura times. In 1333 a "spontaneous" uprising had destroyed the Kamakura Shogunate,[26] by then a thoroughly unworthy governing body. Circumstances had demanded a new and vigorous reassertion of court rule. Godaigo, however, had erred by granting exorbitant rewards in lands and ranks to warriors such as Ashikaga Takauji and his brother Tadayoshi. In fact, Chikafusa maintained, it was the gods, and not at all the military, who had made possible the Restoration.[27] Takauji and his kind, who had rejected hereditary obligations to the Hōjō in order to participate in their overthrow, were hardly the type of men now to render unswerving loyalty to the throne. Ministerial direction in the new age could come only from the great courtier families, whose leaders must once again combine in themselves the civil and military functions of rule. Chikafusa's prototype of the new civil-military man was his own son, Akiie.

In discussing Akiie's appointment to the governorship of Mutsu

[25] Hayashiya Tatsusaburō cites a letter by Yūki Munehiro, later a stalwart of the southern cause, at the time of the antishogunate scheme in 1324 in which he speaks of the emperor's *go-muhon*. *Namboku-chō*, pp. 22–23.
[26] Chikafusa saw the enemies of the shogunate arising miraculously as one "from the provinces of Kyushu to Mutsu and Dewa" in the north. *Jinnō Shōtōki*, p. 175.
[27] *Ibid.*, p. 177.

in the tenth month of 1333, he observed that, although the Kitabatake had served the court for generations, their experience had been entirely in the field of central affairs. They knew nothing of provincial administration and had had no occasion to pursue the military arts. Yet conditions now demanded greater versatility on the part of the minister: "The court has already unified the land and civil and military ways can no longer be kept separate. In ancient times descendants of princes and officials of state were generals of the armies. The courtier must again take on the function of the warrior and become the bulwark of the court." [28]

Godaigo, as we have seen, contended that he had transferred false treasures to the northern emperor Kōmyō and had retained possession of the real regalia during his flight to Yoshino in 1336. Whether true or not, this contention was used by Chikafusa as the basis of his claim for legitimacy of the southern court. If he intended thereby to make possession of the regalia the *ultimate* test of imperial legitimacy, however, he had already weakened his argument by acknowledging the succession of Gotoba in 1185 as legitimate. Both Kōgon and Kōmyō of the northern branch of the imperial family had, like Gotoba, ascended the throne solely on the basis of authorization by cloistered emperors.

Perhaps the strongest claim of the southern court to legitimacy lay in the simple fact that Godaigo never willingly relinquished his imperial position. The behavior of Ashikaga leaders toward the southern emperors throughout the period of war between the courts suggests that they, by and large, recognized this fact to be true and realized the weakening effect it had upon the pretensions of the northern court. It remained their goal, until actual unification in 1392, not to exterminate the southern branch but somehow to persuade it to return to the former practice of alternate succession, which in their minds would have settled conclusively the theoretical problem of the locus of imperial legitimacy.

It has been stated that Chikafusa's was the last voice of any significance to speak out for courtier supremacy during the last stage of transition to a fully warrior-oriented society in Japan.[29] His views

[28] *Ibid.*, p. 176.
[29] See page 96 above.

on the question of court families versus military families must inevitably seem to us a curious combination of practical adjustment to the times and highly reactionary insistence upon the defense of traditional rights and privileges that had become largely indefensible. He joined a long line of nobles, from Jien to Prince Morinaga, who recognized the need for some type of merger of civil and military functions of rule; yet he remained far more insistent than most of the others that the court nobility retain strict supremacy in the state over the provincial military. This can be seen clearly in his policies as effective leader of the southern court during the 1340s and early 1350s.

The southern court seems from the outset to have been a very limited establishment. The great majority of courtiers remained in Kyoto, and of those who fled with Godaigo to Yoshino, many later returned to the northern court. For practical purposes all but the last vestiges of political power of the courtier class vanished at this time. Although many courtiers were able to maintain economic interests in the estate system for another century or more, they held little hope of once again mounting a collective challenge to warrior rule. The northern court came completely under the dominance of the Ashikaga Shogunate, while the southern court, after perhaps a decade or so of offensive warfare, found itself reduced to a near fugitive existence in the hill country in and around Yoshino.

Little is known of administrative organization or operation at Yoshino, although it appears that rule by direct imperial edict (*rinji*), which Godaigo had always cherished, was its principal characteristic.[30] We do know that Godaigo and his successors found it increasingly difficult to secure adequate military and financial support. In the early years the southern court was able to compete for the allegiance of warriors in the central provinces; it also received the backing of certain religious institutions and merchant groups[31] in the Yamato-Kii-Ise region. But mounting skepticism about its

[30] Yomiuri Shimbun Sha, *Nihon no Rekishi*, V, 130.
[31] These groups were known as *sanjo* and appear to have emerged within various estates in the central provinces, especially those belonging to great court families and religious institutions. Members originally engaged in menial tasks, but later branched into teamster activities and became a vital part of the developing economy of exchange during the post-Heian period. For a discussion of the *sanjo*, see Hayashiya, *Namboku-chō*, pp. 48–53.

prospects hampered the southern court's efforts to recruit new followers or to acquire new sources of revenue.[32]

The most pressing problem was to maintain military activities on a national scale. For perhaps the first time in Japanese history warfare raged from one end of the country to the other. Outside the central provinces, the principal regions of strategic contention between the shogunate and the southern court were the northwestern circuit (Hokurikudō), the provinces of the east and far north, and the island of Kyushu. Nitta Yoshisada had transferred his activities to the Hokurikudō after the fall of Kyoto in 1336. But a series of defeats climaxed by Yoshisada's own death in 1338 dashed any hopes the southern court may have had of inaugurating a major offensive in that region. Meanwhile, in 1337, Kitabatake Akiie had departed from his base in the north to undertake a second expedition to the central provinces. His death in battle the following year (actually some two months before the demise of Nitta) not only removed another leading general from the southern ranks, but also cast grave doubts on the likelihood of the Yoshino regime's ever recapturing the position of hegemony which Akiie had long held in the north.

About the time of his departure from Mutsu, Akiie submitted to Godaigo a memorial on government,[33] which is highly critical of the emperor's policies during and after the Restoration period. Among the matters the young Kitabatake leader commented on were the indiscriminate distribution of rank and position to "up-starts" and warriors (echoing his father's line of opposition to inclusion in the ruling elite of members of the lesser nobility as well as of the provincial military such as Ashikaga Takauji, Nitta Yoshisada, and Nawa Nagatoshi); extravagance at court; the granting of preferment to sychophantic concubines, monks, and the like, whose meddling in the affairs of state had become the subject of gossip even in the northern provinces; and the disregard for established laws and customs which had resulted in "decrees issued in the morning that are changed in the evening" (chōrei bokai). Government by

---

[32] One source of revenue that became important to the southern court about Gomurakami's time was assessment of commissariat rice (known as chōyōbun to the southern court, hyōrōmai to the military).

[33] Cited and discussed in Satō, Namboku-chō no Dōran, pp. 92–98.

caprice, Akiie implied, had caused great uncertainty among the people, so that they scarcely knew how to act or where to turn for guidance. To underscore his grave concern over the decline of Restoration ideals, Akiie vowed that unless reforms were undertaken by the southern court he would resign from imperial service and would retire into the mountain forests.

The most successful move of the southern court in its national strategy about this time was the dispatch of Prince Kanenaga (1329–83), one of Godaigo's many sons, to Kyushu in 1336 as general for pacification of the west.[34] Kanenaga established a base in Kyushu which he was able to hold for more than forty years, until it was finally destroyed by the distinguished general of the shogunate, Imagawa Ryōshun. Kanenaga's victories in Kyushu, however, must be regarded as an exception to the general trend of fighting. Even before the decade of the 1330s was over the southern court found itself increasingly restricted in its range of action against the supporters of the shogunate. It was, as we have seen, for the purpose of reopening a front in the north that Chikafusa set out by sea for Hitachi Province in the ninth month of 1338.

Chikafusa's principal aim was to secure the support of the northern chieftain Yūki Chikatomo, who held a key position at Shirakawa in the province of Mutsu. Chikatomo's father, Munehiro (d. 1338),[35] had joined the imperial cause in 1333 at the time of Nitta Yoshisada's attack on Kamakura. He was later stationed with Kitabatake Akiie in Mutsu and joined the young commander on the two occasions, in 1336 and 1338, when he led armies back to the fighting in the central provinces. In the absence of his father and Akiie, Yūki Chikatomo was supposed to be caretaker of the Yoshino court's northern base. But as Chikafusa was to discover, Chikatomo, like other chieftains of the region, had no intention of committing himself to the southern cause unless such an act should be more beneficial than other alternatives open to him and his family.

It is recorded that Chikafusa wrote some seventy letters to Chikatomo alone in his attempt to persuade the Yūki chieftain to side with the southern court. His tone in these and other messages

---

[34] *Seisei taishōgun.*
[35] See the chapter on Munehiro in Hayashiya, *Namboku-chō*, pp. 16–46.

to warrior leaders in the east and north, however, was far more imperious than it was persuasive. In response to inquiries about the amount of reward those who joined the southern court could expect, Chikafusa replied that in the past men who had "surrendered" were lucky to retain even a half or a third of their holdings. At this time the court would be especially generous and would confirm in their entirety the holdings of all who vowed allegiance. But reward was out of the question. Indeed it was a disgrace to think in such crassly material terms. One would expect a merchant thus to seek profit in return for loyalty, but not a warrior.[36]

During his stay of more than five years in the east, Chikafusa was forced to move his base of operations from one fortification to another. While he sought desperately to gain the backing of reluctant chieftains like Chikatomo, the shogunate dispatched Kō no Morofuyu with a large force from the capital to attack him. Under constant pressure from Morofuyu, Chikafusa was barely able to hold on until 1343. Hence, when Yūki Chikatomo finally opted to join the Ashikaga, Chikafusa saw the futility of persisting further, and in the eleventh month of that year he returned to Yoshino.

After Chikafusa's return from the east, the military activities of the southern court, apart from those of Prince Kanenaga in Kyushu, became sporadic at best: a new general would appear briefly and win some impressive victories or someone would defect from Kyoto and help temporarily to give Yoshino an advantage. In 1347, for example, Kusunoki Masashige's eldest son, Masatsura (1326?–48), took charge of the southern forces in the central provinces and defeated several of the shogunate's leading commanders before meeting his death in the first month of 1348 in an encounter with Kō no Moronao (d. 1351) in Kawachi. And between 1350 and 1352 both Ashikaga Tadayoshi and Takauji submitted on separate occasions to Yoshino and led military expeditions in the name of the southern court.

The temporary submissions of the Ashikaga brothers came about from a fierce struggle for power that raged for several years within the shogunate.[37] Enmity between Tadayoshi and the Kō brothers,

---

[36] See the discussion in Satō, *Namboku-chō no Dōran*, pp. 229–31.
[37] See the discussion in Varley, *The Ōnin War*, pp. 30–32.

Moronao and Moroyasu (d. 1351), had flared into the open in 1349. This enmity stemmed in part, no doubt, from a clash of personalities and the sheer lust for power; but on another level it appears also to have arisen from an ideological dispute between a group of great eastern chieftains, led by Tadayoshi, who wanted strong central control within the shogunate and a new class of warriors of the home provinces, including the Kō, who desired more latitude in the building of personal bases in their respective provinces.

When Takauji took the side of the Kō brothers in 1350, Tadayoshi departed from Kyoto and joined the Yoshino court. After gathering a force under the southern standard, he had the Kō brothers murdered, reentered the capital and effected a reconciliation with Takauji. For reasons that are not at all clear in the records, this reconciliation did not last and in the eighth month of 1351 Tadayoshi was forced once again to leave the capital. Takauji now went over to the southern court and obtained a commission to pursue and attack his brother. He captured Tadayoshi within a few months and had him killed at Kamakura early in 1352.

While Takauji was in the east tracking down Tadayoshi, Yoshiakira remained at Kyoto in charge of the shogunate. Yoshiakira's job was to keep negotiations going with the southern court in his father's absence. The Yoshino regime took a characteristically hard line in these negotiations. It demanded, among other things, that the Ashikaga use the year-period designation of the southern court and have the northern court both surrender the "false regalia" which it held and cancel all courtier appointments it had made since 1336. We have seen that the "false regalia" had supposedly been given to the northern emperor Kōmyō by Godaigo shortly before the latter's flight to Yoshino. Although the southern court always claimed possession of the real regalia, it apparently wished now to deprive the northern court of even these allegedly ersatz symbols of imperial legitimacy.

With Takauji in Kamakura, the shogunate's military position in the central provinces was weakened. Seeing that Yoshiakira was simply attempting to stall time, the leaders of the southern court soon decided, instead of negotiating further for the shogunate's "surrender" and a reunification of the courts, to attack the capital. Early in 1352 southern troops with Chikafusa himself at their head entered Kyoto and forced Yoshiakira to withdraw temporarily to nearby Ōmi. Chikafusa and his men held the capital for only a few weeks. When they left in the third month of 1352 they took with them not only the "false regalia" but also three former emperors of the northern court—Kōgon, Kōmyō, and Sukō (who had been obliged to abdicate the previous year when Takauji and Yoshiakira had first made peace overtures to the southern court) —as well as the crown prince, Naohito.

The coronation of the next northern emperor, Gokōgon (r. 1352–74), was carried out under the most extraordinary circumstances. In the absence of any regalia (whether false or not) and with no former emperor to issue an enthronement decree, Gokōgon was given as a token of his imperial office the box (kokarabitsu) which was said to have until recently held the sacred mirror.[38]

Not until 1357, some five years later, were the three former emperors and Prince Naohito finally allowed to return to Kyoto. During these years the southern court was seldom at Yoshino, but kept shifting to different locations in the central provinces south of the capital as changes in strategic conditions dictated.

In the eleventh month of 1352 the southern court received the allegiance of a powerful new commander in Ashikaga Tadafuyu (d. 1400). Tadafuyu was Takauji's own son (and was probably older than Yoshiakira, although his birth date is not precisely known), but had been adopted and brought up by his uncle, Tadayoshi. In the struggles that occurred within the shogunate during the early 1350s Tadafuyu took the side of Tadayoshi against Takauji. It was the execution of Tadayoshi in 1352 that caused him to go over to the southern court. He brought with him at that time several important captains who had also backed Tadayoshi.

With the added strength of Tadafuyu, the southern court was able to reoccupy Kyoto for a second and a third time in 1353 and 1355. Between these dates two important events occurred: Chikafusa died and the southern court granted Tadafuyu the title of sōtsuibushi. All indications are that Chikafusa had been the one best able to hold

---

[38] Satō, Namboku-chō no Dōran, p. 276.

together the differing factions within the southern court.[39] His death was, politically at least, an incalculable loss.

The nearly simultaneous appointment of Tadafuyu as *sōtsuibushi*, moreover, may be interpreted as a grave admission by the southern court of its military decline about this time. From the days of Godaigo and the Kemmu Restoration it had been a cardinal principle of the junior branch of the imperial family that the two highest military titles—*sōtsuibushi* and *seii taishōgun*—should not be granted to a chieftain of the *buke*. Ashikaga Takauji, it will be recalled, had requested both titles from Godaigo in 1336 and had been refused them. Inasmuch as the emperor Gomurakami seems to have been as fully imbued with the restorationist spirit as his father,[40] the southern prospects must have been dim indeed at this time to oblige him to designate as *sōtsuibushi* Tadafuyu, who had no abiding loyalty to Yoshino and had simply joined the southern court because of his alienation from the shogunate.

Takauji died in the fourth month of 1358. He had never wanted a showdown fight with the southern court and had always held to the hope that reconciliation between Kyoto and Yoshino could be arranged. The new shogun Yoshiakira, on the other hand, seems to have decided almost immediately upon the kind of all-out attack that his father had repeatedly hesitated to launch. His plans backfired, however, when discord erupted among his generals. Chieftains of the Yūki and Hosokawa families even defected to the enemy and joined Ashikaga Tadafuyu in occupying Kyoto on behalf of the southern court for the fourth and last time in 1361.

Shortly before Yoshiakira's death in 1367 another important attempt was made by people on both sides to reconcile the courts peacefully. The chief negotiator for the southern court in this instance was Masashige's third son, Kusunoki Masanori, who had played a similar role some sixteen years earlier when Ashikaga Tadayoshi had temporarily submitted to Yoshino. This latest effort at reunification became stalled when the southern emperor Gomurakami in his correspondence with Yoshiakira called upon the latter to "surrender" to the southern court. Whether or not these two

[39] *Ibid.*, p. 291.
[40] *Ibid.*, p. 295.

leaders could eventually have come to some agreement can only be speculated upon, for by the third month of the following year, 1368, both Yoshiakira and Gomurakami were dead.

Yoshiakira was succeeded by his infant son Yoshimitsu (1358–1408), who during his minority was ably assisted by the shogunal deputy (*kanrei*) Hosokawa Yoriyuki (1329–92) and who later became a forceful shogun in his own right. The southern throne went to Gomurakami's eldest son, Chōkei. Much mystery surrounds Chōkei's reign, which is generally believed to have lasted from 1368 until 1383. Not only are his accession and abdication dates not precisely known, there are no records to identify his mother, his offspring (if any), or the place and time of his death. The main reason appears to be that from Chōkei's reign on the Yoshino court and its remnant supporters withdrew ever more deeply into the hill country of the southern Kansai and became veritable fugitives. What records it kept were probably lost in its constant moving about.[41]

A number of scholars have hypothesized that Chōkei and his younger brother, who succeeded him as the emperor Gokameyama (r. 1383–92), came to be rivals within the southern court over the issue of reunification. Chōkei has been seen as the head of the anti-unification faction and Gokameyama of the pro-unification group. There is in fact no convincing evidence of a personal rivalry between the two brothers; but the southern court certainly became once again receptive to negotiations with Kyoto after Chōkei's abdication and Gokameyama's accession about 1383.

The person who seems to have worked hardest for reunification of the courts was Kusunoki Masanori. After he failed to bring Yoshiakira and Gomurakami together and after Chōkei became emperor of the southern court, Masanori in 1369 even went over to the side of the shogunate and the northern court. This suggests that Chōkei as emperor assumed a hard line toward Kyoto that was intolerable to Masanori, a view that gains further credence from the fact that Masanori, after leading shogunate forces in at least one major assault on the temporary position of the southern court at Kongōji

---

[41] Murata, *Namboku-chō Ron*, 121.

in Kawachi in 1373, eventually returned to the southern side when Chōkei transferred imperial authority to Gokameyama.

Masanori has been much maligned by historians of the Tokugawa period. As we shall see in the next chapter, it was during this epoch that sympathy for the lost cause of the southern court was widely aroused by the growth in popularity of the tales of the *Taiheiki*. Supporters of the southern court came to be seen in a new historical light and Kusunoki Masashige, in particular, was converted into a great national folk hero. In the eyes of Japanese of the Tokugawa period the defection of Masashige's son, Masanori, was the only stain on the otherwise exemplary loyalist record of the Kusunoki family during the fourteenth century.

Of the scanty materials extant on Chōkei there are three edicts, known as *insen*, or "edicts of the cloistered emperor," which he issued after his abdication. The proof here that the southern court under Chōkei reopened the long-abolished office of cloistered emperor, combined with other evidence that the southern court about this time began once again to designate imperial regents of the Fujiwara family, reveals how far it had drifted from Godaigo's original Restoration ideals.[42]

I shall not attempt to analyze in detail the conditions that gave rise to the final reunification of the courts in 1393; for this would necessitate, at the very least, a discussion of those institutional developments in military society during the fourteenth century which enabled Yoshimitsu and his advisers to stabilize the shogunate and to impose their rule on most of the central and western provinces of Honshu and, to a lesser degree, the Kantō and Kyushu. Yoshimitsu came to preside over a new balance of power between the shogun in Kyoto and a group of some ten or eleven constables (or constable-daimyos, as modern historians label them) in the provinces. Unlike the constables of the Kamakura period, who had only limited police powers, the constable-daimyos of Yoshimitsu's era were nearly autonomous regional barons who exercised decisive authority over large territorial blocs.

Yoshimitsu proved himself a forceful shogun and must personally

---

[42] *Ibid.*, p. 125.

be credited with much of the political success of the Ashikaga Shogunate in the last quarter of the fourteenth century. In 1392, after lengthy negotiations, he finally persuaded the emperor Gokameyama and the southern court to accept his reunification overtures and to return to Kyoto. The conditions he set were: (1) that Gokameyama transfer the regalia to the northern court and go through the formalities of "abdicating" to the northern emperor, Gokomatsu (1377–1433); (2) that henceforth the junior and senior lines alternate in succession to the throne as they had before the Kemmu Restoration; (3) that the remaining lands attached to the office of governor in the various provinces be given to the junior line; and (4) that the extensive Chōkōdō holdings, already in the possession of the senior line, be retained by it.

In his negotiations with the southern court Yoshimitsu seems to have made no effort whatsoever to consult the wishes of Gokomatsu and his ministers. His sole concern was to have the regalia returned to Kyoto and he apparently saw no need to discuss the matter with a puppet northern court that he dominated completely.

Most likely Yoshimitsu never intended to allow a return to alternate succession as provided in article two above. In any case, it became increasingly clear to Gokameyama and his followers that, after they had relinquished the regalia, their claims to the throne were to be completely ignored. Yoshimitsu, apparently against the wishes of the northern court, had Gokameyama given the honorary title of *dajō tennō* or "retired emperor." But Godaigo had granted the same title to Kōgon of the senior line in 1333 and, as in this former instance, there was no official recognition that the recipient had in fact ever been a legitimate emperor.

In 1410 Gokameyama suddenly left Kyoto and returned to Yoshino. It is not certain why he did this; but most likely it was because he had learned that Emperor Gokomatsu, in contravention of the agreement to return to alternate succession, planned to abdicate in favor of his own son, Shōkō (r. 1412–28), and not Gokameyama's son. Shōkō assumed the emperorship in 1412. Two years later a warrior named Kitabatake Mitsumasa, who was descended from Chikafusa, took up arms on behalf of Gokameyama. But Mitsumasa's rising was not successful and in 1416 the shogunate persuaded Gokameyama to return to the capital, where he lived quietly until his death in 1424.

When Gohanazono (r. 1428–64), also of the senior line of emperors, succeeded to the throne in 1428, Gokameyama's son, Ogura-no-Miya (d. 1443), departed from the capital and went to Ise, where Kitabatake Mitsumasa once again sought to revive the cause of the southern court by a resort to arms. On this occasion, however, Mitsumasa was killed by troops of the shogunate and Ogura-no-Miya, like his father, was obliged to return to Kyoto and to end his days in obscurity.

The records provide only a scattered account of the activities of the southern court from this time on.[43] Yet a few months after Ogura-no-Miya's death in 1443 southern adherents engineered a spectacular robbery of part of the regalia (the jewel) from the imperial palace in Kyoto. The jewel remained in the hands of the southern court until 1457, when retainers of the Akamatsu family recovered it and, in the process, slew the southern pretender (whose precise identity is not known).

The last appearance of the southern court in the pages of history was during the Ōnin War (1467–77). The Yamana, who headed the so-called western army, briefly displayed a man purported to be the "southern emperor" as a backer of their side in a rather futile effort to offset the advantage of the Hosokawa, leaders of the eastern army, who had custody of the emperor Gotsuchimikado (r. 1464–1500). But after the Ōnin War there is only silence. The great movement for the recovery of imperial prerogatives undertaken by Godaigo a century and a half earlier had at length come to an end.

[43] A thorough discussion of information available on the southern court following reunification in 1392 may be found *ibid.*, pp. 160–80.

V

Changing Views of the Past

THE LONG-STANDING DEBATE, stemming from the time of Chikafusa and the *Jinnō Shōtōki*, over the respective claims to legitimacy of the northern and southern courts reached its climax in the textbook controversy of 1911, when the Japanese government authorized the revision of primary school history texts and the establishment of an "orthodox" line of interpretation in regard to fourteenth-century imperial legitimacy. This controversy was in part the outgrowth of an increasing tendency from the 1880s among Japanese authorities to use history as a means to inculcate morality among school-age youth. In 1910 a sensational anarchist plot to assassinate the Meiji emperor had been uncovered and fear of the deterioration of public morals, a periodic concern of all societies, became a burning issue in Japan. To those who ascribed special value to the sanctity and continuity of Japan's imperial line, revelation of the assassination plot quite naturally came as a tremendous shock. When public attention was called the following year to the fact that government-authorized primary school history texts taught that once, for more than a half-century, there had been two lines of reigning emperors in Japan, this seemingly indisputable historical truth was sharply challenged and the events of nearly six hundred years earlier suddenly became a matter of pressing concern to people in widely differing walks of national life.

In this chapter and the next I shall seek to examine the background of the 1911 textbook controversy by tracing changing views of the Japanese toward the events of the great dynastic schism of the fourteenth century. My aim will be to record the evolution of both scholarly interpretation and popular sentiment in regard to this controversial epoch in premodern Japanese history.

Any historiographic study of the Kemmu Restoration and the war between the courts must appropriately begin with the *Taiheiki*, which, for all its many exaggerations and digressions, is by far the

[124]

single most important source of information on the age. A lengthy and episodic work covering some fifty years of the momentous events of the fourteenth century, the *Taiheiki* consists of three parts: (1) the period from Godaigo's succession in 1318 to the overthrow of the Hōjō in 1333; (2) from the early days of the Restoration to the death of Godaigo at Yoshino in 1339; and (3) from the middle years of the war between the courts to the death of the second Ashikaga shogun, Yoshiakira, in 1367.

Regrettably we know very little of either the authorship or the date of composition of the *Taiheiki*. From the endless speculations of Japanese scholars on these matters, however, it seems safe at least to conclude that it was not written at one time and that more than one person participated in its composition. There is strong reason to believe that the original manuscript consisted of only the first third mentioned above; that it was compiled near the time of the events themselves; and that very likely the Buddhist priest Gen'e (d. 1349), who appears in its pages and who at different times in his career was a confidant both of Godaigo and the leaders of the Ashikaga Shogunate, was its principal, if not sole, author.[1]

The title of the work may be literally translated as "chronicle of great peace," a seemingly incongruous appellation for the record of a time of almost constant warfare and struggle. Some commentators have speculated that it was meant to express the yearning of the *Taiheiki*'s author or authors for a return to peace and order. Others, on the grounds that the original work may only have covered events up to the inauguration of the Kemmu Restoration, have proposed that the meaning of *Taiheiki* is closer to "chronicle of great pacification."

Whether or not the first third once stood alone as the "chronicle of great pacification," there do appear to be distinct differences in style and outlook between it and the other parts of the *Taiheiki*. The opening narrative of the overthrow of the Hōjō and Godaigo's triumph has, for example, been told with a kind of exhilaration and epic sweep that was very likely inspired by great expectations of a renaissance in court rule. Despite its characteristically Japanese theme

---

[1] See, for example, the discussion in Ichiko Teiji, ed., *Taiheiki*, pp. 458–59.

of impermanence, so frequently used to account for vicissitudes in the lives of individuals, Part One offers an undeniably optimistic view of things to come. Part Two, on the other hand, introduces a new element of uncertainty and disillusionment. Godaigo's Restoration policies had obviously not been the panacea for accumulated ills of the late Kamakura period that many had hoped they would be, and the authors of the *Taiheiki* did not hesitate to criticize them. Their guidelines in judging human behavior, whether of emperors or of lowly subjects, remained strongly Confucian. Yet increasingly we find these chroniclers willing to assess the course of events in terms of practical results, whether these results were achieved by virtue or by force. Perhaps it was at this point that the informed mind of medieval Japan abandoned the chimera of antiquated imperial rule and at length accepted the fact of warrior supremacy. We could not, of course, expect to draw such a conclusion from the *Jinnō Shōtōki*, since Chikafusa composed his work to rally the spirits of those who were supporting a waning cause. The authors of the *Taiheiki* seem to tell us that this cause is lost.

Part Three is the least well organized and the least valuable portion of the *Taiheiki* as a historical source. Significantly, the focus of the narrative in this part is on the Ashikaga Shogunate and the affairs of the military houses. The *Taiheiki*, which began with events leading to the glorious restoration of the court to power, ends with a somber recitation of struggle among warrior chieftains for position within the new Ashikaga hegemony.

There is one further piece of information about the possible authorship of the *Taiheiki*. In Kyoto on the third day of the fifth month of 1374 the courtier Tōin Kinsada (1340–99) made the following entry in his diary: "I have heard that sometime between the twenty-eighth and twenty-ninth of last month the priest Kojima died. He was author of the *Taiheiki*, which is popular with people these days. Although Kojima was of low birth, he was renowned for his literary skills. It is indeed a pity to hear of his passing." [2] Since there does not appear to be another scrap of information about the identity of "the priest Kojima," we can derive very little

[2] *Tōin Kinsada Nikki*, in Tōkyō Teikoku Daigaku, *Bunka Daigaku Shishi Sōsho*, XLVIII, 27.

from these remarks. Perhaps Kojima was editor of the edition of the *Taiheiki* that was best known in Kinsada's day; or perhaps he collaborated in its writing with his fellow cleric, Gen'e. It is, in any case, interesting to learn that the book enjoyed favor among witnesses or near-witnesses to the events with which it dealt.

The *Taiheiki* has held a kind of popularity through the centuries that can be matched or exceeded by only a few other Japanese books. It is certainly not the equal, in literary merit, of the earlier war-tale, *Heike Monogatari*; but it has probably had a more profound influence on the thinking of later generations.

The *Heike Monogatari* and the *Taiheiki*, quite apart from their factual value, together constitute the chief repository of the legend and sentiment from which we must draw our impressions of medieval Japan. The contrast between elegant courtier and vigorous fighting man, the loyalties, betrayals, and passions of the age are all most vividly portrayed in these works. Without them the medieval setting and medieval attitudes would be immeasurably more difficult to discern. The special significance of the *Taiheiki* lies in the fact that it deals with the delicate question of loyalty to the throne during a time of raw struggle for power and of disorder within the imperial house itself. Later commentators, particularly in the Tokugawa period, were to lavish praise on the behavior of men like Kusunoki Masashige and Nitta Yoshisada, whom they saw to possess a spirit of imperial loyalty that transcended the petty allegiances of other warriors to their feudal overlords. Kusunoki, especially, has been pictured as a paragon of loyalist virtue. We might even say that Kusunoki has been the *Taiheiki*'s greatest legacy to the Japanese people.

This does not mean that all Japanese of all periods have held uniform opinions of the *Taiheiki*. Scholars have constantly debated its value as factual history. In 1891 Kume Kunitake (1839–1931) wrote a series of articles entitled The *Taiheiki* Is Worthless as a Historical Source,[3] and another prominent historian of the day, Hoshino Tadashi (1839–1917), labeled it "fiction." The contempt of these men for the *Taiheiki* seems to have been generally shared by their

---

[3] Kume Kunitake, "*Taiheiki* wa Shigaku ni Eki Nashi," in *Shigaku Zasshi*, I (1891).

fellow academicians of the Meiji period.[4] Yet it was precisely at this time that the Meiji government began to intensify its efforts to inculcate among the people, through primary school history and morals courses, the spirit of a Kusunoki-like loyalism to the throne that was so powerfully delineated in the *Taiheiki*. Kume, Hoshino, and others, as we shall see, opposed this kind of loyalism as reactionary and illiberal. They singled the *Taiheiki* out for special attack because of its importance to the Mito scholars of the Tokugawa period, who had formulated in their great historical work, *Dai Nihon Shi* (History of great Japan), the rhetoric of modern Japan's mystical reverence for the throne.

These Meiji historians, perhaps out of a desire to counter the government's efforts to resuscitate what they regarded as an irrational and "feudalistic" type of loyalism, were unduly harsh on the *Taiheiki*. Historians of the twentieth century have largely reversed their unflattering appraisal of it. One of the first and most prominent scholars to upgrade the work's historicity was Tanaka Yoshinari (1860–1919) of Tokyo Imperial University. Through careful comparison and collation with other documentary materials of the fourteenth century, Tanaka demonstrated that a number of accounts in the *Taiheiki*, previously supposed to be fanciful, were basically factual.[5] He was also chiefly responsible for the inclusion of many of its passages in *Dai Nihon Shiryō* (Historical source materials of great Japan), the most prestigious and exhaustive compendium of primary source materials on Japanese history. Today most scholars accept the *Taiheiki* as generally reliable and discount its hyperbole as essentially stylistic.

At the same time that the Meiji authorities of the early twentieth century rewrote primary school textbooks to exalt Kusunoki and other supporters of the southern court for their peerless loyalty, they slanted the accounts of these textbooks to picture the Ashikaga as among the vilest traitors in the country's history. These authorities

[4] For the views of these scholars see Ōkubo Toshiaki, "Yugamerareta Rekishi" in Sakisaka Itsurō, ed., *Arashi no Naka no Hyakunen*, especially pp. 36–42.

[5] Tanaka's most important study of the period with which we are concerned is *Namboku-chō Jidai Shi*.

certainly could not have derived such a harsh view of the Ashikaga from the *Taiheiki*; and it is important to make this point clear before we turn to an examination of how the *Taiheiki* came to be regarded as something of a scriptural source for modern Japanese loyalism.

Loyalism, like any term that deals with ethical value, is obviously open to differing interpretations; but we can define it as that combination of awe, respect, and transcendental allegiance which the Japanese seem traditionally to have held toward their sovereign. Although in most periods of Japanese history the appropriate focus of imperial loyalty has been clear, during the early medieval age this was not so. Political relations were unusually complex and often the location of "sovereignty" was not manifest at all. Men could sincerely question who should be the recipient of an allegiance that was supposed to transcend the duty and responsibility they owed to their direct overlords. Undoubtedly most people, locked in the hierarchy of feudal relations, never actually faced the need to decide between a cloistered emperor and an emperor or between a northern emperor and a southern emperor. A number of warrior leaders showed themselves to be quite agile in jumping from one side to the other in the war between the courts. But we cannot deduce, without further evidence, that these chieftains did not retain a sense of awe and allegiance toward the imperial institution itself.

There seems little doubt that Ashikaga Takauji was, in the strictest sense, disloyal to Godaigo, a rightful emperor whose will he flouted on several important occasions. Nevertheless, it is possible to view Takauji's kind of disloyalty as almost unavoidable in an age when the imperial family was so deeply divided. Chikafusa forcefully argued in the *Jinnō Shōtōki* that there was one and only one line of legitimate sovereigns and that no subject should be in doubt as to where legitimacy lay. At the same time he frankly acknowledged that the reason he felt compelled to argue the point was precisely because there was doubt among the people.

The *Taiheiki*, far from picturing Takauji as a heinous traitor, even seeks to arouse our sympathy for him because he was faced with the dilemma of choosing between the throne and his own family. In 1335, it will be recalled, Takauji established his headquarters in Kamakura after marching eastward to assist his embattled brother

Tadayoshi and to destroy the uprising of Hōjō Tokiyuki. The court shortly thereafter declared Takauji a rebel and commissioned Nitta Yoshisada to destroy him. Takauji, apparently appalled at the imperial declaration, entered a temple in Kamakura, cut his hair, and made preparations to take holy vows. According to the *Taiheiki* account, his brother and several of his generals forged an imperial decree which declared that priestly status would not protect Takauji from chastisement. Only then did the Ashikaga leader reluctantly ride forth to do battle with Yoshisada. We are told that the men of his army all cut their hair so that Takauji would not appear conspicuous in their ranks.[6]

Most leading chieftains of the early medieval period, including Takauji, were basically conservative men with strong commitments to traditional institutions and to the special privileges of both courtier and warrior elites. They were enmeshed in certain historical processes of sociopolitical change that were radically to alter these institutions and ultimately to dissipate these elite privileges. Yet the leaders of both the Kamakura and Ashikaga Shogunates (until the Ōnin War of 1467–77) adopted policies that were protective of traditional rights. We have noted, for example, how Hōjō Yasutoki and the compilers of the Jōei Code forbade the stewards from intruding upon estates to which they were not assigned. Through much of the mid- and late fourteenth century the Ashikaga also sought to minimize the seizure by local warriors of lands and harvests belonging to courtiers and religious institutions. It is clear that the Hōjō, the Ashikaga, and other senior military families were virtually the only ones who shielded these representatives of the *ancien régime* from complete economic and social dispossession before the fifteenth century.

Two oft-cited incidents in the *Taiheiki* suggest, by contrast, the extraordinary personal disrespect and contempt with which certain newly risen provincial warriors of the post-Restoration period appear to have regarded even ranking members of the imperial family and court society.

At dusk one day in the ninth month of 1341 a warrior from Mino

[6] *Taiheiki*, II, 57.

Province, Toki Yoritō, rode through the capital with a companion after a round of archery practice and revelry. When the riders encountered a procession which included the cloistered emperor Kōgon, an attendant of the latter came forward to demand that they dismount and make proper obeisance. Although his companion promptly complied, Yoritō, who was apparently inebriated, refused. In response to outraged remonstrances that he was an ignorant country boor who did not know how to behave before a cloistered emperor, Yoritō replied: "Did you say 'cloistered emperor' (in) or 'dog' (inu)? If it's a dog, perhaps I'd better shoot it!" So saying, he let loose an arrow that pierced the carriage in which Kōgon was riding and provoked a general commotion which ended with the carriage overturned and the former emperor sprawled on the street. The Ashikaga, who regarded such behavior as intolerable, ignored all pleas for leniency and had Yoritō summarily beheaded.[7]

About the same time Sasaki Dōyo from Ōmi Province burned the Myōhōin, a temple in eastern Kyoto which was headed by a monzeki or abbot of the imperial blood. Dōyo, whose name appears frequently in the pages of the Taiheiki, had earned notoriety as a conspicuously extravagant parvenu in the post-Restoration society of the capital that was dominated by leaders of the shogunal, rather than the imperial, court. Sometime in the autumn of 1338 his servants trespassed on the grounds of the Myōhōin to gather branches from its lushly foliaged maple trees and were driven off by the priests. Incensed that anyone, even though he might be acting for a monzeki, would have the temerity to treat his men in this fashion, Dōyo gathered a force of some three hundred riders, attacked the Myōhōin, and set it ablaze.

Since the Myōhōin was a branch temple of the Enryakuji, the monks of that great monastic center joined the imperial court in demanding Dōyo's punishment. And when the Ashikaga in this instance hesitated, the monks issued orders for the cessation of religious services at Tendai temples throughout the land. The Ashikaga finally ordered Dōyo into exile in the eastern provinces; but at the time of the Sasaki chieftain's departure from the capital he was

[7] Ibid., pp. 403–5.

escorted by some three hundred gaily dressed and frolicsome riders who lent the occasion the kind of festive air one would expect at the outset of a holiday journey rather than a trip into exile.[8]

It would of course be foolish for us to argue whether Takauji was a "good" or a "bad" man. But since our central concern is with the value judgments which later Japanese have made of their leaders of the fourteenth century, it is important to attempt some assessment of his character and personality. We may begin by observing that Takauji seems to have been unexceptional as a military leader. Although he appears to have had sufficient warrior prowess and tactical skill to prevail over his opponents, who did not have his advantage in family backing, we could not rank him with the first captains of Japanese history.

Recent scholars have made much of Takauji's relationship with his brother, Tadayoshi. A popular theory is that the two actually shared the responsibilities of the office of shogun in the newly formed Ashikaga government, Takauji as the personal leader of the Ashikaga vassals and Tadayoshi as the political administrator and maintainer of the shogunate's territorial hegemony.[9] Of the two brothers Tadayoshi was the more forceful and fixed in his views. He certainly opposed with greater vigor the *nariagari* or "upstart" behavior of men like Toki Yoritō, Sasaki Dōyo, and the Kō brothers, Moronao and Moroyasu, who are generally regarded as the most antipathetic of the Ashikaga generals to the rights and privileges of the old *kuge* and *buke* elites and hence the real revolutionaries of this age.[10] Tadayoshi was also more insistent in dealings with Godaigo and the southern court that any settlement between Kyoto and Yoshino be based on a recognition of warrior rights (i.e. the continuance of a shogunate) and a return to the system of alternate succession to the throne. Takauji, on the other hand, was inclined to compromise.

Takauji tended also to be more emotionally volatile than his brother. At least one writer has suggested that on occasion he suffered from fits of extreme irrationality or mental depression and

---

[8] *Ibid.*, pp. 337–39.
[9] Satō, *Namboku-chō no Dōran*, pp. 153–56.
[10] See the comments in Varley, *The Ōnin War*, pp. 25–26.

has offered, among other pieces of "evidence," the incident mentioned above of his attempted escape from reality into a Kamakura temple on the eve of his first great military confrontation with Nitta Yoshisada.[11] The breach between the brothers that finally led to the poisoning of Tadayoshi in 1352 was part of a very complex set of events and personal relationships among the Ashikaga and their leading followers. Although we can scarcely applaud Takauji for murdering his brother, we know too little of the details of these events and relationships to determine precisely why he committed this ghastly act.[12]

Perhaps the most favorable assessment of Takauji by one of his contemporaries is that attributed to the eminent Zen prelate, Musō Soseki (1275–1351):

Takauji possesses three great virtues. The first is his courage. Although he has been near death in battle many times, he has invariably remained cheerful and has shown not the slightest trace of fear. Takauji's second virtue is his compassion: he hates no one and has on many occasions shown vengeful enemies the same leniency he would show children. Third, Takauji is magnanimous and not in the least niggardly. He makes little distinction among material things; and when he bestows weapons, horses, and the like, he does not even try to match the gift to the recipient but simply passes things out as they come to hand.[13]

Musō may not have been the most impartial observer of Takauji's character inasmuch as he, like a number of other leading members of the Zen clergy of Kyoto, appears to have adroitly shifted his personal allegiance from Godaigo to the Ashikaga after the failure of the Kemmu Restoration. Nevertheless, it seems unlikely that Musō's laudatory remarks about Takauji's personal courage, compassion, and generosity were entirely factitious. At Musō's suggestion Takauji even sponsored construction of the Zen temple, Tenryūji, to be dedicated to the memory of Godaigo. Musō himself, as first abbot of the Tenryūji, made the dedicatory address for the temple. He spoke of Takauji's great grief over the fact that the

[11] Satō, *Namboku-chō no Dōran*, pp. 121–23.
[12] For a brief discussion of the Takauji-Tadayoshi quarrel see Varley, *The Ōnin War*, pp. 30–32.
[13] Quoted in Satō, *Namboku-chō no Dōran*, p. 120.

slander of others had brought about his (Takauji's) estrangement from the late emperor and had, in Takauji's words, consigned him to the fate of an ignominious rebel without any real chance to explain his innocence.[14]

There is considerable evidence to show that Takauji was exceptionally pious even during an age of widespread religious fervor. Through his close relations with Musō, he acquired a particular interest in Rinzai Zen and Musō claims that even after a night of heavy drinking Takauji never went to bed until he had devoted an hour or more to Zen practice.[15] Yet Takauji's religious interests were by no means restricted exclusively to Zen. In common with a great many of his contemporaries, he approached Buddhism eclectically. He examined the various sects and incorporated those elements of each that he found most satisfying into his personal body of religious belief.

There is also little doubt that Takauji, in keeping with his clearly discernible religious sensibilities, was profoundly moved by the great human suffering and seemingly endless process of social and political disorder he witnessed during a lifetime of fighting. If he was not unique in being so moved, he certainly was more demonstrative about it than most of his fellow chieftains of the mid-fourteenth century. Even in the flush of great military victory over Nitta and and Kusunoki at Minatogawa in 1336, for example, Takauji submitted a written prayer to the Kiyomizudera temple in Kyoto in which he likened this world to a world of dreams and declared his intention of retiring from it to seek the path to salvation. He expressed, furthermore, the wish that Tadayoshi might be allowed to replace him as warrior hegemon of the country. Without attempting to attach any overriding significance to this prayer, we can, I believe, see in it an aspect of Takauji that contrasts strikingly with the stereotyped image of him as a ruthless and cynical opportunist.[16]

Although Takauji was not a man of exceptional learning or

[14] I have paraphrased this from the translation of Musō's address in Tsunoda, de Bary, and Keene, eds., *Sources of Japanese Tradition*, p. 257.

[15] Takayanagi Mitsutoshi, *Ashikaga Takauji*, p. 420.

[16] Sir George Sansom gives, in colorful terms, the more traditional view of Takauji in *A History of Japan, 1334–1615*, pp. 98–102.

erudition, he left nearly seven hundred *waka* poems that attest to his unusually keen interest in that perennially popular form of artistic composition. One scholar has noted that Takauji's poems, though far inferior to those of Minamoto Sanetomo (1192–1219), the literarily inclined shogun of the early Kamakura period, reflect an honesty of expression that had become rare in the overly refined and restricted world of *waka* poetizing.[17] However trivial the distinction may be, Takauji stands foremost among the great founders of military regimes in Japanese history in the composition of *waka*. Minamoto Yoritomo and Oda Nobunaga (1534–82) left none; and those of Tokugawa Ieyasu (1542–1616) have been judged "atrocious."[18] Only Toyotomi Hideyoshi (1536–98), who had the least formal education or training of any of these men, produced *waka* that approach in quality those of Takauji.

Unsatisfying though it is, we have a clearer picture of the personality and character of Takauji (and also his brother, Tadayoshi) than we do of any of the other protagonists of the Restoration period with the possible exception of Chikafusa, who we can observe through the *Jinnō Shōtōki*. Most of the great figures of the very early years of the medieval age, such as Taira Kiyomori (1118–81), Taira Shigemori (1138–79), Minamoto Yoshitsune (1158–89), and the cloistered emperor Goshirakawa, have been brought vividly to life and made memorable by the *Heike Monogatari*. The key personalities of the fourteenth century, on the other hand, are much dimmer to our view because the *Taiheiki*, our main source, is markedly weaker in its character delineation than the *Heike Monogartari*. Indeed, many of the lesser characters of the *Taiheiki* seem to merge one into the other. We have been able to detect some interesting, lifelike traits of Takauji, which appear to tally with comments made in other sources, and we are therefore able to envision him as a fairly real personality. But other leaders, such as Godaigo, remain disappointingly indistinct.

Godaigo is invariably handled in highly stylized or rhetorical terms by the authors of the *Taiheiki*. He is always pictured as an emperor and never really as a mere man. Hence we simply cannot know the personal emotions or uncertainties that may have lain

---

[17] Takayanagi, *Ashikaga Takauji*, p. 430.
[18] *Ibid.*

behind his actions and decisions. Virtually the only unshakable impression we have of Godaigo is that of an enormously stubborn individual determined to have his own reactionary way.

One of the most important portrayals in the *Taiheiki* is that of Kusunoki Masashige. Masashige is presented not in the plausibly human form of Takauji nor in the remotely aloof image of Godaigo, but as the repository of those ethical qualities of loyalty and constancy that the authors of the *Taiheiki* most esteemed. His brief career of prominence is inextricably linked with Godaigo's imperial restoration. Although such powerful and influential warriors as Takauji and Nitta Yoshisada undoubtedly played more significant roles in its initial success and later failure, Masashige was the very embodiment of this cause.

Masashige first appears in the *Taiheiki* under unusual and prophetic circumstances. In 1331 the emperor Godaigo, his anti-Hōjō plot prematurely revealed, had fled to Mt. Kasagi. Although some armed monks and warriors from neighboring locales had begun to gather about him, Godaigo had not yet received the support of any leading stalwarts. One night, in a dream, he saw an enormous evergreen tree standing before one of the main buildings of the imperial palace in Kyoto. Beneath this tree were seated the great ministers of state and in their midst was a raised and unoccupied seat facing south. Suddenly two children appeared and beckoned Godaigo to sit in this seat of honor.

When the emperor awoke he was perplexed by his dream, although he was certain that it carried an important message for him. He considered the tree and the fact that the seat he was asked to occupy faced south: by placing the written character for "tree" next to that for "south" he formed the combined character for camphor tree, which in Japanese is *kusunoki*. Godaigo enquired of one of his aides and learned that there was a man in the nearby province of Kawachi named Kusunoki Masashige, who was noted for his fighting skill. The emperor immediately dispatched a messenger to summon Masashige and, upon the latter's arrival, asked him how to destroy the enemies of the throne and restore order to the land. Masashige replied that the imperial forces could not hope to rely upon strength alone to overthrow the Hōjō and their allies. Only through careful planning and clever strategy could they destroy these "eastern barbarians." He implored the emperor to disregard the outcome of any single battle and swore that "so long as Your Majesty hears that Masashige alone still lives, be assured that the imperial cause will in the end prevail." [19]

Although Godaigo was shortly thereafter taken by the Hōjō and sent into exile in the Oki Islands, Masashige and Prince Morinaga continued their resistance to Kamakura rule through sporadic guerrilla raids and harassments in the central provinces. Masashige seems to have been a first-rate fighter, even though the *Taiheiki* accounts of his stratagems and exploits are outrageously exaggerated.[20] In 1331, shortly after joining the loyalist cause, Masashige took a stand on Mt. Akasaka in Kawachi and repeatedly repulsed attempts by numerically superior forces to dislodge him. Although he was finally forced to abandon Akasaka, Masashige had by then done much to establish his reputation as a skillful and daring tactician.

The following year he took up another defensive position against the Hōjō armies at Chihaya on Mt. Kongō in southern Kawachi. The inability of the Hōjō to destroy Masashige's Chihaya fortress was not only a great military, but also a psychological, setback for them. Many people who were still wavering between loyalty to Godaigo and to Kamakura were undoubtedly inspired by Masashige's example to cast their lot with the former.

When victory over the Hōjō was finally achieved in 1333, Masashige was in the forefront of the retinue that accompanied Godaigo back to the capital. Among the rewards he received for his faithful service to the throne were the governorships of Settsu and Kawachi and appointment to the records office and the settlements board. Despite these honors, Masashige does not appear to have played a prominent role in affairs again until the final days of the Restoration

[19] *Taiheiki*, I, 98. Very little is known about Masashige's background, although it has been suggested that he may have been a steward of the Kamakura Shogunate or perhaps an official of an estate in Kawachi held directly by the emperor. The various possibilities are discussed in Uemura Seiji, *Kusunoki Masashige*, pp. 26–34.

[20] For example, see the section entitled "The Battle of Akasaka Castle" in Helen C. McCullough, tr., *The Taiheiki*, pp. 85–91.

period. After Takauji had gone into revolt against Godaigo and had been forced to retreat to Kyushu, Masashige was directed by the court to go to Hyōgo on the shore of the Inland Sea to join Nitta Yoshisada in repulsing any attempt by the Ashikaga to return to the central provinces. According to the *Taiheiki*, Masashige, always the canny tactician, advised against an immediate showdown fight with the newly strengthened forces of the Ashikaga. Better, he said, to allow the enemy temporarily to occupy Kyoto. Later he and Nitta could cut the supply lines to the city and rout the Ashikaga and their supporters with a coordinated attack from Mt. Hiei in the northeast and from Kawachi to the south.

Whether or not the *Taiheiki* account of Masashige's advice at this time is historically true, it is certainly plausible. One of the most remarkable features of warfare in fourteenth-century Japan was the general disinclination of military commanders to seek decisive victories in single battles. Almost invariably, if they found conditions unfavorable or if they saw the tide of battle going against them, these commanders preferred to withdraw and fight again another day. Conflict in this epoch was often widely scattered and few positions or sites were deemed important enough to warrant risking great loss for temporary possession of them. Kyoto seems to have been particularly difficult to hold, partly because its supply lines were so vulnerable to disruption. For these reasons alone Masashige's strategy was probably sound; but the court rejected it and reiterated the order that he join Yoshisada in Hyōgo.

According to the *Taiheiki*, Masashige now resigned himself to the fact that he would die in the coming battle. In one of the most famous and moving scenes in Japanese literature, he informed his young son, Masatsura (1326?–48), that he would not see him again in this life. He told the boy, then only nine or ten years of age, that he had no alternative but to go to his death in the service of his emperor. The greatest duty that Masatsura could perform for his father would be to return home and await the time when he himself could lead the struggle against the Ashikaga.

Kusunoki Masashige died at the battle of Minatogawa in Hyōgo on the twenty-fifth day of the fifth month of 1336. He had fought stoutly for many hours against the combined sea and land attack of the Ashikaga. When the battle was clearly lost, he and a number of his kinsmen and followers retired from the field and disemboweled themselves. It is recorded that just before the end Masashige asked his brother, Masasue, what his final wish might be. Masasue, to the delight of Masashige, replied that his only desire was to be reborn "seven times" (again and again) in order to continue the fight against the enemies of the court. Centuries later Tokugawa Mitsukuni (1628–1700), second lord of Mito and founder of that domain's famous historical project, visited the site near the battlefield at Minatogawa where Masashige was purportedly buried. Stirred by the memory of this medieval warrior's selfless loyalism, Mitsukuni left a marker with the simple inscription: "Ah, the resting place of Kusunoki, a loyal subject."[21]

After the battle of Minatogawa, Masashige's head was severed and taken to Kyoto where it was displayed at the river bed at Rokujō. The *Taiheiki* records that Takauji, who was genuinely grieved at the loss of a former ally whom he much admired, later had the head removed and returned to the Kusunoki family in Kawachi. In another famous scene from the *Taiheiki*, the youthful Masatsura, overwhelmed with emotion at viewing the badly decomposed head with its distorted features, withdrew to a nearby temple building and prepared to cut into his stomach. He was prevented from doing so only at the last moment when his mother rushed in to seize his sword arm and tearfully remind him of his vow to grow into manhood in order to fight on behalf of the cause for which his father had perished.

A recent scholar, Watsuji Tetsurō (1889–1960), sees the *Taiheiki*'s account of the life and death of Masashige as the epitome of the loyalist movement of the fourteenth century.[22] When he first summoned Masashige to Mt. Kasagi in 1331, Godaigo was a fugitive from the capital and in very difficult straits. Masashige, who thus took up the emperor's cause when it was at its lowest ebb, counseled careful strategy against the Hōjō and gave fully of his own skill and resources to make possible the loyalist victory two years later. Yet, when Masashige was called upon to serve the throne

---

[21] "Aa Chūshin Nanshi no Bo."

[22] Watsuji, *Nihon Rinri Shisō Shi*, II, 69–79.

again in battle against the Ashikaga in 1336, Godaigo refused to accept the kind of advice that had previously been so valuable. Perhaps the authors of the *Taiheiki*, as Watsuji suggests, wished to link the failure of the Restoration to this refusal to heed the military advice of the most unswerving of loyalist generals. The seemingly invincible Masashige could be understood to have gone to his death because of a kind of "betrayal" of faith by the emperor. It was indeed the spirit of Masashige, and not of Godaigo, that most truly exemplified the ideals of the loyalist movement as set forth in the *Taiheiki*. One might further interpret the parting scene between Masashige and Masatsura as designed to show Masashige's desire to bequeath this spirit to future generations of the Kusunoki family.

The *Taiheiki* gives no hint of conflict or enmity between Masashige and his fellow commander at Minatogawa, Nitta Yoshisada. It was clearly Yoshisada's idea that the loyalist stand be made there. In the *Taiheiki* Masashige acknowledged the Nitta chieftain's desire to win an important battle after the setbacks of recent months, but expressed the opinion that Yoshisada would in the final analysis agree with his plan to relinquish Kyoto for the time being and await a later opportunity to turn the tables on the Ashikaga. Another source, however, casts an entirely different light on the relationship between Masashige and Yoshisada. In the *Baishōron* Masashige is quoted as advising the court in the spring of 1336 to recall Takauji from Kyushu and to recognize that its real enemy was Yoshisada, whose slanderous remarks had originally been responsible for the alienation of the Ashikaga.[23] Since the *Baishōron* is a work generally biased in favor of the Ashikaga, perhaps we should not give too much credence to its version of Masashige's advice to the court at this time. Nevertheless it does suggest that we can never hope to understand fully the complexity of the personal relationships among the leading figures of the Restoration period.

We have already reviewed briefly the war between the courts, which was brought to a conclusion in 1392 with the return of the

[23] *Baishōron*, p. 197.

southern emperor Gokameyama to Kyoto and the transference of the regalia to the northern emperor Gokomatsu. The denouement of this great struggle between branches of the imperial family was decidedly anticlimactic. The northern emperors had been nothing more than puppets of the Ashikaga from the first and now Gokameyama abandoned the feeble southern resistance to the spreading hegemony of the third Ashikaga shogun, Yoshimitsu. Henceforth the imperial family was to enjoy no real political power whatsoever. Gokomatsu's branch became sole possessor of the imperial succession simply because Yoshimitsu chose to allow it in contravention of his promise to return to the former system of alternate succession.

The nominal victor in the war between the courts, then, was the northern court and the loser was the southern court. Although, as noted, several pretenders attempted to rekindle the southern cause during the fifteenth century, these and their adherents never became more than a handful of veritable desperados who struggled to maintain a precarious existence in the provinces south of the capital.

During much of the remainder of the medieval age the prevailing view was that Godaigo, and his followers and successors, had been chiefly responsible for the strife and disorder which the war between the courts had brought. The memory of those warriors who had fought most faithfully for the Yoshino regime came to be held in low esteem. Although we have only scattered references to rely on, it appears that persecution of the descendants of southern "loyalist" heroes was not uncommon. The Kusunoki seem to have been especially detested and, during the fifteenth century, a number of real or assumed members of Masashige's line were harshly treated by the authorities. In 1429, for example, one Kusunoki Mitsumasa was seized in Nara for an alleged attempt to assassinate the sixth Ashikaga shogun, Yoshinori (1394–1441), and was promptly beheaded.[24] Eight years later, in 1437, some men known as the "Kusunoki brothers" were murdered as enemies of the court.[25] And in 1460 a man called Kusunoki was taken and executed, as we learn in the following vivid description from a contemporary chronicle:

[24] *Kammon Gyoki*, 1429:9:18, 9:24.
[25] *Ibid.*, 1437:8:3.

A certain Kusunoki, a descendant of the general of the southern court, secretly planned rebellion with his cohorts. When his plot was prematurely revealed, Kusunoki was seized and turned over to the police. Today he was beheaded at Rokujō-Kawara. The records tell us that the Kusunoki family once held great military power in the land and that they slaughtered untold tens of thousands, the majority of whom were innocent people. Since the fall of the southern court, descendants of the Kusunoki have been taken by the authorities and have all been put to death. This is retribution for their accumulated evils.[26]

Despite these denunciatory remarks, however, there are indications that the popular view of the southern court and its supporters was beginning to change even during the final years of the fifteenth century. This change in view was closely related to the compilation and distribution of new editions of the *Taiheiki*. Tōin Kinsada has informed us that the *Taiheiki* was much read as early as the 1370s; but its readership at that time must surely have been restricted largely to Kyoto society. It was not until the fifteenth century that people of all classes came to be familiar with it. Probably the most important reason for this widening familiarity was the increasing adoption of the *Taiheiki* as a source by itinerant priestly chanters, who played such a significant role also in the popularization of the *Heike Monogatari*. These chanters carried the tales of the *Taiheiki* into every village and hamlet in the land and stamped them indelibly on the folk consciousness.

The increasing popularity of the *Taiheiki* during the sixteenth century is attested by the various commentaries and glosses on it that appeared from about 1504 on.[27] Certainly by the Tokugawa period the work had established itself as one of the best-loved in Japanese history. With the advantage of new printing techniques, greater numbers of copies of the *Taiheiki* could be published and circulated to meet the reading public's consistently high demand for it. Moreover, it was during Tokugawa times that attempts were made to study and collate the variant editions of the *Taiheiki* in order to produce newer, more authoritative versions. The most

---

[26] *Hekizan Nichiroku*, 1460: 3: 28.
[27] Kubota Osamu, *Kemmu Chūkō*, p. 196.

important of the latter was the *Sankō Taiheiki* of the Mito scholars, which even today is one of the most widely consulted versions.

So popular did both the reading aloud and the recitation of the *Taiheiki* become by the Tokugawa period that the phrase *Taiheiki-yomi* (*Taiheiki*-reading) entered common usage. We learn from various diaries that courtiers of the fifteenth century had enjoyed having passages of the book read aloud to them.[28] Later generations of Japanese simply continued and expanded this pleasurable practice. The *Taiheiki* thus became, along with the *Heike Monogatari*, one of the principal sources for a new literary experience in which the response of various audiences was as much a part of the total effect as the delivery of the reader or chanter. We have no way of knowing, of course, the precise extent to which *Taiheiki-yomi* brought alterations in the written texts of the work. The textual development of the *Taiheiki* has not received nearly the attention given that of the *Heike Monogatari*. But we can note at least one important difference in the historical evolution of the two books. Whereas the *Heike Monogatari* was not committed to writing until approximately a century after the Taira-Minamoto war and then was constructed of tales that had already been orally composed,[29] from what we have observed of the *Taiheiki* most of it was probably written by eyewitnesses to the events covered. The *Taiheiki* was therefore well established as a written work long before it was adapted for recitative purposes and, for this reason alone, is surely of greater historicity than the *Heike Monogatari*.

The passages of the *Taiheiki* that appealed most to audiences of the late medieval and Tokugawa periods were those that dealt with the Kusunoki. People admired especially the great exploits of Masashige: his rise from obscurity to inspirational leadership of the imperial cause; his tenacious defenses of Akasaka and Chihaya; his gallant death at Minatogawa. We can imagine the emotional impact on rapt audiences of Masashige's stirring words to Godaigo at Kasagi or of his poignant farewell to Masatsura on the eve of

[28] See *ibid.*, pp. 195–96; see also Murata, *Namboku-chō Ron*, p. 184.
[29] Kenneth D. Butler, "The Textual Evolution of the *Heike Monogatari*," in *Harvard Journal of Asiatic Studies*, XXVI (1965–66), contains a detailed discussion of this subject.

Minatogawa. Not only were people impressed with Masashige's *élan*, they were struck by the extraordinary sacrifices which the entire Kusunoki family had made for the cause of Godaigo and the southern court.

The growing public sentiment in favor of the Kusunoki was perhaps best demonstrated by an incident which occurred in the early 1560s. A man named Kusunoki Masatora, who claimed to be Masashige's descendant, appealed to the throne through his feudal overlord to have the family name of Kusunoki historically cleared. In response, the emperor Ōgimachi (r. 1557–86) issued a proclamation in 1563 granting full posthumous pardon to Masashige for alleged "crimes" he had committed that had made him an "enemy of the court" (i.e., the northern court) and that had brought his house to ruin.[30]

By the Tokugawa period a kind of cult of Masashige had evolved that was to continue into modern times. The *Taiheiki*, in which Masashige was seen both as a warrior genius and as an exemplar of public morality, was adopted as a primary text for military studies; and the strategy, tactics, and conduct of the Kusunoki chieftain became the core of several schools of samurai training.[31] A number of documents circulated by these schools were purportedly Masashige's own statements on warfare, soldierly behavior, and the like, but these were apparently without exception spurious. One of those who founded a "Kusunoki school" (*nanryū*) was a man called Kusunoki Masatatsu, who according to one tradition was the son of the above-mentioned Masatora. Of the samurai of the Tokugawa period who professed to be adherents of the teachings of Kusunoki, one of the most prominent was Yui Shōsetsu (1605–51), who led an unsuccessful revolt against the shogunate in 1651.

Masashige was thus transformed in the minds of the Japanese from the historical villain of the late fourteenth and fifteenth centuries to the object of widespread veneration in the Tokugawa period. This shift in attitude toward one of the key supporters of

---

[30] Murata, *Namboku-chō Ron*, pp. 184–87.

[31] A discussion of the various Kusunoki schools and the textual materials used by them may be found in Ishioka Hisao, ed., *Shoryū Heihō(jō)*, vol. VI in *Nihon Heihō Zenshū*.

Godaigo was, quite predictably perhaps, accompanied by a re-evaluation of the whole issue of the war between the courts. The sentiments toward Masashige which a revival and expansion of interest in the *Taiheiki* evoked worked similarly in favor of the cause he championed. Yet the process by which the southern court ultimately came to be seen as the rightful or legitimate seat of imperial authority during the fourteenth-century dynastic schism was, by the very nature of the larger issues involved, much slower and much more considered than the rather spontaneous rise of sympathy and admiration for Masashige.

After Kitabatake Chikafusa, no writer of the late medieval period took up the cause of the legitimacy of the southern court.[32] At least one commentator, Otsuki Harutomi, even composed a brief tract about the mid-fifteenth century entitled the *Zoku* [later] *Jinnō Shōtōki*, in which he sought to refute Chikafusa's argument and to stress the legitimacy of the northern court.[33] Other than Otsuki, no one apparently felt the need to argue what, for all practical purposes, had ceased to be an issue. Historical works written during the fifteenth, sixteenth, and even the early seventeenth centuries invariably listed the northern emperors in genealogical tables of the imperial family and restricted their comments about the heads of the Yoshino court to the context of the events in which they participated.

One obvious difficulty in any consideration of whether the southern, rather than the northern, court should be regarded as legitimate was the fear of offending the imperial family, which since the fourteenth century had been descended from the northern emperors. The Tokugawa, no less than the Ashikaga, had obtained their legitimization as military hegemons from these very descendants of the northern court. Although the throne enjoyed no political power during the Tokugawa period, it remained, in formal terms, the highest office of the state; and the Tokugawa shoguns were not inclined to favor any questioning of the theo-

---

[32] A convenient book for excerpts from primary sources over the centuries which have touched upon the northern and southern courts issue is Yamazaki Fujiyoshi and Horie Hideo, eds., *Namboku-chō Seijun Ronsan*.

[33] See the excerpted passage from this work *ibid.*, pp. 98–102.

retical source of their own authority. For this reason the shogunate never encouraged, and indeed often attempted to suppress, the historical debate that arose over fourteenth-century imperial legitimacy.

Curiously, it appears to have been one of the Tokugawa Shogunate's stanchest supporters—the Confucian adviser Hayashi Razan (1583–1657)—who first cast doubt on the commonly held assumption that the southern court had simply been a kind of political aberration whose existence did not affect the northern court's legitimacy. In the preface to the great historical work of the Hayashi family, *Honchō Tsugan*, Razan stated:

During the Juei and Genryaku periods [1182–85] there were two emperors, one in the east and one in the west; and from the era of Ryakuō [1338–41] until Meitoku [1390–93] there were two imperial lines, the northern and the southern. These were certainly unusual times for the imperial dynasty of this country and it will not do to judge arbitrarily in either case which emperor or line was legitimate and which was not.

Razan was the first of many writers to draw the analogy, which I have commented on in an earlier chapter, between the situation of the mid-1180s—when Gotoba was enthroned by order of the cloistered emperor Goshirakawa even while the emperor Antoku, in possession of the regalia, was still alive in the western provinces—and the fourteenth-century rivalry between the senior and junior emperors of the Kyoto and Yoshino courts.

Razan's son, Hayashi Shunsai (1618–80), suggested that it might be appropriate to consider Godaigo, who had never willingly abdicated, as the rightful emperor until his death at Yoshino in 1339 and to regard the northern emperors as legitimate only from that date.[34] This would mean the deletion of the first three years of the reign of the northern emperor Kōmyō, whom Takauji placed on the throne in 1336, from the list of official reign years.

The opinions of the two Hayashi, although interesting to note as attestations of growing doubts about the legitimacy question of the fourteenth century, were never developed into formal, revisionist proposals. This was perhaps only natural, inasmuch as the Hayashi

[34] *Zoku Honchō Tsugan*, excerpted *ibid.*, pp. 122–23.

were official Confucian advisers and historians of the Tokugawa Shogunate. The first to assert unequivocally the legitimacy of the southern court was, in fact, Tokugawa Mitsukuni.

Mitsukuni was a member of a cadet branch of the Tokugawa family and the second daimyo of Mito, a *han* located to the north of Edo. He is best remembered as the founder of a center of historical studies known as the Mito School. The scholars whom Mitsukuni gathered at the Mito School devoted themselves chiefly to compilation of the *Dai Nihon Shi*, a history of Japan (composed in Chinese and modeled on the Chinese dynastic histories) from its mythical origins until reunification of the northern and southern courts in 1392. Although the ideology of the Mito scholars was basically Confucian, they, like virtually all Japanese of the premodern period, accepted as articles of faith the Shinto accounts of the divine origins of Japan and the imperial family as recorded in the *Kojiki* and the *Nihon Shoki*. The *Dai Nihon Shi* is an *imperial* history in that its focus is on the throne and its successive occupants. Like Kitabatake Chikafusa, the Mito scholars stressed in their discussions of government and rulership the unique character and continuity of Japan's imperial line. It was precisely because Japan had maintained one uninterrupted dynasty at its head through the ages that she differed from, and was superior to, China and other countries.[35]

Owing to their special interest in the imperial line, the Mito scholars addressed themselves to specific problems of dynastic legitimacy in Japanese history. In the *Dai Nihon Shi* they took positions on three major dynastic issues. They asserted, first, that the empress Jingū, who according to tradition reigned from 200 to 269, had not been a true sovereign; second, that the emperor Kōbun, who was killed in the Jinshin conflict of 672, had on the other hand rightfully occupied the throne; and, finally, that the southern emperors had been the legitimate sovereigns during the period 1336–92. Several of the leading Mito scholars have reported that Mitsukuni himself formulated the basic Mito position on each of

[35] For my comments on the Mito school and Tokugawa period attitudes toward imperial legitimacy in general I am indebted to Herschel Webb, *The Japanese Imperial Institution in the Tokugawa Period*, especially chapter 3, "Imperial Loyalism."

these issues. In the case of the legitimacy of the Yoshino emperors we can hypothesize from the incident of Mitsukuni's moving tribute to Kusunoki Masashige at the old battle site of Minatogawa that the Mito lord based his formulation at least partly on personal sentiment and emotional response to the memory of the southern cause.[36]

The Mito scholars regarded national unity under the throne as an essential prerequisite to good government. Following the dictum drawn from Chinese political thought that "there are not two suns in heaven, nor two lords on earth," they rejected as unthinkable the proposition that sovereignty in Japan might be divisible. To those so predisposed, the very designation of *namboku-chō jidai*—Period of the Northern and Southern Courts—would be anathema. Although there is ample evidence that this phrase, taken from Chinese history, was commonly used by Japanese chroniclers as early as the fourteenth century (that is, during the *namboku-chō* period itself),[37] it was later widely rejected by theorists who regarded it as utterly inapplicable to any situation in Japanese history.

To Mitsukuni and the Mito scholars it was necessary at all times to identify the legitimate sovereign of Japan according to certain criteria. They determined that the southern emperors were legitimate during the fourteenth century because: (1) Godaigo had been properly enthroned and had been widely recognized as a rightful emperor; and (2) he had never relinquished the regalia to the northern emperors. The Mito scholars held that the real regalia had remained uninterruptedly in the possession of the southern emperors until 1392, when they were transferred by Gokameyama to Gokomatsu. It was their view that the location of the regalia always determined the locus of imperial legitimacy: hence the southern emperors were rightful sovereigns until 1392 and only at that time did legitimacy shift to the northern line of Gokomatsu.

In fact, it is unlikely that we shall ever be able to determine

[36] See Murata, *Namboku-chō Ron*, pp. 187–92, for a discussion of the circumstances under which Mitsukuni first visited Minatogawa.

[37] Tanaka Yoshishige gives as the earliest known use of this phrase in Japanese history an entry in a diary dated 1392 (*Namboku-chō Jidai Shi*, pp. 2–3).

whether or not the southern emperors retained possession of the "real" regalia until 1392.[38] Moreover, it is not especially important to the argument of the Mito scholars. A number of commentators have pointed out that someone could steal the regalia, yet this could hardly be construed as the assumption of imperial authority. The regalia could only be transferred from one emperor to another by a *free act* on the part of the former, including the act of appointing a crown prince before one's death. As we have noted, there is no evidence to show that Godaigo ever freely gave the regalia and all they symbolized to anyone other than one of his own sons.

The Mito scholars praised Godaigo for refusing to allow the Ashikaga to force him into relinquishing his legitimate authority to the northern court. They noted at the same time that, although Godaigo had succeeded in bringing about an imperial restoration, he had been unable to sustain it. This was because he had erred in his selection of ministers: that is, he had trusted and rewarded people like Ashikaga Takauji. We see Takauji, at the hands of the Mito scholars, taking on the image of opprobrium that he was to carry into modern times. Takauji had helped Godaigo overthrow the Hōjō and restore order to the land in 1333. For this he deserved praise. But when in 1336 he forced the emperor to flee to Yoshino and established the puppet northern court in Kyoto, Takauji sowed the seeds for more than a half century of discord and disunity.

It becomes clear in various writings of the Tokugawa period that Takauji's new historical unpopularity arose not so much from how he acted toward the throne per se, but because his actions were seen to have caused disunity. Historians of the seventeenth and eighteenth centuries in Japan were uniform in the stress they placed on national order. They could, for example, forgive Minamoto Yoritomo much bad personal behavior toward the imperial family and toward members of his own family because he had been the "virtuous founder" of a strong warrior regime. They could not, on the other hand, so forgive Takauji, since far from establishing or sustaining order he had disrupted it.

The foremost interpretive historian of the Tokugawa period was

[38] See Appendix 3.

Arai Hakuseki (1657–1725), the Confucianist adviser to the shogunate in the early eighteenth century. In his best-known study of Japanese history, *Dokushi Yoron* (which covers the period from the mid-ninth century to Hideyoshi's unification at the end of the sixteenth), Arai is surprisingly modern in his use of source materials and in his analyses of the events and people of the Kemmu Restoration. He states that political "restoration" is always a difficult business, since by definition it involves patching up rather than starting afresh. In seeking to "repair the cow's horns," one is likely to "kill the cow." [39] Arai, with the heightened puritanical sense of the eighteenth-century Japanese Confucianist, heaps criticism on the extravagance, waste, and judicial inequities of Godaigo's Restoration government. He also speaks accusingly of Godaigo's failure to support his son, Prince Morinaga, and his allowing the prince to be taken by the Ashikaga. [40]

The great hero of the Restoration in Arai's mind was Kusunoki Masashige. If he had not held out against the armies of the Hōjō during the critical period from 1331 until 1333, none of the other warrior leaders—Nitta, Ashikaga, Akamatsu—would ever have been drawn into the struggle. The Ashikaga, in fact, never contributed anything to the overthrow of the Kamakura Shogunate. By the time Takauji declared himself to be a loyalist, victory over the Hōjō was a foregone conclusion. Moreover, the Ashikaga had for generations thought only of becoming warrior masters of the country and Takauji joined in the Restoration simply to realize that aspiration. [41] But Arai was not as critical of Takauji as he might have been. Rather, he adopted the line of interpretation, which has since become popular with many writers, that Tadayoshi was the one responsible for most of the dark scheming which led to such things as the murder of Prince Morinaga and the refusal of the Ashikaga to return to Kyoto after putting down the Hōjō counteruprising in the Kantō in 1335. [42]

Although neither the shogunate nor the Kyoto court ever took

---

[39] Muraoka Tsunetsugu, ed., *Dokushi Yoron*, p. 183.
[40] *Ibid.*
[41] *Ibid.*, p. 185.
[42] *Ibid.*, p. 207.

official note of it, the scholarly debate over fourteenth-century imperial legitimacy continued throughout the Tokugawa period. Among those who took sides was the Confucian scholar Yamazaki Anzai (1618–82). Anzai asserted the legitimacy of the southern court and indeed several of his disciples later became scholars of the Mito School. Some people, especially members of the courtier class in Kyoto, continued to argue in favor of the northern court; others suggested that both courts ought to be regarded as legitimate. But, by and large, the *Dai Nihon Shi* view that the southern court was legitimate because it had retained the regalia carried the day.

One prominent person who assumed a view somewhat at variance with the Mito position was the Confucian writer and poet Rai San'yō (1780–1832). While he fervently eulogized the southern court and its valiant followers, especially the Kusunoki, San'yō held that it was not possession of the regalia that mattered in determining Yoshino's legitimacy, but the "will of the imperial ancestors."[43] He presumably meant by this that the southern court enjoyed its legitimacy more as a result of divine blessing than owing to what might be construed as the chance fact that it had physically retained the regalia.

San'yō was not the most careful of scholars, but his works, especially the *Nihon Gaishi*, were widely read and his historical views were highly influential in the molding of public opinion during the late Tokugawa period. The kind of popular loyalism that permeated the Meiji Restoration received its impetus from such writings as San'yō's idealized accounts (based on the *Taiheiki*) of the Kemmu Restoration and not from the *Dai Nihon Shi*, which by itself, without commentary, is simply a dry recitation of historical events.[44]

How memories of the great events of the fourteenth century were rekindled during the final, tumultuous years of the Tokugawa Shogunate can perhaps most strikingly be seen in the case of Yoshida

[43] *Nihon Seiki*, excerpted in Yamazaki and Horie, eds., *Namboku-chō Seijun Ronsan*, pp. 214–16.

[44] The finished text of the *Dai Nihon Shi* was not actually published until 1906, although there were incomplete manuscripts available throughout the eighteenth and nineteenth centuries.

Shōin (1830–59), the Chōshū samurai who was one of the leading loyalist thinkers and activists of this period. On a trip to Edo in 1851 Yoshida stopped off at Minatogawa and visited the site where Masashige had fallen and where Tokugawa Mitsukuni had paid simple tribute to "a loyal subject." Yoshida, in common with a great number of Japanese by this time, saw in the legend of Kusunoki Masashige the most splendid and unsullied example of devotion to the throne in Japanese history. Several years later, in 1856, he wrote a tribute to Masashige entitled *Shichishō Setsu* (a discussion of seven lives), the title of which alludes to the final wish of Masashige and his brother Masasue that they be reborn "seven times," or again and again, in order to give their lives in the fight against the enemies of the court. To Yoshida it was preeminently the spirit of the Kusunoki that must be made to galvanize the nation during his own troubled age.[45]

The Meiji Restoration of 1868 was hailed as the next great imperial restoration in Japanese history. No attempt, even supposing it would be worthwhile, to compare the political and social issues of the Kemmu and Meiji Restorations can be undertaken here. In the case of the Meiji Restoration, it is obvious that very little of the past was "restored" and in fact many profound changes in Japanese government and society were wrought. Nevertheless the Japanese, at least before World War II, never entirely lost the restorationist spirit. Periodically, in times of stress or concern about national drift, leaders sought to reassert traditional values and to glorify certain venerable native institutions. They could do this most directly by demonstrating how these values and institutions had functioned in Japan's past, an approach which in turn brought the need to "control the past," that is, to make sure that the past taught the lessons it ought to teach.

How the government of the late Meiji period sought to control through the revision of primary school history texts the lessons it wished the Japanese citizenry to draw from the Kemmu Restoration and the war between the courts is the subject of the next chapter. I would like in conclusion here to comment briefly on the general

---

[45] See the comments on this in David Earl, *Emperor and Nation in Japan*, p. 188.

tenor of sentiment toward the events and leading figures of the fourteenth century that had evolved among the Japanese by the early years of the modern era.

We have been observing two processes in this chapter: the steady growth from at least the sixteenth century on in enthusiasm for the loyalist supporters of Godaigo and the southern court as national folk heroes; and the accompanying emergence of a scholarly, or at least quasi-scholarly, historical debate over fourteenth-century imperial legitimacy. The debate over imperial legitimacy did not become a matter of widespread interest until the rise of the text-book issue in 1911. What strikes us most forcefully in the early Meiji period is the degree to which popular imagination had been kindled, during the years of Japan's opening to the West and of Imperial Restoration, by the concept of men like Prince Morinaga, Nitta Yoshisada, and especially Kusunoki Masashige as possessors of the finest qualities of the Japanese character of the past that were now to be borne by the Japanese people into the future. That these men who now stood foremost in the historical consciousness of the masses of the Japanese (if not, as we shall see, of the intellectuals of the early Meiji Enlightenment) were remembered chiefly for their martial virtues, is an important testament to the high position of the *bushidō* (way of the warrior) ethic in the Japanese ethos.

Perhaps more revealing than any statements by Japanese concerning their folk heroes of the fourteenth century are the remarks of a foreign observer, the American educator William Griffis. In 1876 Griffis wrote the following about Nitta Yoshisada:

The tomb of this brave man stands, carefully watched and tended, near Fukui, in Echizen, hard by the very spot where he fell. I often passed it in my walks, when living in Fukui in 1871, and noticed that fresh blooming flowers were almost daily laid upon it—the tribute of an admiring people.

Of Kusunoki he said:

Of all the characters in Japanese history, that of Kusunoki Masashige stands pre-eminent for pureness of patriotism, unselfishness of devotion to duty, and calmness of courage. The people speak of him in tones of reverential tenderness, and, with an admiration that lacks fitting words, behold in him the mirror of stainless loyalty. I have more than once asked my Japanese

[153]

students and friends whom they considered the noblest character in their history. Their unanimous answer was "Kusunoki Masashige." Every relic of this brave man is treasured up with religious care; and fans inscribed with poems written by him, in fac-simile of his handwriting, are sold in the shops and used by those who burn to imitate his exalted patriotism.

In a footnote to this statement Griffis added:

I make no attempt to conceal my own admiration of a man who acted according to his light, and faced his soldierly ideal of honor, when conscience and all his previous education told him that his hour had come, and that to flinch from suicidal thrust was dishonor and sin.[46]

The cult of *nankō sūhai* (worship of Lord Kusunoki) seems to have attracted at least one foreign convert in Griffis.

The affection and respect which the Japanese government and people held toward the loyalist adherents of Godaigo and the southern court were publicly demonstrated during the Meiji period (1868–1911) both in the granting of posthumous court ranks and in the construction of special shrines to institutionalize the offering of prayers to their spirits. Some thirty-five loyalists—including Nitta Yoshisada, Kusunoki Masashige, Kusunoki Masatsura, Nawa Nagatoshi, Kitabatake Chikafusa, Hino Suketomo, and Hino Toshimoto —received posthumous promotions in court rank during the years 1868–1911.[47] Of these only three—Chikafusa, Yoshisada, and Masashige—were granted the highest grade of senior first rank. Since Chikafusa was descended from the prestigious courtier clan of Murakami Genji, such rank was not inappropriate to his social standing; and Yoshisada was at least a branch member of the great military family of Seiwa Genji. But Kusunoki, as we have seen, came from very humble, indeed obscure,[48] provincial origins and in his own day would not have been considered for this supreme honor.

Chikafusa, for one, would have been horrified. In the *Jinnō Shōtōki* he took little more than passing note of Masashige's contributions to the loyalist cause. With his formalistic views toward

[46] William Elliot Griffis, *The Mikado's Empire*, I, 190–92.
[47] A list of these posthumous ranks and the dates of their bestowal may be found in Murata, *Namboku-chō Ron*, pp. 209–10.
[48] See n. 19 above.

[154]

status and rank, Chikafusa undoubtedly regarded the Kusunoki chieftain as unworthy of excessive praise by the court for his heroics in the field of battle.

The Meiji government, in its desire to encourage the organization and propagation of Shinto, sponsored the construction of numerous shrines to be dedicated to former sovereigns, other members of the imperial family, and subjects who had been conspicuously loyal to the throne. Seven shrines were built for emperors, including Antoku, Gotoba, and Godaigo, who had in one way or another been deprived of their imperial prerogatives and who were felt to deserve special commiseration from later generations of their countrymen. Another group of eleven shrines was dedicated to imperial princes who had distinguished themselves in military service and who, in most cases, had died in battle. Of these, five were sons of Godaigo.[49]

Nearly all the leading warrior chieftains who had served Godaigo and the southern court were also honored at one time or another during the Meiji period by the construction of shrines in their names. In many cases these shrines were located in the places where the various heroes had fallen. Masashige's, to note the most famous, was completed at Minatogawa in 1872.

[49] D. C. Holtom comments on the construction and dedication of these shrines in *The National Faith of Japan*, pp. 174–76.

VI

History Revised

THE PERIOD FROM THE ACCESSION of the Meiji emperor in 1867 until 1871 was an "imperial restoration" at least insofar as it brought the overthrow of the Tokugawa regime and the temporary revival of ancient court institutions of rule. Yet a variety of measures undertaken in 1871, including dissolution of the feudal domains or *han* and dispatch of the Iwakura mission to America and Europe, pointed up clearly that the real course the Meiji government intended to pursue was one not of going backward at all but of forward progress (as the youthful emperor had already intimated in his Charter Oath of 1868). To leading intellectuals of the day, such as Fukuzawa Yukichi (1834–1901), this course was envisioned in terms of "civilization and enlightenment" (*bummei kaika*).

Most of the early advocates of civilization and enlightenment believed that modernization and Westernization were one and the same. They were ashamed of what they regarded as Japan's backward, feudal past and unabashedly admired the progressive ways of Europe and America. In their more extreme moments, the new Japanese enlighteners even suggested such things as the abandonment of their own language in favor of English and the adoption of a policy of mass miscegenation to transform their descendants gradually from Mongoloids to Caucasians. The high point of the Japanese Enlightenment was the founding in 1873 of the Meiji Six Club (Meirokusha), an organization of intellectuals dedicated to discussing the modernization of Japan, which had among its charter members Fukuzawa, Mori Arinori (1847–89) and Nishimura Shigeki (1828–1902).

Probably the strongest philosophical current that entered Japan from the West in the early Meiji period was British empiricism. The Japanese already had in their Confucian background the pervasive concept of the perfectibility of society through the cultivation and exercise of man's inherent rational faculties. Empiricist philosophy seemed simply to place this concept in a modern and "enlightened" setting: the rational faculties of *all* men must be cultivated; and true rationality could only be realized through the acquisition of scientifically and technologically up-to-date knowledge.

The earlier experiences of the Japanese also made them receptive to the belief then widely held in the West that, since ignorance was the chief cause of evil and wrongdoing, the spread of education would eventually lead to social utopia. With a literacy rate of more than 40 percent for males and 15 percent for females at the end of the Tokugawa period, the Japanese appear, in fact, to have accomplished more by that time in terms of rudimentary national education than most of the advanced Western nations. It is therefore no surprise that they could readily share in the prevailing Western optimism about the rewards to be gained from the universal acquisition of knowledge.

We shall be mainly concerned in this chapter with one aspect of Meiji education, the teaching of Japanese history, particularly as it was undertaken among the mass of the people through the system of universal primary education which was inaugurated in 1872. But before turning to this, let us briefly note some of the new attitudes toward history that emerged in Japan in the opening years of the Meiji period.

Fukuzawa Yukichi was one of the first modern writers to attack the traditional methods of history-writing in Japan. He maintained that earlier histories had not been accounts of the Japanese people and Japanese society at all, but of the wielders of political power. These histories had, moreover, been blatantly used for the Confucian didactic purpose of inculcating in the people the values of submissiveness and group subservience. Along with Taguchi Ukichi (1855–1905), Fukuzawa was instrumental in urging that "histories of civilization" (*bummeishi*) be written with the aim of showing the past in the broadest possible perspective and of dealing with specific problems of historical cause and effect. Taguchi even adopted a substantially materialist interpretation of Japanese history in his *Nihon Kaika Shōshi* (short history of Japanese enlightenment).[1] Although neither Fukuzawa nor Taguchi was an exceptionally

---

[1] Tōyama Shigeki and Satō Shin'ichi, eds., *Nihon Shi Kenkyū Nyūmon*, I, 8. See also Iwai Tadakuma, "Nihon Kindai Shigaku no Keisei," in Iwanami Shoten, *Iwanami Kōza Nihon Rekishi*, XXII, for an excellent discussion of Fukuzawa, Taguchi, and the *bummeishi* writers; and Carmen Blacker, *The Japanese Enlightenment*, pp. 90–100.

meticulous scholar, their writings opened the way in the early Meiji period for the composition of history from viewpoints and styles other than the restrictive orthodox ones of the premodern era. At the same time, like so many others who criticize and seek to change dogmatic methods of the past, they produced their own dogmas in urging that history be adjusted to practical, modern learning and that historians adopt Western positivist techniques in searching for underlying laws of historical progress similar to the laws that had been found to govern the physical and natural sciences.

In addition to attacking traditional historiography, Fukuzawa showed scant respect for the sacred cows of Japanese history. In order, for example, to demonstrate his contempt for the centuries-old practice of blind personal loyalty toward superiors, which he believed had made impossible the cultivation in Japan of the individualistic spirit so essential to modernization, Fukuzawa created a character in one of his books called "Kusunoki Gonsuke," a servant who hangs himself because he cannot face his master after losing a small sum of the latter's money.[2] We have seen that Kusunoki Masashige had become one of the greatest of Japanese folk heroes by the Meiji Restoration; it was apparently for this very reason that Fukuzawa, in this early iconoclastic stage of his thinking, employed the great loyalist samurai's name for the purpose of social ridicule.

Whatever the Meiji enlighteners' attitudes toward historical interpretation, they were not reflected in primary school training during the period immediately following the Restoration. One practical problem was the unavailability of suitable new history texts for youngsters. Tokugawa books on Japanese history, such as Rai San'yō's *Nihon Gaishi*, which had been used to instruct samurai children before 1868 (children of commoners had received almost no formal exposure to history in their schools), continued to be generally employed in Meiji classrooms until 1872 and in some places until much later.[3]

History, moreover, was not yet regarded in the early Meiji period as something that needed to be taught to children as a

[2] *Gakumon no Susume*, in *Fukuzawa Yukichi Senshū*, I, 145.
[3] Kaigo Muneomi, ed., *Nihon Kyōkasho Taikei*, XX, 525–27.

separate and distinct discipline. History books were apparently used more as primers for instruction in reading and writing than for the study and analysis of their contents. And in those cases where "history learning" was encouraged, it seems to have amounted to little more than having students memorize the names of emperors and calendrical eras.

Not until the establishment of a Ministry of Education (Mombushō) in 1871, which coincided with the end of the "restoration" phase of the Meiji political change and the beginning of the Japanese government's open drive toward modernization, did the need for dealing systematically with public education in general (and the teaching of history in particular) receive important official attention. In its Education Act (Gakusei) of 1872, which was strongly Western and utilitarian in tone and which contained the vow that there would be "no community with an illiterate family nor family with an illiterate member," the new Ministry of Education placed itself squarely in the van of Japan's modernization.[4]

The chief concern of the Education Act was with primary schooling, where the campaign for universal education was to be undertaken. According to the act's provisions, some 53,760 primary schools (shōgakkō)—one for every six hundred people—were to be set up throughout the country. Each was to be divided into a lower level of four years for children aged six to ten and an upper level, also of four years, for children aged ten to fourteen. Initially only the lower level was to be universal; and indeed, for financial and other reasons, compulsory education in Japan was not raised above four years until 1907, when it was made six.

Also in 1872 the Ministry of Education published a world history textbook entitled Shiryaku (Concise history) which it recommended, but did not make mandatory, for use in primary schools.[5] The most significant thing about Shiryaku, in the light of later Japanese ethnocentrism toward history, was the geographical distribution of

[4] Herbert Passin has called the Gakusei of 1872 "a complete victory for the Westernizers" (Society and Education in Japan, p. 69).

[5] The complete texts of Shiryaku, as well as Nihon Ryakushi mentioned in the paragraph after next, can be found in Kaigo, Nihon Kyōkasho Taikei, XVIII.

its treatment of the world's past: it devoted eighteen pages to Japan, eighteen to China, and eighty to the West. Chinese history had, of course, always been of great interest to the Japanese and we should not be surprised if even more space had been given to it. On the other hand, the extraordinarily large dose of Western history contained in *Shiryaku* was important testimony of the extent to which the Japanese of the early Restoration period had become enamored with the dominant modern world outside East Asia.

The section in *Shiryaku* dealing with Japanese history began with a few sentences about the founding of the country by the gods, and then, in the chronological style (*hennentai*) of traditional Japanese historiography, listed the emperors, giving their basic genealogical data and, very briefly, the most important events of their reigns. It provided little that by itself could have inspired or stimulated the interest of even the most motivated student; and its use for teaching history at the primary school level could scarcely have resulted in much more than the rote memorization of dry facts.

In 1875 the Ministry of Education published two more history texts for school children, one devoted entirely to Japan, entitled *Nihon Ryakushi* (Concise history of Japan), and the other treating the histories of China and the West. Although *Nihon Ryakushi* was considerably longer—ninety pages—than the Japan section of *Shiryaku*, it too was arranged in the old chronological style of discrete events linked together by imperial reigns and revealed no true concern on the part of its compilers for illustrating the principles of cause and effect in history, which the *bummeishi* writers so fervently believed to be a prime function of the modern historian. At the same time, *Nihon Ryakushi* was not overtly didactic in tone. Emperor Nintoku's legendary benevolence toward his subjects was, for example, recorded in the same matter-of-fact way as the purportedly evil behavior of the later emperor Buretsu.

Other primary school texts, written privately about this time, were by and large of the same colorless type as the Ministry of Education publications. The fact is that, despite the polemics of the *bummeishi* writers about the need for new interpretations of history, very little serious thought was given in the 1870s to the teaching of this subject in schools, and the authors of history texts apparently felt no particular need to experiment with progressive methodologies.

Although the teaching of history may not have received the attention that historians would consider appropriate, the new public education of the 1870s was otherwise quite liberal, individual-centered, and modern; and the man most responsible for making it so was Tanaka Fujimaro (1845–1909), who became vice minister of education in 1873. In that year Tanaka brought David Murray of Rutgers University to Japan and together they set about introducing American methods and ideas into the Japanese educational system. Tanaka became a strong advocate of American-style decentralization in education, although the government's intent in the 1872 Education Act had been to assert centralized control on the French model. Pushing his views forcefully from about 1875 on, Tanaka brought about the issuance in 1879 of an Education Ordinance (Kyōikurei) which was aimed at granting considerable autonomy to individual teachers and at permitting them to adjust their courses of instruction to meet special needs in local settings.[6]

Yet, even as Tanaka pressed to liberalize and Americanize public education still further in Japan, conservative forces were at work that were largely to vitiate his efforts and ultimately to force his withdrawal from the Ministry of Education in 1880.

The decade of the 1870s was a time of sweeping change in Japan, distinguishable as clearly in education as in any other field. Dissolution of the samurai class had been a particularly drastic break with the past. It had resulted, on one hand, in the convulsion of the Satsuma Rebellion of 1877 and, on the other, in the beginnings of the people's rights movement, which many Japanese regarded as a manifestly subversive activity. Although there was not the widespread reaction to a sense of "over-Westernization" that occurred ten years later, a number of leaders in intellectual circles and elsewhere in the late 1870s began to fear that Japan was moving at too reckless a pace in her modernization. Many began to suspect, more-

[6] Discussed by J. G. Caiger in Education, Values and Japan's National Identity: A Study of the Aims and Content of Courses in Japanese History, 1872–1963 (Unpublished doctoral dissertation for the Australian National University), pp. 15–16.

over, that in the first flush of enthusiasm for the West the Japanese had cavalierly rejected certain traditional values and institutions whose absence now threatened the stability of Japanese society. The attack on the overly liberal educational policies of Tanaka was a first step in what was to become an increasingly vigorous movement to "re-traditionalize" Japanese society, a movement which reached its peak in 1889–90 with promulgation of the Meiji Constitution and issuance of the Imperial Rescript on Education.

The attack was first launched in the form of an imperial edict entitled The Great Principles of Education (Kyōgaku Taishi) in which the emperor stated that, after visiting a number of public schools on a trip to the provinces the previous year, he had become profoundly disturbed over the adoption of improper ideas by the people. It was his wish that the teaching of heterodox thinking in the schools now be checked and that Confucian principles once again be made the basis of education for the young.

Although issued in the imperial name, The Great Principles of Education was actually written by Motoda Eifu (1818–91), the emperor's Confucian lecturer, who exercised great influence at court from the beginning of the Meiji period until his death in 1891. Motoda had been a stern critic of the new education system from its inauguration in 1872, when the decision had been made to omit from the public school curricula instruction in Confucian ethics as an independent subject. He persistently sought to prejudice the emperor against the foreign-style, liberal training that was being given to Japanese youth and found in Tanaka's proposed ordinance, which would provide even greater freedom in education, an excellent opportunity for open attack upon the "liberals" in the Ministry of Education.[7]

Motoda, however, encountered unexpectedly sharp opposition from Itō Hirobumi (1841–1909), one of the leading oligarchs and then home minister, who strongly resented what he considered Motoda's attempts to bring the throne into politics. Itō had no enduring commitment to liberal education; indeed as prime

[7] See Donald Shively's discussion of Motoda's views on education policy in "Motoda Eifu," in David S. Nivison and Arthur F. Wright, eds., Confucianism in Action, pp. 326–31.

minister a few years later he presided over the first major moves
taken to reorient public education to give primacy to state, rather
than individual, goals. In backing Tanaka's Ordinance at this time
(after making certain amendments to it) Itō was motivated, rather,
by personal hostility to Motoda and by a determination to keep the
emperor above the actual administration of governmental affairs.[8]

Although the Tanaka Ordinance was made into law in 1879, it
was never fully enforced. Itō was apparently satisfied with his
political victory and did nothing to prevent Tanaka's forced departure from the Ministry of Education the following year and the
implementation of a series of measures under a new minister—Kōno
Togama (1844–95)—during the period 1880–82 which reasserted
the principles of centralized public education and generally carried
out the suggestions contained in The Great Principles of Education.

The most significant change in the actual content of education at
this time was the ranking of "ethics" (shūshin) at the head of a list of
compulsory primary school subjects (a ranking it was to hold until
1947). Ethics, like history, had received no special priority in the
educational reforms of the early 1870s. Its texts—many of which
were translations of Western books—were often used, as were history texts, simply as primers for practice in reading and writing.
From this time on, however, ethical training was to receive first
consideration in the public schools. The Ministry of Education was
to set national standards for ethics courses and only books based on
Oriental moral principles (particularly the Confucian principles of
"benevolence, righteousness, loyalty, and filial piety") were to be
used in classrooms.[9]

The new emphasis on moral training in the early 1880s was
accompanied by a reevaluation of the teaching of history. In a
General Plan of Regulations for Primary Schools (Shōgakkō
Kyōsoku Kōryō) issued in May, 1881, the Ministry of Education

---

[8] Naka Arata also suggests that Itō may have felt at the time that the decentralization of education would deprive the people's rights movement of an
issue and would also save the central government considerable money at a
time of financial difficulty following the Satsuma Rebellion. Meiji no Kyōiku,
p. 205.

[9] Kaigo, Nihon Kyōkasho Taikei, XX, 550–51.

decreed that henceforth only Japanese history was to be taught in the elementary grades and that teachers were to aim at cultivating among their pupils, through instruction in history, a spirit of "reverence for the emperor and love of country" (sonnō aikoku). In addition, teachers were to assess the personal qualities of the great figures of the past, to trace important changes in manners and customs through the ages and to try to make understandable the major processes of historical cause and effect.[10] Taken together, these instructions proposed the adoption of more progressive historical methodology for conservative, value-indoctrinating purposes.

The teaching of history was thus to be incorporated in a general program of education to inculcate in primary school children a uniform set of ethical precepts taken chiefly from the Oriental tradition. Since the chronologically arranged (and unquestionably dull) narrative texts then widely in use in primary school history courses were hardly suitable for this purpose, the Ministry of Education proposed the writing of new books on Japanese history that would deal more topically with the past. In its General Plan of 1881 the ministry even provided a list of suggested topics that it deemed appropriate for presenting primary school children with their first formal exposure to Japanese history.

The official in the Ministry of Education who was chiefly responsible for drawing up the General Plan and its list of historical topics was Egi Kazuyuki (1853–1932). After completing a first draft, Egi sent a copy to the emperor, who had retained a keen interest in the implementation of moral training in the public schools following his initial advocacy of it in the 1879 Great Principles of Education edict. The emperor, no doubt with Motoda at his side, examined the draft carefully and then had Egi summoned to the palace. It was His Majesty's feeling that Egi's suggested historical topics placed too much stress on warfare and disorder, as observable in headings such as Emperor Jimmu's Subjugation of the East, The War Between the Minamoto and the Taira, and The Conflict of the Northern and Southern Courts. Struggle and fighting should not be made appealing to children; rather, the emphasis in

[10] *Ibid.* See also Matsushima Eiichi, "Rekishi Kyōiku no Rekishi," in Iwanami Shoten, *Nihon Rekishi*, pp. 246–50.

historical instruction to them should be on the great achievements for good in Japan's past. Moreover, the emperor commented to Egi, it might be appropriate to have the founding of the country by the gods as the first topic in a suggested list, rather than Jimmu's eastward campaign as Egi proposed.

Egi attempted to incorporate the emperor's suggestions in the final draft of the General Plan. As the first topic in his revised list for the study of Japanese history, for example, he placed The Founding of the State and, as the second, Emperor Jimmu's Accession to the Throne. Egi also eliminated several topics he had earlier suggested that dealt with wars and changed the one treating the fourteenth-century dynastic dispute to read The Coexistence of the Northern and Southern Courts. Finally, Egi inserted topics such as Emperor Nintoku's Frugality and The Achievements in Government of the Engi and Tenryaku Periods with the intent of satisfying the emperor's wish that great achievements for good in the past be given special attention.[11]

The inclusion of the founding of the state as the first topic in Egi's revised list was symptomatic of an important change in the official attitude toward history that was just beginning to take place at this time but would ultimately exert a profoundly inhibiting influence on research into the humanities and social sciences in modern Japan. The first important books by post-Restoration Japanese on subjects such as archaeology, philology, and the beginnings of religion were written during the 1880s. Yet, even as these books were in the process of preparation, popular as well as official sentiment was coming increasingly to view as taboo the origins of Japan and the Japanese (and particularly the imperial family) upon which such studies invariably touched.

Another significant change in the teaching of history in primary schools after 1881, as reflected in textbooks, was the avoidance of reference to the conduct of "bad" sovereigns of the past. Such

[11] Egi's revised list of topics may be found in Matsushima, "Rekishi Kyōiku no Rekishi," p. 248. The Engi and Tenryaku periods were calendrical eras of the tenth-century emperors Daigo and Murakami. Daigo, of course, was the emperor whose reign Godaigo so much admired and Murakami was the sovereign from whom Chikafusa's branch of the Genji clan was descended.

things as the iniquity of Buretsu and the murderous behavior of Yōzei, although they had been freely recounted in the earlier Ministry of Education publications, *Shiryaku* and *Nihon Ryakushi*, were now systematically omitted from history texts prepared for use in the elementary grades.[12] There was clearly a growing feeling that there should be no tainting of the imperial institution or its sacred character in the minds of impressionable youngsters through "improper" instruction in Japanese history or in the Shinto mythology that was henceforth to be officially regarded as a part of history.

The reindoctrination through public education of traditional ethical values and of reverence for the throne was, of course, enthusiastically endorsed by Motoda Eifu, who had fulminated throughout the 1870s on the original failure to give preference to ethics in the new Meiji education. At the same time other prominent Japanese, with intellectual orientations and political views quite different from Motoda's, were also more and more inclined to look favorably upon such reindoctrination.

Fukuzawa Yukichi, the great pro-Western and antifeudal enlightener, had, for example, undergone a radical shift in his attitudes by the late 1870s and early 1880s. Whereas he had previously viewed the world as a place of cooperative striving toward a higher civilization based on "natural law," which he believed the advanced Western countries had nearly achieved, Fukuzawa now regarded the world more as an arena of struggle for power among nations and as a testing ground in which the fittest might demonstrate their right to survive.[13] Fukuzawa, in other words, had come to feel that the teachings of Herbert Spencer made more sense than those of J. S. Mill; and that the slogan "enrich the nation and strengthen its arms" (*fukoku kyōhei*) was a better guide for modernizing Japan than the vaguer goal of "civilization and enlightenment." Furthermore, in order to cultivate the nationalism necessary for Japan to compete successfully in the imperialism of the late nineteenth century,

---

[12] Kaigo, *Nihon Kyōkasho Taikei*, XX, 554.

[13] Albert Craig presents an analysis of the transitions in Fukuzawa's attitudes in "Fukuzawa Yukichi: The Philosophical Foundations of Meiji Nationalism," in Robert E. Ward, ed., *Political Development in Modern Japan*.

Fukuzawa came increasingly to extol the moral code of the premodern samurai, based chiefly on the ethic of loyalty, which he had a decade earlier so vociferously mocked.

Another Meiji enlightener who had experienced an important change in his views by the 1880s was Mori Arinori, a former chargé d'affaires to the United States, minister to England, and founder, along with Fukuzawa and others, of the Meiji Six Society. Mori was perhaps the most enthusiastic and extreme of the Westernizers of the early Restoration period. It was he who most prominently urged the adoption of English as the national language of Japan. Mori was also one of the first to advocate abolishment of the exclusive samurai privilege of wearing swords; he vigorously espoused the causes of religious freedom and women's rights; and in 1875 he created a sensation by having his own wedding conducted in the Western fashion.

Yet, despite his early progressiveness, Mori is best recollected in history for the conservative and statist-oriented reforms he initiated as Minister of Education in the first Itō cabinet. Actually Mori's reforms, which were contained mainly in a series of enactments of 1886, did not constitute so much a radical shift in educational policy as a continuation of the changes begun in the 1880–82 period. Most important, perhaps, were the steps he took to concentrate control over education even more completely than before in the central ministry in Tokyo and to standardize teaching curricula and materials.[14]

Mori, like Fukuzawa, had become concerned with the matter of ethics in education; but he summarily rejected what he regarded as the outmoded Confucianism of Motoda, and laid plans to provide in the schools ethical instruction based more on German principles. Mori's assassination in 1889 brought an end to these plans, however, and a return to the kind of Confucian moral training that Motoda had pressed for so strenuously since at least 1879. The Imperial Rescript on Education issued in 1890 was Motoda's final triumph.

One of Mori's most significant measures was the institution of a system of textbook authorization, whereby all texts for use in

---

[14] Naka, *Meiji no Kyōiku*, pp. 244–45.

public schools were required to have the authorization or official approval of the Ministry of Education. This measure, so far as history textbooks were concerned, in fact brought little immediate change in the kinds of textual materials then being employed in the schools. The ministry's stipulations about what should be covered in Japanese history were very general and most of the current texts, which had by and large been compiled to conform to Egi's list of suggested topics published some five years earlier, were easily able to qualify for authorization.[15]

Yet, in spite of the apparently casual manner in which authorization was granted to texts in the period 1886–90, it is clear that the Ministry of Education was coming to look upon the teaching of history with considerably more interest than it had previously. In 1887, for example, the ministry appointed a board of scholars to conduct a competition for the writing of textbooks on Japanese history for primary school use. The board drew up a proposed table of contents which it recommended to authors planning to enter the competition, but did not insist on their following.

In effect, this proposed table of contents came to replace the Egi list as the official (although not rigidly orthodox) scheme for the ordering of Japanese history for presentation in the public schools. It was far more detailed than Egi's list and showed a marked tendency to encourage the presentation of Japanese history in terms of the people most prominent in its making. Thus one of the proposed chapters, dealing with the fourteenth century, included the following subheadings: The Emperor Godaigo, The Northern and Southern Courts, Kusunoki Masashige, Nitta Yoshisada, Ashikaga Takauji, and Unification of the Courts. For the purpose of ethical indoctrination such an incipient "great man" approach to history—four of the six subheadings here are the names of individuals—was most useful, since delineation of the lives and conduct of important people was a convenient and direct means of illustrating morality or the lack of it.

What has been said thus far about the teaching of history in primary schools and the preparation of textbooks for that purpose during

[15] Kaigo, *Nihon Kyōkasho Teikei*, XX, 560.

the 1870s and 1880s in Japan does not constitute an exceptional record of the use of a national past for the purpose of public indoctrination. The aim of having history serve as a means of nourishing in the breasts of young Japanese a spirit of "reverence for the emperor and love of country" (reiterated in the prefaces to most primary school history texts written during the 1880s) is probably comparable to the use of American history in elementary schools of the United States to foster civic pride and patriotism. Even the incorporation within the discipline of history of the Shinto myths of creation and the divine descent of the Japanese imperial family, never absolutely insisted upon even in the late 1880s,[16] probably did not differ greatly from the widespread handling of the Bible in its entirety as factual truth in Western schools. Perhaps the most questionable aspect of history instruction to Japanese youngsters in the elementary grades during the first two decades or so of the modern era was the restriction of it from 1881 on solely to Japanese history.

But from the early 1890s the teaching of history in Japanese primary schools came under much more stringent control and was more closely integrated with training in ethics. Rigid orthodoxies of historical interpretation were imposed, orthodoxies that were not arbitrarily contrived for indoctrination of the young but emerged from strong sentiment periodically aroused over public morals, as in 1892 when Professor Kume Kunitake was forced to resign from the faculty of Tokyo Imperial University for publishing an article that labeled Shinto a primitive form of heaven-worship, and in the political furor of 1911 over the fourteenth-century imperial legitimacy issue.

The Kume incident must be seen against the background of the development of the mainstream—the so-called academic—school of Meiji historiography, which arose under governmental sponsorship shortly after the Restoration and later came to be centered at Tokyo University.

In April, 1869, Sanjō Sanetomi (1837–91), then chancellor (*dajō*

[16] One history text published in 1888 and authorized by the Ministry of Education, for example, omitted the age of the gods and presented archaeological material on the origins of Japanese civilization. *Ibid.*, p. 568.

[169]

daijin) of the Great Council of State, was instructed by imperial edict to organize a Bureau of Historical Compilation[17] within the new Meiji government. The Japanese court from the eighth through the tenth century had, under Chinese influence, sponsored the compilation of "six national histories" (*rikkokushi*) covering the period from the age of the gods until the end of the reign of Emperor Kōkō in 887. Discontinuance of the writing of national histories occurred in the shift from rule by the throne to rule by Fujiwara regents in the tenth century. To the Meiji government, flushed with the restorationist spirit of its early years, the reinstatement of this practice after a lapse of more than a millenium must have seemed an eminently fitting act of rulership.

The original intent of the emperor's edict was to have the Bureau of Historical Compilation gather materials for an official history of Japan from 887. But it was later decided to make the starting point of this history—which in 1881 was designated *Dai Nihon Hennen Shi* (Chronological history of great Japan)—1392, or the date of the reunification of the northern and southern courts. The reason for this change was the general desire of the bureau's scholars to undertake their work as a sequel not to the ancient six national histories but to the more recent and highly admired (although not imperially authorized) *Dai Nihon Shi* of the Mito school, which covered Japanese history until the end of the war between the courts.

Among the principal scholars assigned to the Bureau of Historical Compilation were Shigeno Yasutsugu (1827–1910), Kume, and Hoshino Tadashi.[18] These men were known at the time as scholars of Chinese studies (*kangakusha*) from the fact that their background in historical training was in the "empirical research" or "textual collation" school (*kōshōgaku*; in Chinese, *k'ao-cheng hsüeh*) of scholarship which had originated in China during the seventeenth and eighteenth centuries and had strongly influenced historians in Tokugawa Japan.

In China, the empirical research school began as a reaction against

[17] Kokushi Henshū Kyoku; renamed Shūshi Kyoku in 1875 and Shūshi Kan in 1877.

[18] For a relevant article in English on the Bureau of Historical Compilation and its principal scholars see Jiro Numata, "Shigeno Yasutsugu and the Modern Tokyo Tradition of Writing," in W. G. Beasley and E. G. Pulleyblank, eds., *Historians of China and Japan*.

the orthodox Neo-Confucian interpretations of the Chinese classics that had evolved during the Sung and Ming periods. The desire of its adherents was to reevaluate the past more objectively through rigorous textual criticism and analysis; yet the tendency in both China and Japan was for scholars of this school to restrict themselves almost exclusively to the gathering and authentication of materials, without venturing into historical interpretation.

In 1888 the work of the Bureau of Historical Compilation was transferred to the newly established history department of Tokyo University, and Shigeno, Kume, and Hoshino were given professorships there. The German historian Ludwig Riess, disciple of the great Leopold von Ranke of Berlin, had also recently accepted a position at the university and through him the Japanese scholars now came in direct contact with German historical methodology. Actually, Shigeno and his associates had already had some exposure to Western historiography; and with their background in "empirical research" they had taken readily to the attitude that the study of the past should be treated as a science, that primary source materials should be painstakingly collected and verified and presented so as to make clear their underlying historical principles.

An important result of the cultivation of a modern, scientific attitude toward history by Shigeno and the others was that they became increasingly critical of the very record, *Dai Nihon Shi*, which they were using as the point of departure for their own historical work. The *Dai Nihon Shi* had been undertaken by the Mito scholars with a deliberate didactic intent: to demonstrate the functioning of the ethical principle of *taigi-meibun*[19] in Japanese history. Yet it was precisely against such an ethical bias in the interpretation of the past that Shigeno and Kume, in particular, now began boldly to speak out. They did so at a time when the Meiji government was preparing to undertake with more vigor than before the implementation of morals education in primary schools and when the Japanese public was showing a marked revulsion to excessive Westernization, a revulsion that became especially intense after the breakdown of the efforts to secure revision of the unequal treaties of 1889. The *bummeishi* writers of the early Meiji period had been allowed to criticize

[19] See pp. 69–70 above.

with impunity Japan's feudal past and the venerated works in which it was recorded. Yet similar, although far more carefully marshaled, criticism by historians of the academic school in the late 1880s and early 1890s was not to be granted the same license by either Japanese government or public.

Shigeno and Kume made their attacks on the *Dai Nihon Shi* chiefly through critiques of the historicity of the *Taiheiki*, extensive portions of which were reproduced in the Mito work in its treatment of the fourteenth century. Kume, as we observed in the last chapter, categorically dismissed the *Taiheiki* as historically worthless in a series of articles published in 1891 in *Shigaku Zasshi*, the journal of the historical society (Shigakkai) established at Tokyo University in 1889 with Shigeno as its first president. Even earlier, Shigeno himself had challenged the historical validity of certain portions of the *Taiheiki* that dealt with a specific loyalist chieftain from Bizen Province named Kojima Takanori.[20]

Kojima, like Kusunoki Masashige, had purportedly been one of the earliest to announce his support of Godaigo in the 1331 uprising against the Hōjō. He reappears periodically throughout the *Taiheiki* in a lengthy career, first as a loyalist and then as a backer of the southern court, that extended at least into the 1350s. Kojima is best remembered in history for the attempt he made to intercept and free Godaigo when the latter was sent into exile in 1331 by the Hōjō. In this he was foiled, because the route of the imperial party was changed at the last minute, but Kojima was able a short while later to steal into the garden in front of a residence the emperor was temporarily occupying and to carve on a tree a poem pledging his undying loyalty to the throne.

Shigeno claimed that he could find no mention whatever of Kojima in any other source from the fourteenth century, and asserted that he was probably a fictional character. Hoshino Tadashi, Shigeno's colleague, noted that Kojima's name was the same as "the Priest Kojima," reported in one journal to have been the author of the *Taiheiki*,[21] and suggested that this priest may have

[20] "Kojima Takanori Kangae" in Satsuma Shi Kenkyū Kai, ed., *Shigeno Hakushi Gakuron Bunshū*, vol. II.
[21] See pp. 126–27 above.

invented Kojima Takanori in order to write himself into the book. In any case, by questioning the historical existence of Kojima, Shigeno and Hoshino implied that the entire *Taiheiki* might be factually unreliable. Shigeno, who at one point went so far as to challenge the authenticity of the famous scene (recorded only in the *Taiheiki*) in which Kusunoki Masashige bade farewell to his son, Masatsura, before the battle of Minatogawa in 1336, gained particular notoriety as a historical "obliterator" and was even unflatteringly dubbed "Professor Obliterator" (*massatsu hakushi*). It was he who chiefly set the stage for Kume's public rejection of the *Taiheiki* in 1891 as worthless.

(In fact, as we noted in the last chapter, the academic historians of this time were unduly harsh in their evaluation of the *Taiheiki*. One of their successors at Tokyo University, Professor Tanaka Yoshinari, discovered several references to Kojima Takanori in other fourteenth-century sources, and used this and additional evidence to upgrade the work's standing as history).

The academic historians were unquestionably touching upon delicate issues in the atmosphere of the late 1880s and early 1890s and opposition to them was not long in coming. One of the groups that attacked them most vociferously was the national scholars (*kokugakusha*), who traced their descent from the Neo-Shinto revival of the mid-Tokugawa period, which had been concerned with such matters as Japanese philology and the search for a true Japanese spirit (i.e., one uncorrupted by Confucianism or Buddhism) in the literature of the nation's antiquity.

The national scholars had enjoyed a brief spell of glory at the time of the Meiji Restoration when they were employed by the Department of Religion (which was officially ranked above the Grand Council of State) for the purpose of launching a movement of Shinto evangelism. But as the early Meiji enthusiasm for Shinto waned and the Department of Religion was phased out of existence along with other anachronistic offices that had been patterned on the Taihō Code of 701, the national scholars employed by the government had either been released or relegated to minor posts.

These men deeply resented the fact that their rivals, the former scholars of Chinese studies, were permanently engaged by the government in historiographic work and, in some cases, had even been given professorships at Tokyo University. They claimed that it was improper for such patronage to be granted solely to one school of historians. The national scholars maintained, moreover, that the supposedly scientific methodology of the academic historians ran precisely counter to the proper function of historical research, which (in their view) was to identify and make clear the unique ethical qualities of the Japanese people. Finally, the national scholars made the charge—and this was an especially potent one in the xenophobia of the times in Japan—that the academic historians were remiss in continuing to write in classical Chinese rather than in Japanese.[22]

Kume became a chief target of attack of the national scholars in 1891 when he published both his essay on Shinto as a primitive form of heaven-worship and the series of articles debunking the *Taiheiki*, all in the academic journal *Shigaku Zasshi*. The Shinto essay would not have received such wide publicity if it had not been reissued the following year in the more popular magazine *Shikai*, edited by the former *bummeishi* writer Taguchi Ukichi. Within months the Meiji government, under intense criticism from the national scholars and others that Kume in his analysis of Shinto had demonstrated a flagrant disrespect for the sacred origins of the imperial family, felt constrained to dismiss the academic scholar from the faculty of Tokyo University. A year later Shigeno also withdrew from the university, the Historical Compilation Bureau was closed, and work was permanently suspended on the government-sponsored official history of Japan, *Dai Nihon Hennen Shi*.

A new Office for the Compilation of Historical Materials (Shiryō Hensan Gakari; later, Shiryō Hensan Jo) was opened at Tokyo University in 1895 and undertook work on several long-term projects, including the great historical source compendium *Dai Nihon Shiryō*. But the academic scholars in this office, with few exceptions, henceforth devoted themselves exclusively to "textual collation" and conspicuously avoided becoming involved in disputes over interpretations of Japanese history.[23]

[22] Iwai, "Nihon Kindai Shigaku no Keisei," pp. 85–86.
[23] *Ibid.*, p. 90.

The Kume affair, which resulted in the first major instance in modern Japanese history of the imposition of official censure for the expression of unorthodox or unpopular scholarly views, occurred almost simultaneously with the dismissal from Tokyo's First High School in 1891 of the noted Japanese Christian, Uchimura Kanzō (1861–1930), for his refusal to bow before the Imperial Rescript on Education. Both Kume and Uchimura were victims of the indignation of a society which a few decades earlier had tolerated the most extreme diversities of personal opinion and behavior but had now become increasingly determined to enforce conformity to a national code of ethics drawn from its earlier feudal-Confucian tradition. The fundamental elements of this code, including filial piety and loyalty to the sovereign as the father of the state, were set forth in imposingly formal terms in the Education Rescript and were henceforth to be inculcated in the mass of the Japanese citizenry in more systematic fashion than before through the system of authorized morals and history textbooks in primary schools.

A significant characteristic of the elementary grade history textbooks authorized by the Ministry of Education after issuance of the Education Rescript was the increased stress on the lives of great men. One book published in 1892,[24] for example, had as the headings in its table of contents for the early medieval period: Taira Kiyomori and Taira Shigemori; Minamoto Yoritomo and Minamoto Yoshitsune; Hōjō Tokimune and the Mongol Invasions; and Kusunoki Masashige and Kusunoki Masatsura. The two pages devoted to the last heading included no mention whatsoever of the Kemmu Restoration and simply noted Takauji's rebellion and the founding of the northern and southern courts; rather, they dealt almost exclusively with the activities of the Kusunoki, father and son, who were held to be exemplars of bravery and loyalty for the Japanese people.

From about 1890 on, the Ministry of Education clearly aimed at ever greater control over and standardization of the contents of primary school history texts. In 1903 it finally abandoned altogether the practice, inaugurated by Mori Arinori in 1886, of authorizing

[24] *Teikoku Shōshi*, reproduced in Kaigo, *Nihon Kyōkasho Taikei*, vol. XIX.

privately written texts for school use and assumed responsibility for the composition of such books by specialists directly under its jurisdiction. The first ministry text, *Shōgaku Nihon Rekishi* (Japanese history for primary schools), was produced in 1904 and was revised and reissued five years later on the basis of recommendations made by a ministry-appointed advisory board, which included such prominent scholars as Mikami Sanji (1865–1939), Tanaka Yoshinari, and Kida Teikichi (1871–1939). It was the section The Northern and Southern Courts in this revised edition that came under widespread criticism in 1911 and precipitated a near political crisis for the administration of Prime Minister Katsura Tarō (1847–1913).

The earliest expressions of discontent with the treatment of the fourteenth-century war between the courts in the Ministry of Education's primary school history text, however, appear to have been raised in the fall of 1910 at one of a series of refresher-type courses for public school teachers sponsored by the ministry and held periodically in Tokyo.[25] The instructor in charge of this particular course was Kida Teikichi, who had been the principal author of the ministry's history text and who chose in his lectures to talk about the problem of historical interpretation of the northern and southern courts period. At this time, as well as later, Kida made his position as a scholar forthrightly clear.[26] He acknowledged that, owing primarily to the influence of the Mito School and the *Dai Nihon Shi*, the view had come to be widely held that the southern court, which supposedly retained uninterrupted possession of the regalia, had been the sole source of imperial authority during its existence from 1336 to 1392. He noted, moreover, that memory of the gallant fighters for the Yoshino cause had come to occupy a very special place in the hearts of the Japanese people. This latter fact had been publicly confirmed on numerous occasions by the Meiji government's bestowal of posthumous rank on such great loyalists as Kusunoki Masashige, Nitta Yoshisada, and Kitabatake Chikafusa and by its construction of shrines dedicated exclusively to the worship of their spirits.

Nevertheless, Kida pointed out, no definitive public position had

---

[25] Yamazaki and Horie, eds., *Namboku-chō Seijun Ronsan*, pp. 28–29.
[26] The following views of Kida may be found *ibid.*, pp. 322–35.

ever been taken by the government since the Meiji Restoration as to which line of emperors—the northern or the southern—should be considered historically "legitimate." In an imperial genealogy issued by an office of the government (Genrōin) in 1877, for example, although the southern emperors were given primacy in the order of official listing, the occupants of the northern throne were also included as "secondary" *tennō* or emperors. In addition, the mausolea of the northern emperors had been cared for and treated in the same fashion as those of the Yoshino sovereigns throughout the Meiji period. Finally, although it was believed by many people that at some time about 1891 the Department of the Imperial Household (Kunaishō) had decided at last to take the official stand that the southern emperors had been legitimate (and therefore that the heads of the northern court had not been emperors at all), again there had been no public pronouncement to this effect.

Kida stressed that he and his colleagues had attempted to be extremely circumspect in their presentation of the medieval dynastic schism in the Ministry of Education's primary school history text. They had finally decided that the most appropriate thing to do was to recognize the objective fact that there had been two lines of emperors who claimed legitimacy and maintained separate courts for a period of fifty-six years during the fourteenth century. Kida, in a later statement, added the wry personal observation that to have regarded the southern court as legitimate and the northern court as illegitimate would have been tantamount to acknowledging that wrong had triumphed over right, certainly not an edifying historical conclusion to present to elementary grade youngsters.[27]

On January 9, 1911, Tokyo's Yomiuri newspaper published an editorial sharply criticizing the Ministry of Education for allowing the theory of the "two courts"—which implied that imperial

[27] Beasley and Blacker discuss the problem which the Tokugawa period writer, Rai San'yō, faced in attempting to apply the Confucian "praise and blame" theory to his interpretation of Japanese history inasmuch as "most of the persons he wished to praise had been remarkable for their failures and early deaths, while those on whom he heaped most abuse had been rather conspicuously successful as rulers and long-lived as dynasties" ("Japanese Historical Writing in the Tokugawa Period (1603–1868)," in Beasley and Pulleyblank, *Historians of China and Japan*, p. 262).

sovereignty was divisible—to be expounded in its primary school history text. Such a theory, the paper asserted, could only upset the sentiments of the people and serve to obscure their sense of responsibility and loyalty to the throne.[28]

Of course, the ministry's text had by 1911 been in use in primary schools throughout the country for some seven years. That it should suddenly be attacked by a leading newspaper for containing an allegedly improper interpretation of the history of the imperial family was owing largely to especially heightened fears at the time in Japan over what was widely regarded as the rapid spread of dangerous foreign political ideologies, such as the anarchism that had inspired a plot to assassinate the Meiji emperor the year before. In fact, the outcome of the secret trial of those accused in the anarchist or Great Treason plot of 1910 was carried in the press on the very same day as the Yomiuri editorial attacking the two courts theory. Five days later, on January 24, 1911, twelve of the men who had stood trial were executed, including Kōtoku Shūsui (1871–1911), who, though in fact falsely charged and convicted of participation in the plot, was, nevertheless, a leading left-wing radical and theorist of the day. In the acrimonious public debate that soon raged over the northern and southern courts issue, Kida Teikichi was even charged with having secretly conspired with Kōtoku to subvert the morals of the Japanese people through the public education system.

Although socialism and left-wing thought in Japan had had their origins in the 1880s as offshoots of the people's rights movement, it was not until the period following the Sino-Japanese War of 1894–95 that, as a result of factory shutdowns and general economic distress in the cities, their appeal became potentially significant. However, the first important socialist party, founded in 1901, was forced by the authorities to disband on the same day it declared its existence.[29] As a result of this and other acts of harassment and suppression, many socialists soon despaired of achieving their aims through

---

[28] Reproduced in Ōkubo Toshiaki, "Yugamerareta Rekishi," in Sakisaka, ed., *Arashi no Naka no Hyakunen*. This is probably the best single account of the northern and southern courts issue of 1910–11.

[29] Shakai Minshutō.

parliamentary, legal means in Japan and became advocates of more radical doctrines, such as anarchism, syndicalism, and Marxism.

Yamagata Aritomo (1838–1922) and other Meiji leaders, vastly exaggerating in their minds the threat of radicalism, turned to increasingly harsh legislation and police measures to deal with it. In addition, they became more concerned than ever with the moral training of Japanese youth and took the initiative in bringing about in 1903 the Ministry of Education's "nationalization" of the writing of ethics, as well as history and other, textbooks for primary schools.

It was also during the first decade or so of constitutional government that the ancient concept of *kokutai* ("national entity" or "national essence"), which had been largely ignored in the early Meiji period, came more and more to be invoked as the central component of ideological orthodoxy for the modern Japanese state. To Kitabatake Chikafusa, writing in the fourteenth-century, *kokutai* had signified above all else the awe-inspiring fact that Japan, alone among the nations of the world (as he knew it), had been ruled from the time of the gods by a single, unbroken dynastic line of sovereigns. By Tokugawa times the interpretation of *kokutai* had been broadened to include the feudal-Confucian idea of a harmonious society based on the ethics of filial piety and loyalty and the irrational Neo-Shintoist belief in the unique spiritual or emotional quality of the Japanese folk. The latter belief made modern *kokutai* in certain ways similar to the *Weltanschauung* of some German Romanticists. Both concepts rejected Western individualism and liberalism and glorified the racial vitalism of the Japanese and German peoples; moreover, both became imbued with a strident martial character derived from the *bushidō* and Prussian military traditions.

The orthodox nationalistic thinking based on *kokutai* that ultimately evolved in Japan before World War II differed, however, in at least one very important respect from what became the European ideology of fascism. Fascism denied the ideas of evolutionary change and historical determinism and insisted that the maker of history is the great leader who, unfettered by the conventional restraints of society, rises to power by means of his resolute will and inherent superiority as an individual. Yet such a concept of the "superman" could scarcely have been more alien to the Japanese;

[179]

indeed, a Duce or Führer could not conceivably have arisen in Japanese society. The greatest heroes of Japan's past, apart from emperors themselves, were no olympians but men who served others (whether feudal overlords or sovereigns) with self-abnegating devotion and loyalty. Thus the emphasis placed on great men in primary school ethics and morals texts during the late Meiji period was in no sense aimed at encouraging the wills of individuals to power; rather it was to teach children through the examples of their forebears their responsibilities to society and especially to inspire in them an overriding sense of loyalty and duty to the emperor, the "non-acting" father of a great family-state.

In the political rhetoric of pre-World War II Japan the most heinous offense of which a person could be accused was the desecration or violation of *kokutai*, an offense that was simultaneously *lèse majesté*, since the imperial institution was inseparable from the national entity. In 1911 such "desecration of *kokutai*" was one of the charges leveled against Kida Teikichi; and in fact a Society for the Protection of the Japanese National Entity (Nihon Kokutai Yōgo Dan) was even formed to oppose him and to support the cause for official recognition of the historical legitimacy of the southern court.

Two men who took the initiative in escalating to the level of the national government criticism of the manner of presentation of the history of the northern and southern courts in the Ministry of Education's primary school history text were Makino Kenjirō and Matsudaira Yasukuni, members of the faculty of Waseda University in Tokyo. They persuaded Fujisawa Genzō, a relative of Makino's, who was a member without party affiliation of the House of Representatives, to raise the issue publicly in the Diet.

Originally, Fujisawa planned to make the following "statement of inquiry" (*shitsumon sho*) to the House of Representatives: (1) Are the regalia meaningless as determinates of imperial sovereignty? (2) Was Ashikaga Takauji not a rebel? (3) Were Kusunoki, Nitta, and the other adherents of the southern court not loyal subjects? (4) Is it not regrettable that the history textbook for primary schools prepared under the auspices of the Ministry of Education has implanted doubts about these matters in the minds of the Japanese people, offended the imperial dignity, and destroyed the basis of education?[30] Later, Fujisawa deleted the first three questions and, with the supporting signatures of fifty-one other representatives, presented only the fourth to the House on February 4, 1911.

Yet this single, crudely inflammatory inquiry was more than sufficient to cause great alarm within the Katsura administration. The minister of education, Komatsubara Eitarō (1852–1919), personally attempted to dissuade Fujisawa from his announced intent to discuss the "northern and southern courts issue" (*namboku-chō mondai*) in an official speech in the House on February 16. Komatsubara even brought Kida together with Fujisawa and the two Waseda professors on the tenth for a discussion of the problem, but at the time achieved no solution.[31]

Fujisawa Genzō, however, appears to have been a person of only the slightest significance in the Japanese government of 1911 who suddenly and uncomfortably found himself at the center of a potentially explosive national controversy. In the days that followed in early February he behaved in a manner that caused many people to believe he was either emotionally unstable or exceptionally irresolute. The Katsura government was in any case soon able successfully to pressure him into abandoning a course of action that could have called into question its entire conduct of public education precisely at a time, following the Great Treason plot, when the Japanese people were highly sensitive to what they regarded as a real decline in national morals.

A few days before his proposed address in the Diet, Fujisawa returned to his home in Osaka to consult his father, a respected Confucian scholar, and to visit and, apparently, seek spiritual guidance at the Great Shrine of Ise. When he returned to Tokyo on the fifteenth, he was met at Shimbashi station by government officials and was taken directly to a conference with Prime Minister Katsura and General Terauchi Masatake (1852–1919), one of whose former aides-de-camp was a pupil of Fujisawa's father. The precise details of this conference are not known, but Katsura in essence told Fujisawa that he would be willing to have any objectionable passages

[30] Listed in Murata, *Namboku-chō Ron*, p. 233.

[31] An article on this discussion appeared in the journal *Nihon Oyobi Nihonjin*, no. 554.

in the Ministry of Education's primary school history text altered if the representative would agree not to pursue his plan to put the "northern and southern courts issue" before the Diet in open debate. Katsura sought to strengthen his appeal by suggesting that such a debate would very likely bring about attacks not only on the Ministry of Education, but also on the Department of the Imperial Household, which in its genealogies had not made perfectly clear the relationship in terms of legitimacy of the rival lines of emperors in the fourteenth century.[32]

Apparently Katsura was most persuasive. For, much to the dismay of his backers, many of whom were undoubtedly strongly motivated by a desire to embarrass the Katsura administration politically, Fujisawa in his appearance before the House of Representatives on February 16 stated that, because of government assurance that the primary school history text would be revised, he had decided to withdraw his earlier statement of inquiry into the matter of the northern and southern courts. At the same time Fujisawa dramatically announced his resignation from the House.

This backing down on the issue by Fujisawa, as his performance before the House was widely interpreted in the press and elsewhere, did not however bring to an end the discomfort of the Katsura government. Within days many individuals and a variety of organizations[33] issued demands calling for absolute clarification of the historical fact of the southern court's legitimacy. Among the general assertions made in these demands were the following: that the *Dai Nihon Shi* had conclusively proved such legitimacy on the basis of possession of the regalia; that the Japanese people idolized Kusunoki and the other great loyalists and despised the treacherous Ashikaga Takauji; and that proper loyalty to the throne, devotion to duty, and understanding of *kokutai* must be taught to school children by praising the examples of the former and condemning the conduct of the latter.

One of the strongest attacks made on the government about this

[32] Ōkubo, "Yugamerareta Rekishi," p. 57.

[33] One of these organizations was the Education Society of Mito City. A detailed statement issued by it is contained in Yamazaki and Horie, eds., *Namboku-chō Seijun Ronsan*, pp. 33–37.

time was by Inukai Tsuyoshi (1855–1932), president of the Kokumintō, in a resolution presented to the House of Representatives on February 23, which just barely failed to get the necessary number of votes for passage. Among other things, Inukai criticised the Ministry of Education for mishandling, in its primary school history text, the explanation of the process of imperial succession through the ages and of the criteria traditionally used to determine legitimacy of emperorship. He asserted that this mishandling had caused grievous distress and uncertainty among the people and insisted that ultimate responsibility for it lay with the entire Katsura administration. Inukai also alluded darkly to a connection between this textbook issue and the Great Treason plot.

On February 27 Kida Teikichi resigned his position on the textbook advisory board of the Ministry of Education. The following day Prime Minister Katsura petitioned the throne through the Privy Council to issue a decree making official the interpretation that the emperors of the Yoshino court had been the sole legitimate sovereigns during the period 1336–92. This decree was duly made public on March 3. Almost simultaneously the Ministry of Education revised the title of chapter 23 of its primary school history text from "The Northern and Southern Courts" to "The Yoshino Court" and made appropriate changes in its contents.

It is reported, in conclusion, that Yamagata Aritomo, who was at the time president of the Privy Council, became so distraught over the issue of the northern and southern courts when it came to light nationally that he went directly to the emperor to plead that the latter take an immediate and uncompromising stand in favor of the southern court's legitimacy. The emperor, who was himself of course descended from the northern line of sovereigns, assured Yamagata that it had always been his understanding that this was a generally acknowledged fact: indeed, had not the great work of the Meiji Restoration been undertaken simply as a continuation of the earlier Restoration of Kemmu? According to one source, Yamagata later told an acquaintance that, if the emperor had not held this view, he, Yamagata, was prepared to commit "admonitory suicide." [34]

[34] This anecdote is related in Murata, *Namboku-chō Ron*, pp. 238–41.

Concluding Remarks

IT IS BEYOND THE LIMITS of this study to examine further the political implications or repercussions of the northern and southern courts issue of 1911. But from the standpoint of freedom of expression in education and even in scholarly historical research the effects of the issue as it was officially settled were indisputably harmful.

Throughout the year 1911 there was a vast outpouring of opinion in the mass media concerning the "legitimacy" question, which, academically speaking at least, was at the heart of the issue; and indeed many of the most prominent scholars of the day came forth to take one stand or another in journal and newspaper articles.[1] Among those who, for example, supported Kida Teikichi's position that, simply from an objective examination of the facts, the northern and southern courts should be regarded as having been rival centers of imperial authority were Kume Kunitake (whose former colleague in the Bureau of Historical Compilation, Shigeno Yasutsugu, had died the year before) and Mikami Sanji, who had worked closely with Kida on the Ministry of Education's textbook advisory board.

Probably the most distinguished proponent of the view that the northern court had been legitimate was Yoshida Tōgo (1864–1918), while those who argued on behalf of the southern court's legitimacy included Inoue Tetsujirō (1855–1944), Hozumi Yatsuka (1860–1912), Anesaki Masaharu (1873–1949) and Kuroita Katsumi (1874–1946). A number of the latter group disputed the issue purely from ethical positions with scant regard for the available historical facts. The eminent historian Kuroita, although he agreed in his personal conclusion that the southern court had the stronger claim to legitimacy, went to great lengths to point out the necessity in any analysis

---

[1] Statements by many of these scholars may be found in Yamazaki and Horie, eds., *Namboku-chō Seijun Ronsan*, pp. 321–653; also in Shigaku Kyōkai, ed., *Namboku-chō Seijun Ron*.

of first examining the period of the great dynastic schism in the light of historical objectivity. Kuroita was especially critical of those who regarded the *Dai Nihon Shi* as a source of unassailable scriptural truth and who insisted upon reducing historical inquiry to a "praise and blame" exercise conducted solely in terms of the ethic of *taigi meibun*.[2]

Yet however one assesses the personal views of scholars and others of 1911, the fact remains that an orthodox line of interpretation of a particular period of Japanese history was established by the government, was sanctified by imperial decree, and was incorporated into primary and other school textbooks. And in time it made difficult, and finally impossible, impartial scholarly research into the period in question.

I have referred to Professor Tanaka Yoshinari for his work in reevaluating the historicity of the *Taiheiki* after the withering attacks made on it by Shigeno, Kume, and others. For some years prior to his death in 1919, Tanaka was responsible for lecturing on the period of the fourteenth-century war between the courts at Tokyo University. He had remained silent during the 1911 debate on the legitimacy question and had even acquiesced when his departmental chief, Ueda Mannen (1867–1937), suggested that he alter the title of his lectures on this particular topic from "The Northern and Southern Courts" to "The Yoshino Court."[3] But from the content of his lectures, which were published posthumously as *Namboku-chō Jidai Shi*, it is clear that Tanaka was a fierce advocate of freedom of academic expression and continued to regard "the period of the northern and southern courts" as the most appropriate designation for the era that extended from 1336 until 1392. Moreover, Tanaka expressed to his students the view that possession of the regalia was by itself an academically unsatisfactory determinant of imperial legitimacy. Like Kuroita, he furthermore insisted that pure historical research be kept strictly separate from application of the *taigi meibun* test to the conduct of individuals in history.[4]

---

[2] Kuroita's views are well set forth *ibid.*, pp. 263–326.
[3] Reported by Mikami Sanji in his eulogistic introduction to Tanaka's *Namboku-chō Jidai Shi*, p. 13.
[4] Tanaka, *ibid.*, pp. 139–40.

In the general liberality of the 1920s other scholars were also able to work on the northern and southern courts period without incurring unusual criticism or inviting molestation. Noteworthy publications during this decade were Nakamura Naokatsu's *Namboku-chō Jidai* (1922), which was the first important attempt to deal with the age in terms of economic, social, and cultural as well as political history, and Uozumi Sōgorō's *Namboku-chō* (1927).

But the rise of a militant nationalism in the 1930s was accompanied by a new popular interest in the Kemmu Restoration and the epoch of war between the courts—as seen in the orthodox light of the righteousness of Godaigo's cause and of the legitimacy of the Yoshino court—that sharply curtailed open research into and even free discussion of the period. In December, 1933, an Organization in Commemoration of the Six-Hundredth Anniversary of the Kemmu Restoration (Kemmu Chūkō Roppyaku-nen Kinen Kai) was formed to conduct a gala celebration on March 13, 1934, the day when six centuries earlier the calendrical designation of Kemmu had been adopted. And in 1936 a Kemmu Council (Kemmu Kaigi) was founded to gather and publish materials on the Restoration. The leading figure of this council was Professor Hiraizumi Kiyoshi, whose fervently aroused nationalistic sentiments led him to abandon scholarly objectivity and to produce books such as *Kemmu Chūkō no Hongi* (The true significance of the Kemmu Restoration) that were not genuine histories at all but simply propaganda tracts.

One of the most significant developments to note in the period after about 1930 was the great intensification by schoolteachers and others, for the purpose of moral indoctrination, of the hero-villain interpretation of the protagonists of the fourteenth-century dynastic struggle. Kusunoki, Nitta, and their comrades in arms were fully apotheosized, whereas Takauji was relegated to the status of the most loathsome of traitors in Japanese history.

In 1934 Nakajima Kumakichi, commerce minister in the cabinet of Saitō Makoto (1858–1936), was even obliged to resign his post because, as a history buff, he had published an article in the magazine *Gendai* (February, 1934, issue) that praised Takauji; and, during the Pacific War, Professor Tsuji Zennosuke (1877–1955) was widely berated for an article of his that had appeared nearly thirty years earlier (1917) in *Shigaku Zasshi* entitled *Ashikaga Takauji no Shinkō* (The faith of Ashikaga Takauji), which was an attempt to analyze, in some measure sympathetically, the character and beliefs of this controversial warrior chieftain of the fourteenth century. Richard Ponsonby-Fane, an eccentric Englishman who lived for years in Japan before the Pacific War and assiduously studied things Japanese, had this to say about Takauji: "Of him it is difficult to write in temperate tones, for he was that most detestable of human beings, a traitor, and, like so many of his kind, once a traitor, always a traitor." [5]

Since the end of the war, old attitudes concerning the imperial institution have been drastically altered, and research in Japan on the Kemmu Restoration and the struggle between the courts has been undertaken from completely fresh viewpoints. Freed from the restraints of official orthodoxies of interpretation, scholars have been at liberty to deal with the period as they see fit. The legitimacy issue, no longer a subject to arouse passions, has been reexamined in purely dispassionate terms; and I have attempted in this study to make use of the most recent findings and views. It may be helpful in conclusion to summarize the issue as it evolved over nearly six centuries.

We cannot presume to know precisely the feelings of Japanese of the fourteenth century toward the legitimacy quarrel. Nevertheless, the evidence that the Ashikaga themselves believed the southern court's claim to the throne to be the more rightful suggests that this view may well have been shared by most Japanese leaders at the time. After the southern court agreed to reunification in 1392, however, its cause came to be retrospectively denigrated. Those who sought to revive it were regarded as outlaws in a way in which members of the Yoshino court and its supporters had not been regarded up to 1392, even by the shogunate and the northern court in Kyoto. For nearly a century they were relentlessly hounded by shogunate authorities.

Yet the spread in popularity of the *Taiheiki* from about the end of the sixteenth and beginning of the seventeenth century set in motion a process whereby belief in the legitimacy of the southern,

---

[5] *Sovereign and Subject*, p. 163.

over the northern, court was widely restored. I am convinced that it was the enshrinement of Kusunoki Masashige, Nitta Yoshisada, and other loyalist leaders as supreme folk heroes that most fundamentally determined the subsequent course of the legitimacy issue. The Mito scholars and others argued that the southern court had been legitimate on the basis of various criteria—e.g., possession of the regalia, or the fact that Godaigo never willingly abdicated. Yet in the final analysis it was the popular feeling that Kusunoki, Nitta, and their comrades in arms could not have fought and died as gloriously as they did for a cause that was not just or rightful which ultimately brought official recognition of the southern court's historical legitimacy.

We can see in the great dynastic issue of Japanese history a clearly traceable example of how the rhetoric of a modern state's nationalist ideology can be significantly shaped by changing views of its past.

Appendix 1

Imperial Chronology to 1392

The early dates are traditional. Neither dates nor even the existence of sovereigns before the sixth century A.D. can be accepted as historical facts.*

Posthumous Name	Period of Rule	Posthumous Name	Period of Rule
1. Jimmu	660–585 B.C.	26. Keitai	507–531
2. Suizei	581–549	27. Ankan	531–536
3. Annei	549–511	28. Senka	536–539
4. Itoku	510–477	29. Kimmei	539–571
5. Kōshō	475–393	30. Bidatsu	572–585
6. Kōan	392–291	31. Yōmei	585–587
7. Kōrei	290–215	32. Sushun	587–592
8. Kōgen	214–158	33. Suiko	593–628
9. Kaika	158–98	34. Jomei	629–641
10. Sujin	98–30	35. Kōgyoku	642–645
11. Suinin	29 B.C.–A.D. 70	36. Kōtoku	645–654
12. Keikō	71–130	37. Saimei	655–661
13. Seimu	131–190	38. Tenji	668–671
14. Chūai	192–200	39. Kōbun	671–672
Jingū (Regent)	201–269	40. Temmu	673–686
15. Ōjin	270–310	41. Jitō	690–697
16. Nintoku	313–399	42. Mommu	697–707
17. Richū	400–405	43. Gemmei	707–715
18. Hanzei	406–410	44. Genshō	715–724
19. Ingyō	412–453	45. Shōmu	724–749
20. Ankō	453–456	46. Kōken	749–758
21. Yūryaku	456–479	47. Junnin	758–764
22. Seinei	479–484	48. Shōtoku	764–770
23. Kenzō	485–487	49. Kōnin	770–781
24. Ninken	488–498	50. Kammu	781–806
25. Buretsu	498–506	51. Heizei	806–809

* This chronology is adapted from Herschel Webb, *The Japanese Imperial Institution in the Tokugawa Period* (New York, 1968), pp. 269–73.

Posthumous Name	Period of Rule	Posthumous Name	Period of Rule
52. Saga	809–823	76. Konoe	1141–1155
53. Junna	823–833	77. Goshirakawa	1155–1158
54. Nimmyō	833–850	78. Nijō	1158–1165
55. Montoku	850–858	79. Rokujō	1165–1168
56. Seiwa	858–876	80. Takakura	1168–1180
57. Yōzei	876–884	81. Antoku	1180–1183
58. Kōkō	884–887	82. Gotoba	1183–1198
59. Uda	887–897	83. Tsuchimikado	1198–1210
60. Daigo	897–930	84. Juntoku	1210–1221
61. Suzaku	930–946	85. Chūkyō	1221
62. Murakami	946–967	86. Gohorikawa	1221–1232
63. Reizei	967–969	87. Shijō	1232–1242
64. En'yū	969–984	88. Gosaga	1242–1246
65. Kazan	984–986	89. Gofukakusa	1246–1259
66. Ichijō	986–1011	90. Kameyama	1259–1274
67. Sanjō	1011–1016	91. Gouda	1274–1287
68. Goichijō	1016–1036	92. Fushimi	1287–1298
69. Gosuzaku	1036–1045	93. Gofushimi	1298–1301
70. Goreizei	1045–1068	94. Gonijō	1301–1308
71. Gosanjō	1068–1072	95. Hanazono	1308–1318
72. Shirakawa	1072–1086	96. Godaigo	1318–1339
73. Horikawa	1086–1107	97. Gomurakami	1339–1368
74. Toba	1107–1123	98. Chōkei	1368–1383
75. Sutoku	1123–1141	99. Gokameyama	1383–1392

Emperors of the Northern Court

1. Kōgon	1331–1333	6. Gokomatsu	1382–1392
2. Kōmyō	1336–1348	(became sole emperor upon	
3. Sukō	1348–1351	reunification of the courts in	
4. Gokōgon	1352–1371	1392 and continued to rule	
5. Goenyū	1371–1382	until 1412)	

Appendix 2

Chikafusa's Imperial Chronology*

Imperial reigns are numbered in bold figures

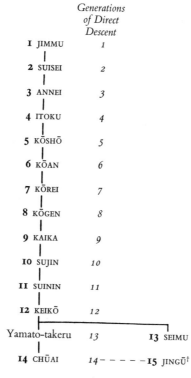

```
                          Generations
                           of Direct
                           Descent
            1 JIMMU            1
               |
            2 SUISEI           2
               |
            3 ANNEI            3
               |
            4 ITOKU            4
               |
            5 KŌSHŌ            5
               |
            6 KŌAN             6
               |
            7 KŌREI            7
               |
            8 KŌGEN            8
               |
            9 KAIKA            9
               |
           10 SUJIN           10
               |
           11 SUININ          11
               |
           12 KEIKŌ           12
             ┌────────────────────────┐
    Yamato-takeru      13            13 SEIMU
               |
           14 CHŪAI      14 – – – – –15 JINGŪ†
```

* Dates of rule may be found in Appendix 1.

† Chikafusa regarded Jingū as the 15th legitimate sovereign, but omitted Kōbun (the 39th emperor in the chronology given in Appendix 1). Under the influence of the Mito School of historiography of the Tokugawa period, however, Jingū was officially eliminated from the list of legitimate sovereigns and Kōbun was added. Hence the numbering of the sovereigns from 15 through 39 differs in Chikafusa's chronology from that given in Appendix 1.

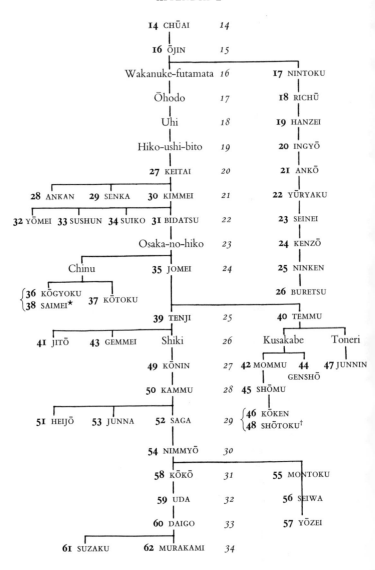

* Empress Kōgyoku reascended the throne as Empress Saimei.
† Empress Kōken reascended the throne as Empress Shōtoku.

APPENDIX 2

62 MURAKAMI 34
64 EN'YŪ 35
63 REIZEI
66 ICHIJŌ 36
65 KAZAN
67 SANJŌ
68 GOICHIJŌ
69 GOSUZAKU 37
71 GOSANJŌ 38
70 GOREIZEI
72 SHIRAKAWA 39
73 HORIKAWA 40
74 TOBA 41
75 SUTOKU
76 KONOE
77 GOSHIRAKAWA 42
80 TAKAKURA 43
78 NIJŌ
79 ROKUJŌ
81 ANTOKU
82 GOTOBA 44
Gotakakura
84 JUNTOKU
83 TSUCHIMIKADO 45
85 GOHORIKAWA
86 SHIJŌ
87 GOSAGA 46
89 KAMEYAMA 47
88 GOFUKAKUSA
90 GOUDA 48
91 FUSHIMI
93 GONIJŌ
95 GODAIGO 49
92 GOFUSHIMI
94 HANAZONO
96 GOMURAKAMI 50

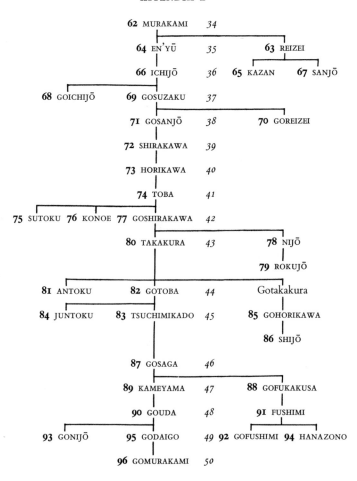

Appendix 3

The Japanese Imperial Regalia*

THE ORIGINS of the imperial regalia—mirror (*yata no kagami*), sword (*kusanagi no tsurugi*), and curved jewel (*yasakani no magatama*)—are unknown, although sets of such objects have been found in a number of burial sites in northern Kyushu dating from the earliest centuries A.D. It is believed that these objects may have served as tokens of tribal headship; and very little imagination is required to suppose that one set was later adopted by the imperial family as symbols of the right to rule the entire country after it had asserted its hegemony over the other clans (*uji*) of ancient Japan, probably between the mid-third and early sixth centuries.

The mirrors found in the Kyushu sites were imported from China of the Han period (206 B.C.–A.D. 220). Cast in bronze, they are round—averaging perhaps a foot in diameter—and are usually covered with embossed designs on their reverse sides. The swords, which are either imports from Korea or fashioned from Korean models, are also made of bronze, whereas the distinctive comma- or kidney-shaped jewels have been carved or molded from a wide variety of materials ranging from semiprecious stones to jade, baked clay, fossilized wood, and even glass.

According to the traditional mythology, the Sun Goddess, Amaterasu, bestowed the regalia on her grandson Ninigi when she sent him down from heaven to rule over Japan, the land of "luxuriant rice-fields." From the time of the first emperor, Jimmu (Ninigi's grandson, r. 660–585 B.C.),† the regalia were supposedly transferred from sovereign to sovereign and, indeed, proper receipt of them was assumed to be an essential prerequisite to emperorship. Until the reign of the tenth emperor, Sujin (r. 98–30 B.C.), the regalia were purportedly kept in the palaces or dwelling places of the various sovereigns. But Sujin, claiming that their presence close-by caused him to "feel uneasy," had replicas made of the mirror and sword (nothing is said about the jewel) and had the originals of these two objects placed in a newly

---

* Two sources in English that provide considerable information on the regalia are R. A. B. Ponsonby-Fane, *Studies in Shintō and Shrines* (Kyoto, 1942) and D. C. Holtom, *The Japanese Enthronement Ceremonies, with An Account of the Imperial Regalia* (Tokyo, 1928).

† These dates and those of Sujin and Suinin below are traditional (see Appendix I).

built shrine at the village of Kasanui in Yamato Province. During the reign of Sujin's successor, Suinin (r. 298 B.C.–A.D. 70), they were transferred to Ise.

The mirror—the most sacred of the regalia, since it is held to represent the body of Amaterasu herself—has according to legend been kept constantly at the Great Shrine of Ise from Suinin's time until the present day. The sword, however, is supposed to have been removed by Suinin's grandson, the redoubtable warrior Yamato-takeru, who took it on a campaign against unruly tribes in the east and left it at the Atsuta Shrine near present-day Nagoya.

With the original mirror at Ise and the original sword at Atsuta, the regalia that the sovereigns of historical times have actually transmitted from one to another have been the real jewel and replicas of the mirror and the sword. In time the replicas came to be regarded as having a sacred quality of their own. When, for example, the young Emperor Antoku (r. 1180–83) drowned at the naval battle of Dannoura in 1185 and carried the sword with him to the bottom of the sea, people acted as though the real object had been lost. Another sword owned by the imperial family was used as a substitute until 1210; in that year a new replica was ceremoniously forged at Ise.

As discussed in the text of this book, the emperor Godaigo reputedly used one and perhaps more false sets of regalia—that is, substitutes for the jewel, the original replica of the mirror, and the replica of the sword made in 1210—to deceive first the Hōjō and then the Ashikaga when these warrior families tried to force him to abdicate imperial authority. In fact, there simply is not sufficient evidence to determine precisely who had the "real" regalia at each stage in the complex succession quarrel of the fourteenth century; but it is generally acknowledged that the southern or Yoshino court held them from 1336 on and that the last southern emperor, Gokameyama (r. 1383–92), returned them to Kyoto in 1392 at the time of the reunification of the courts.

None of the regalia—originals or replicas—may be seen or examined today. They are concealed in various wrappings and receptacles and are never placed on public or private display.

Appendix 4

Imperial Restoration

RESTORATION IN THE TRADITIONS of early China and Japan was basically a Confucian concept, although (as discussed in chapter I of this book) it also had Buddhist connotations derived from the notion of the decline of the Buddhist law in history. Perhaps the most common term for restoration was *ōsei fukko*: literally, "a return to imperial rule of the past." Implicit was the belief that sometime in an earlier era sovereigns of high ethical character had exercised extraordinarily beneficent and harmonious rule, but that in subsequent ages the standards of government had degenerated.

Whereas *ōsei fukko*—or simply *fukko*—expressed the general ideal of restoration, a second term, *chūkō*, was used by the Chinese to describe specific situations in their history. Actually, the meaning of *chūkō* was nearer to "regeneration" than restoration and was inextricably related to the idea of the dynastic cycle. According to the latter, each Chinese dynasty went through a preordained sequence of phases: establishment by vigorous men; flourishing; decline and overthrow. Under special conditions, however, it was possible for the period of decline and overthrow to be checked temporarily by a reinvigoration of rule; that is, by an "Indian summer," which would not solve fundamental problems but would delay the inevitable final phase of the dynastic cycle.★ The archetypal instances of *chūkō* in premodern Chinese history were those of Emperor Hsüan-wang of the Chou Dynasty, 827–782 B.C.; Emperor Kuang-wu of the Han Dynasty, A.D. 25–57; and Emperor Su-tsung of the T'ang Dynasty, 756–62.

Godaigo took a certain pride in likening himself to Kuang-wu. But his idea of the *chūkō* that he was undertaking (discussed in detail in chapter III) was based primarily on the conditions of Japanese, not Chinese, history. The principle of the dynastic cycle could not be applied to Japan—at least at the imperial level—since there were no dynastic changes. Hence Godaigo

---

★ A discussion of restoration in Chinese history may be found in Mary C. Wright, *The Last Stand of Chinese Conservatism: The T'ung chih Restoration, 1862–1874* (Stanford: Stanford University Press, 1957), pp. 43–50. I have taken the expression "Indian summer" from this source. For comments on restoration in the Japanese setting, see Herschel Webb, *The Japanese Imperial Institution in the Tokugawa Period*, pp. 198–209.

assuredly did not conceive of his rule as a temporary postponement of inevitable decline and overthrow. He believed that the first principle of good rule was *direct* rule by the emperor and that the restoration therefore meant the abolition of those offices, such as the imperial regency, the cloistered emperorship, and the shogunacy, which had been used to arrogate the prerogatives of the throne.

Glossary

Akutō 悪党
Rowdy bands.

Bakufu 幕府
Military government or shogunate.

Buke 武家
Military families.

Bumbu kenkō 文武兼行
Union of court and military.

Bummei kaika 文明開化
"Civilization and enlightenment."

Bummeishi 文明史
History of civilization.

Buppō 佛法
Buddhist law.

Bureikō 無礼講
"Free and easy" society formed by a group in Kyoto during the early fourteenth century as a front to plot against the Kamakura Shogunate.

Bushidō 武士道
Way of the warrior.

Chinjufu shōgun 鎮守府将軍
Military commander for the northern provinces.

Chōrei bokai 朝令暮改
"Decrees issued in the morning that are changed in the evening."

Chōyōbun 朝用分
Commissariat rice.

Chūkō 中興
Imperial Restoration (see Appendix 3).

Dai 代
Chikafusa's designation for a legitimate imperial reign.

Daikakuji-tō 大覚寺党
Junior branch of the imperial family descended from Emperor Kameyama.

Dajō daijin 太政大臣
Chancellor of the department of state (or Great Council of State).

Dajō hōō 太上法皇
Retired emperor who has taken Buddhist vows.

Dajōkan 太政官
Department of state or Great Council of State.

Dajō tennō 太上天皇
Retired sovereign.

Dōri 道理
Literally, "principle" or "reason"; a term used with various meanings by Jien, Hōjō Yasutoki, and others.

Fukoku kyōhei 富国強兵
"Enrich the nation and strengthen its arms."

Gekū 外官
Outer shrine of the Ise Shrine.

Goke'nin 御家人
Shogunal houseman or retainer.

Gokoku 護国
Guardian of the state.

Go-muhon 御謀叛
Imperial "rebellion."

Han 藩
Feudal domain.

Hennentai 編年体
The writing of history according to a strict chronology of events.

Higoke'nin 非御家人
Warrior of the Kamakura period who was not a retainer or houseman of the shogunate.

Hikitsukeshū 引付衆
Board of coadjutors.

Honji suijaku 本地垂迹
"The essences (buddhas and bodhisattvas) have left traces (*kami*)."

Hyōjōshū 評定衆
Council of state.

Hyōrōmai 兵糧米
Commissariat rice.

In 院
Cloistered emperor.

Inchō 院庁
Administrative office of the cloistered emperor.

Ise-mairi 伊勢参
Ise visiting; the practice of making a pilgrimage to Ise.

Jihi 慈悲
Compassion.

Jimyōin-tō 持明院党
Senior branch of the imperial family descended from Emperor Gofukakusa.

Jingi sūhai 神祇崇拝
Worship of the Shinto gods.

Jitō 地頭
Steward.

Kami 神
Shinto deity.

Kamikaze 神風
Divine wind.

Kamiyo 神世
Age of the gods.

Kampaku 関白
Imperial regent.

Kangakusha 漢学者
Scholars of Chinese studies.

Kanrei 官領
Shogunal regent of the Kamakura period.

Kantō mōshitsugi 関東申次
Liaison official between the Kamakura Shogunate and the imperial court at Kyoto.

Kenkon tsūhō 乾坤通宝
Coins purportedly minted by Godaigo's Restoration government.

Ketsudan 決断
Decision or resolve.

Kirokujo 記録所
Records office.

Kokarabitsu 小唐櫃
Box used to hold the sacred mirror.

Kokka shugo 国家守護
Protector of the state.

Kokubunji 国分寺
Provincial temples erected during the Nara period.

Kokugakusha 国学者
National scholars.

Kokujin 国人
Local samurai warriors.

Kokutai 国体
National polity or essence.

Kōshōgaku 考証学
School of "empirical research" or "textual collation."

Kōtaishi 皇太子
Crown prince.

Kubosho 窪所
An office of Godaigo's Restoration government.

Kuge 公家
Courtier families.

Kurōdo dokoro 蔵人所
Sovereign's private office.

Mandokoro 政所
Administrative board.

Mappō 末法
Period of the "end of the Buddhist law."

Mikuriya 御厨
Landed holdings of the Ise Shrine.

Miuchi 御内
Direct vassals of the Hōjō family.

Monchūjo 問注所
Board of inquiry.

Monzeki 門跡
Head abbot of a temple who was also a member of the imperial family.

Mushadokoro 武者所
An office of Godaigo's Restoration government.

Naikū 内宮
Inner shrine of the Ise Shrine.

Namboku-chō jidai 南北朝時代
Period of the "northern and southern courts"; in Japanese history, 1336–92.

Nankō sūhai 楠公崇拝
Worship of Lord Kusunoki (Masashige).

Nanryū 楠流
Kusunoki school of military training.

Nembutsu 念佛
Invocation of the name of Amida Buddha.

Ōhō 王法
Imperial law.

Ōkimi 大王
Overlord or leading chieftain.

Onshōkata 恩賞方
Board of rewards.

Ōsei fukko 王政復古
Imperial restoration (see Appendix 3).

Rensho 連署
Co-signer.

Rikkokushi 六国史
"Six national histories" of Japan that cover the period from the age of the gods to 887.

Rinji 綸旨
Imperial edict.

Samurai dokoro 侍所
Board of retainers.

Sanjo 散所
Medieval merchant group.

Sato dairi 里内裏
Literally, "country palace"; the emperor's temporary or non-official residence.

Sei 世
Chikafusa's designation for a generation of imperial descent.

Seichaku 正着
Uprightness.

Seii taishōgun 征夷大将軍
Great general for pacification of the eastern barbarians.

Seisei taishōgun 征西大将軍
Great general for pacification of the west.

Shikken 執権
Shogunal regent.

Shimpon butsujaku 神本佛迹
"The Shinto *kami* are the 'essences' and the buddhas and bodhisattvas are the 'traces'"; reversal of the *honji suijaku* doctrine.

Shingi 新儀
New measures.

Shinkoku 神国
"Land of the gods" or "divine land"; applied exclusively to Japan.

Shō 正
"Legitimate" or "rightful."

Shōen 荘園
Private estates or manors.

Shōhō 正法
Period of the "flourishing of the Buddhist law."

Shugo 守護
Constable or protector.

Shūshin 修身
Ethics

Sonnō aikoku 尊皇愛国
"Reverence for the emperor and love of country."

Sōtsuibushi 総追捕使
Great constabulary or police official.

Taigi meibun 大義名分
Ethical precept meaning, literally, "supreme duty and name-position."

Tandai 探題
Deputy.

Tennō 天皇
Japanese sovereign, either male or female.

Tokusei 徳政
Literally, "virtuous administration"; debt cancellation decree.

Tokusō 得宗
Head of the Hōjō family.

Uji 氏
Family or clan.

Yoriai 寄合
Hōjō family council.

Zasso ketsudanjo 雑訴決断所
Settlements board.

Zatsunin 雑人
Designation for commoners during the Kamakura period.

Zōhō 像法
Period of the "reflected Buddhist law."

Bibliography

Aoki Kazuo. *Nara no Miyako*. In Chūō Kōron Sha, *Nihon no Rekishi*, Vol. III. Tokyo, 1965.

Arai Hakuseki. *Dokushi Yoron*. In Muraoka Tsunetsugu, ed., *Dokushi Yoron*. Tokyo, 1936.

Aston, W. G. *Nihongi, Chronicles of Japan From the Earliest Times to A.D. 697*. London, 1956.

Baishōron. In Hanawa Hokiichi, ed., *Gunsho Ruijū*, Vol. XX. Tokyo, 1929.

Beasley,W. G., and Carmen Blacker. "Japanese Historical Writing in the Tokugawa Period (1603-1868)." In W. G. Beasley and E. G. Pulleyblank, eds., *Historians of China and Japan*. London, 1961.

Bitō Masahide. "Nihon ni okeru Rekishi Ishiki no Hatten." In Iwanami Shoten, *Iwanami Kōza Nihon Rekishi*, Vol. XXII. Tokyo, 1963.

Blacker, Carmen. *The Japanese Enlightenment: A Study of the Writings of Fukuzawa Yukichi*. London, 1964.

Butler, Kenneth D. "The Textual Evolution of the *Heike Monogatari*." In *Harvard Journal of Asiatic Studies*, XXVI (1965–66).

Caiger, J. G. Education, Values and Japan's National Identity: A Study of the Aims and Content of Courses in Japanese History, 1872–1963. Unpublished doctoral dissertation for the Australian National University.

Craig, Albert. "Fukuzawa Yukichi: The Philosophical Foundations of Meiji Nationalism." In Robert E. Ward, ed., *Political Development in Modern Japan*. Princeton, 1968.

Earl, David. *Emperor and Nation in Japan*. Seattle, 1964.

Fujita Seiichi. *Nanshi Kenkyū*. Tokyo, 1933.

Fukuzawa Yukichi. *Gakumon no Susume*. In *Fukuzawa Yukichi Senshū*, Vol. I. Tokyo, 1951.

Gotō Tanji, Kamado Gisoburō, and Okami Masao, eds. *Taiheiki*. 3 vols. Tokyo, 1960–62.

Griffis, William Elliot. *The Mikado's Empire*, Vol. I. New York, 1876.

Hall, John W. *Government and Local Power in Japan, 500 to 1700*. Princeton, 1966.

Hanazono Tennō Shinki. In Zōho Shiryō Taisei Kankō Kai, *Zōho Shiryō Taisei*, Vols. II and III. Kyoto, 1965.

Hayashiya Tatsusaburō. *Namboku-chō*. Osaka, 1957.

Hekizan Nichiroku. In Kondō Keizō, ed., *Kaitei Shiseki Shūran*, Vol. XXV. Tokyo, 1902.

Hiraizumi Kiyoshi. "*Gukanshō* to *Jinnō Shōtōki*." In *Shigaku Zasshi*, September, 1936.

—— *Kemmu Chūkō no Hongi*. Tokyo, 1934.

Hirata Toshiharu. *Yoshino Jidai no Kenkyū*. Tokyo, 1943.

Holtom, D. C. *The National Faith of Japan*. New York, 1938.

Hōryaku Kanki. In Hanawa Hokiichi, ed., *Gunsho Ruijū*, Vol. XXVI. Tokyo, 1929.

Ichiko Teiji, ed. *Taiheiki*. Tokyo, 1965.

Inoue Mitsusada. "*Gukanshō* no Rekishi-kan." In *Kokugo to Kokubungaku*, October, 1954.

—— *Shinwa Kara Rekishi E*. In Chūō Kōron Sha, *Nihon no Rekishi*, Vol. I. Tokyo, 1965.

Ishida Takeshi. *Meiji Seiji Shisō Shi Kenkyū*. Tokyo, 1954.

Ishii Susumu. *Kamakura Bakufu*. In Chūō Kōron Sha, *Nihon no Rekishi*, Vol. VII. Tokyo, 1965.

Ishioka Hisao, ed. *Shoryū Heihō, jō*. In *Nihon Heihō Zenshū*, Vol. VI. Tokyo, 1967.

Iwai Tadakuma. "Nihon Kindai Shigaku no Keisei." In Iwanami Shoten, *Iwanami Kōza Nihon Rekishi*, Vol. XXII. Tokyo, 1963.

Jien. *Gukanshō*. In Okami Masao and Akamatsu Toshihide, eds., *Gukanshō*. Tokyo, 1967.

Kaigo Muneomi, ed. *Nihon Kyōkasho Taikei*, Vols. XVIII–XX. Tokyo, 1962–63.

Kitabatake Chikafusa. *Jinnō Shōtōki*. In Iwasa Masashi, *et al.*, eds., *Jinnō Shōtōki, Masu Kagami*. Tokyo, 1965.

Kitazume Masao. "Namboku-chō Ki no Tennō-sei Ron." In *Rekishi Hyōron*, September, 1960.

Kiyowara Sadao. "Kitabatake Chikafusa no Shisō." In *Shirin*, IX (1924), No. 2.

Kubota Osamu. *Kemmu Chūkō*. Tokyo, 1965.

Kume Kunitake. "*Taiheiki* wa Shigaku ni Eki Nashi." In *Shigaku Zasshi*, II (1891).

Kuroda Toshio. "Chūsei Kokka to Shinkoku Shisō." In Kawasaki Tsuneyuki, *et al.*, eds., *Nihon Shūkyō Shi Kōza*, Vol. I. Kyoto, 1959.

—— "Chūsei no Kokka to Tennō." In Iwanami Shoten, *Iwanami Kōza Nihon Rekishi*, Vol. VI. Tokyo, 1963.

—— "*Gukanshō* to *Jinnō Shōtōki*." In Rekishigaku Kenkyū Kai, *Nihon Rekishi Kōza*, Vol. VIII. Tokyo, 1965.

────── *Mōko Shūrai.* In Chūō Kōron Sha. *Nihon no Rekishi.* Vol. VIII. Tokyo, 1965.

────── "*Taiheiki* no Ningen Keishō." In *Bungaku*, XXII (1954), No. 11.

Maki Kenji. "Buke-hō ni Miyuru Rekishi-kan." In Fuzanbō, *Hompō Shigaku Shi Ronsō*, Vol. I. Tokyo, 1939.

Matsumoto Shimpachirō. "Namboku-chō Nairan no Sho-zentei." In *Chūsei Shakai no Kenkyū.* Tokyo, 1956.

Matsushima Eiichi. "Rekishi Kyōiku no Rekishi." In Iwanami Shoten, *Iwanami Kōza Nihon Rekishi*, Vol. XXII. Tokyo, 1963.

McCullough, Helen C., tr. *The Taiheiki.* New York, 1959.

Miura Hiroyuki. "Namboku-chō Gattai Jōken ni Tsukite." In *Shirin*, VII (1922), No. 1.

Muraoka Tsunetsugu. "Mappō Shisō no Tenkai to *Gukanshō* no Shikan." In *Nihon Shisō Shi jō no Sho-mondai.* Tokyo, 1957.

Murata Masashi. *Namboku-chō Ron.* Tokyo, 1959.

────── *Namboku-chō Shi Ron.* Tokyo, 1949.

Nagahara Keiji. "Chūsei no Sekai-kan." In Kawade Shobō, *Nihon Rekishi Kōza*, Vol. I. Tokyo, 1951.

────── "Chūsei-teki Seiji Keitai no Tenkai to Tennō no Ken'i." In *Nihon Hōken Shakai Ron.* Tokyo, 1955.

────── "Kitabatake Chikafusa." In Satō Shin'ichi, ed., *Nihon Jimbutsu Shi Taikei*, Vol. II. Tokyo, 1959.

────── "Namboku-chō Nairan." In Iwanami Shoten, *Iwanami Kōza Nihon Rekishi*, Vol. VI. Tokyo, 1963.

────── "Nihon Kokka-shi no Ichi Mondai." In *Shisō*, 1964, No. 1.

Naka Arata. *Meiji no Kyōiku.* Tokyo, 1967.

Nakamura Naokatsu. *Ashikaga no Takauji.* Tokyo, 1953.

────── *Kitabatake Chikafusa-kō Keiden.* Kyoto, 1933.

────── *Nanchō no Kenkyū.* Kyoto, 1927.

────── *Yoshino-chō Shi.* Kyoto, 1940.

Naoki Kōjirō. *Kodai Kokka no Seiritsu.* In Chūō Kōron Sha, *Nihon no Rekishi*, Vol. II. Tokyo, 1965.

Numata, Jiro. "Shigeno Yasutsugu and the Modern Tokyo Tradition of Writing." In W. G. Beasley and E. G. Pulleyblank, eds., *Historians of China and Japan.* London, 1961.

Ōkubo Toshiaki. "Yugamerareta Rekishi." In Sakisaka Itsurō, ed., *Arashi no Naka no Hyakunen.* Tokyo, 1952.

Ōta Toshirō, ed. *Kammon Gyoki.* 2 vols. Tokyo, 1930.

Passin, Herbert. *Society and Education in Japan.* New York, 1965.

Ponsonby-Fane, R. A. B. *Sovereign and Subject*. Kyoto, 1962.

——— *Studies in Shintō and Shrines*. Kyoto, 1942.

Sakamoto Tarō. *Nihon no Shūshi to Shigaku*. Tokyo, 1958.

Sansom, George. *A History of Japan, 1334–1615*. Stanford, 1961.

Satō Shin'ichi. "Bakufu Ron." In Chūō Kōron Sha, *Shin Nihon Shi Kōza*. Tokyo, 1949.

——— "Kamakura Bakufu Seiji no Sensei-ka ni tsuite." In Takeuchi Rizō, ed., *Nihon Hōken-sei Seiritsu no Kenkyū*. 2d ed. Tokyo, 1948.

——— *Kamakura Bakufu Shugo Seido no Kenkyū*. Tokyo, 1948.

——— *Kamakura Bakufu Soshō Seido no Kenkyū*. Tokyo, 1938.

——— *Namboku-chō no Dōran*. In Chūō Kōron Sha, *Nihon no Rekishi*, Vol. IX. Tokyo, 1965.

Shigaku Kyōkai. *Namboku-chō Seijun Ron*. Tokyo, 1911.

Shigeno Yasutsugu. "Kojima Takanori Kangae." In Satsuma Shi Kenkyū Kai, ed., *Shigeno Hakushi Gakuron Bunshū*, Vol. II. Tokyo, 1938.

Shimizu Mitsuo. *Nihon Chūsei no Sonraku*. Tokyo, 1942.

Shinoda, Minoru. *The Founding of the Kamakura Shogunate, 1180–1185*. New York, 1960.

Shively, Donald. "Motoda Eifu." In David S. Nivison and Arthur F. Wright, eds., *Confucianism in Action*. Stanford, 1959.

Taga Munehaya. "Hōjō Shikken Seiji no Igi." In *Kamakura Jidai no Shisō to Bunka*. Tokyo, 1946.

Takayanagi Mitsutoshi. *Ashikaga Takauji*. Tokyo, 1955.

Tanaka Yoshinari. *Namboku-chō Jidai Shi*. Tokyo, 1922.

Tōkyō Teikoku Daigaku. *Dai Nihon Shiryō*, Vol. 6^1. Tokyo, 1901.

Tōin Kinsada Nikki. In Tōkyō Teikoku Daigaku, *Bunka Daigaku Shishi Sōsho*. Tokyo, 1897–1908. Vol. XLVIII.

Tōyama Shigeki and Satō Shin'ichi, eds. *Nihon Shi Kenkyū Nyūmon*, Vol. I. Tokyo, 1954.

Toyoda Takeshi. "Chūsei no Tennō-sei." In *Nihon Rekishi*, June, 1952.

Tsuda Sōkichi. "*Gukanshō* oyobi *Jinnō Shōtōki* ni okeru Shina no Shigaku Shisō." In Fuzanbō, *Hompō Shigaku Ronsō*, Vol. I. Tokyo, 1939.

Tsuji Zennosuke. "Ashikaga Takauji no Shinkō." In *Shigaku Zasshi*, September, 1916.

Tsukamoto Yasuhiko. "*Gukanshō* to *Jinnō Shōtōki*." In *Kokugo to Kokubungaku*, September, 1962.

Tsunoda, Ryusaku, Wm. T. de Bary, and Donald Keene, eds. *Sources of Japanese Tradition*. New York, 1958.

Ueki Shin'ichirō. *Goseibai Shikimoku Kenkyū*. Tokyo, 1930.

Uemura Seiji. *Kusunoki Masashige*. Tokyo, 1962.

Uozumi Sōgorō. *Sōgō Nihon Shi Taikei*, Vol. VI. Tokyo, 1926.

—— "Yoshino-chō Jidai Shi." In Yuzankaku, *Dai Nihon Shi Kōza*, Vol. IV. Tokyo, 1936.

Uwayokote Masataka. "Jōkyū no Ran." In Iwanami Shoten, *Iwanami Kōza Nihon Rekishi*, Vol. V. Tokyo, 1962.

Varley, H. Paul. *The Ōnin War*. New York, 1967.

Watsuji Tetsurō. *Nihon Rinri Shisō Shi*. 2 vols. Tokyo, 1952.

—— *Sonnō Shisō to Sono Dentō*. Tokyo, 1943.

Webb, Herschel. *The Japanese Imperial Institution in the Tokugawa Period*. New York, 1968.

Yamazaki Fujiyoshi and Horie Hideo, eds. *Namboku-chō Seijun Ronsan*. Tokyo, 1911.

Yasuda Motohisa. "Hōken Jidai ni okeru Tennō." In *Shisō*, 1952, No. 6.

—— *Nihon Zenshi*, Vol. IV. Tokyo, 1958.

Yomiuri Shimbun Sha. *Nihon no Rekishi*, Vol. V. Tokyo, 1961.

Index

INDEX

Studies of the East Asian Institute

The Ladder of Success in Imperial China, by Ping-ti Ho. New York: Columbia University Press, 1962.

The Chinese Inflation, 1937–1949, by Shun-hsin Chou. New York: Columbia University Press, 1963.

Reformer in Modern China: Chang Chien, 1853–1926, by Samuel Chu. New York: Columbia University Press, 1965.

Research in Japanese Sources: A Guide, by Herschel Webb with the assistance of Marleigh Ryan. New York: Columbia University Press, 1965.

Society and Education in Japan, by Herbert Passin. New York: Bureau of Publications, Teachers College, Columbia University, 1965.

Agricultural Production and Economic Development in Japan, 1873–1922, by James I. Nakamura. Princeton, N. J.: Princeton University Press, 1966.

Japan's First Modern Novel: Ukigumo of Futabatei Shimei, by Marleigh Ryan. New York: Columbia University Press, 1967.

The Korean Communist Movement, 1918–1948, by Dae-sook Suh. Princeton, N. J.: Princeton University Press, 1967.

The First Vietnam Crisis, by Melvin Gurtov. New York: Columbia University Press, 1967.

Cadres, Bureaucracy, and Political Power in Communist China, by A. Doak Barnett. New York: Columbia University Press, 1967.

The Japanese Imperial Institution in the Tokugawa Period, by Herschel Webb. New York: Columbia University Press, 1968.

The Recruitment of University Graduates in Big Firms in Japan, by Koya Azumi. New York: Teachers College Press, Columbia University, 1968.

The Communists and Chinese Peasant Rebellion: A Study in the Rewriting of Chinese History, by James P. Harrison, Jr. New York: Atheneum Publishers, 1969.

How the Conservatives Rule Japan, by Nathaniel B. Thayer. Princeton, N. J.: Princeton University Press, 1969.

Aspects of Chinese Education, edited by C. T. Hu. New York: Teachers College Press, Columbia University, 1969.

Economic Development and the Labor Market in Japan, by Koji Taira. New York: Columbia University Press, 1970.

The Japanese Oligarchy and the Russo-Japanese War, by Shumpei Okamoto. New York: Columbia University Press, 1970.

Documents on Korean Communism, by Dae-sook Suh. Princeton, N. J.: Princeton University Press, 1970.

Japan's Postwar Defense Policy, 1947–1968, by Martin E. Weinstein. New York: Columbia University Press, 1971.

Imperial Restoration in Medieval Japan, by H. Paul Varley. New York: Columbia University Press, 1971.

Li Tsung-Jen, A Memoir. Edited by T. K. Tong. University of California Press (forthcoming).

086693